If You're in a Dogfight, Become a Cat!

Strategies for Long-Term Growth

LEONARD SHERMAN

Columbia University Press
Publishers Since 1893
New York   Chichester, West Sussex
cup.columbia.edu

Library of Congress Cataloging-in-Publication Data
Names: Sherman, Len, 1956– author.
Title: If you're in a dogfight, become a cat! : strategies for long-term
growth / Leonard Sherman.
Description: New York : Columbia University Press, 2017. | Includes
bibliographical references and index.
Identifiers: LCCN 2016021876 | ISBN 9780231174824 (cloth : alk. paper) |
ISBN 9780231174831 (pbk. : alk. paper) |ISBN 9780231542821 (e-book)
Subjects: LCSH: Strategic planning. | Industrial management.
Classification: LCC HD30.28 .S42995 2016 | DDC 658.4/012—dc23
LC record available at https://lccn.loc.gov/2016021876

Columbia University Press books are printed on permanent
and durable acid-free paper.
Printed in the United States of America

COVER DESIGN: Faceout Studio

For Shelly, who has contributed to this endeavor more than she can ever know.

Contents

Preface

PRIOR TO JOINING the faculty of Columbia Business School, I spent more than three decades in management consulting, providing advice on business strategy to senior executives in the automotive, aerospace, and other industries around the world. I also served as a general partner in a corporate venture capital fund and as an investor and board member for a variety of high-tech startups.

My thinking over this time was shaped by a number of emerging theories of business strategy, from Porter's Five Forces and the Boston Consulting Group's growth–share matrix at the beginning of my career, to disruptive technology frameworks in the middle, to new ideas on big-bang disruption and the death of competitive advantage at the end. At each step along the way I approached my consulting assignments and venture capital investment opportunities with messianic zeal, as consultants do, fully committed to the prevailing strategy theory that promised to help solve vexing client problems. I was as guilty as anyone of the old adage: if the only tool you have is a strategic hammer, you tend to see every client problem as a nail.

Looking back over my career, I am gratified to have actually changed the strategic direction of a few troubled clients, who went on to achieve great success. But if truth be known, most of my consulting engagements were less successful. For example, I worked on and off for over a decade for what was once the largest corporation in the world (General Motors), but couldn't alter their steadfast decline into bankruptcy. And at the turn of the new millennium, I enthusiastically recommended investments in promising start-ups, some of which did not survive the bursting of the dot-com bubble.

Along the way, it was easy to rationalize such disappointments by concluding that the client wouldn't accept my wise counsel or that they didn't properly execute the recommended strategy. But the passage of time has tempered my hubris and provided a broader perspective on the challenges of managing a complex business enterprise. Failure is a great teacher.

But perhaps I'm being a bit too hard on myself. After all, being deeply immersed in the workings of business strategy over many decades, it has become increasingly apparent that most companies do not achieve and sustain long-term profitable growth, with or without the help of consultants.

A 2007 study by my former employer, Accenture, showed that only about 5 to 20 percent of companies, depending on industry, were able to consistently outperform competitors across business and economic cycles.[1]

Bain consultants James Allen and Chris Zook examined the annual reports of the *Forbes* Global 2000 and found that on average, CEOs projected that their company would grow at twice the rate and be four times more profitable than the industry average. In other words, as Allen waggishly notes, "the entire world of business is projecting to take share from the entire world of business." But after examining the performance of the Global 2000 over the decade 2001–2011, Bain found that only about 10 percent of companies actually met their growth targets.[2]

And in perhaps the most extensive study of long-term growth rates, researchers at the Corporate Executive Board found that only 13 percent of Fortune 100 companies were able to sustain as little as 2 percent annual real revenue growth from one decade to the next over the past fifty years.[3]

Many of my MBA students find these results surprising, and perhaps even a bit unsettling. After all, they have made a significant personal investment to learn the latest strategy theories, management best practices, and analytical frameworks that hold the promise of driving superior business performance. They have every reason to expect that they can beat the odds and achieve better outcomes over their careers.

I share their conviction and optimism, even after my own chastening experience in discovering that there are no silver bullets or universally applicable business-strategy frameworks or management best practices that ensure superior business performance. While I have been a beneficiary of the insightful strategy thinking contributed by Michael Porter, Bruce Henderson, Clay Christensen, C. K. Prahalad, Paul Nunes, Youngme Moon, Rita McGrath and others that will be reviewed in this book, I have also come to appreciate that effective business strategy is inherently dynamic and context sensitive. No one universal framework or management prescription fits all business circumstances. What works well for one company may actually be quite harmful if applied by another company operating in a different market and competitive environment. And what works well for a company at a given point in time may be counterproductive after its business circumstances change.

Thus the purpose of this book is to share practical advice in addressing two of the most common and vexing questions facing business executives:

- Why is it so hard to achieve and sustain long-term profitable growth?
- How can businesses achieve this?

Answering these questions has been the central focus of two popular MBA courses that I have been teaching at Columbia Business School for the past nine years. After making and observing innumerable mistakes over my own business career, I joined the ranks of academia with the intent of helping next-generation business leaders avoid common pitfalls and showing them how to lead better businesses. This book is similarly motivated, with the hope of reaching a wider audience beyond the cozy confines of Columbia Business School.

The curious title of this book metaphorically captures the competitive challenge eventually faced by all businesses, as well as the management mindset required to overcome the odds against sustained profitable growth. Consider the mental image conjured up by a dogfight, where rival dogs (firms) scratch and claw for territorial dominance (market share), often battling with largely similar tactics (products and services). In business terms, such conditions generally refer to mature, commoditized markets characterized by slow growth, slim margins, and intense competition, making it difficult for any one firm to effectively break away from the pack. In dogfights, as in business, strong players may gain a temporary advantage, but the ongoing fight for dominance usually takes a heavy toll on all combatants, and the prospect for renewed battles remains a constant threat.

Cats are a different breed of animal—clever, solitary hunters who are more inclined to explore new territory and to redefine the game on their own terms than to engage with the pack in a no-win dogfight. Cats are agile and innovative, and seek their prey (customers) with tactics that dogs cannot easily replicate.

Throughout this book, I will feature many firms that emulate cat-like behavior to break away from the pack, even in industries known for intense competition and unfavorable economics. Exemplars can be found in virtually every industry, from high tech (Apple) to low (Yellow Tail wine), selling either products (LittleMissMatched socks) or services (citizenM hotels).

In business terms, these firms avoid competitive dogfights and break away from the pack by embracing the three strategic imperatives required to drive sustained profitable growth.

- Continuous innovation—not for its own sake, but to deliver. . . .
- Meaningful product differentiation—recognized and valued by consumers, enabled by . . .
- Business alignment—where all corporate capabilities, resources, incentives, and business culture and processes are aligned to support a company's strategic intent.

By continuously delivering innovative and meaningfully differentiated products and services, companies can attract and retain customers at favorable prices, while making it difficult for competitors to replicate their business practices. These outcomes are the essential drivers of long-term profitable growth.

While this prescription may seem to draw on a heavy dose of common sense, it turns out to be difficult and rare for companies to actually incorporate these imperatives as the foundation of their business strategy, underscoring the objective of this book to explore why this is, and what to do about it.

If You're in a Dogfight, Become a Cat!

CHAPTER ONE

The Origins of Modern Business Strategy Thinking

THE SEARCH FOR winning strategies and management best practices that drive long-term profitable growth is not new. When I started my business career in the late 1970s, Michael Porter had just published *How Competitive Forces Shape Strategy*,[1] now widely considered one of the most influential pillars of modern business strategy thinking. In this seminal work, Porter established "Five Forces"—essentially the underlying competitive characteristics of companies operating within a given industry—to explain why some enterprises are inherently more profitable than others (figure 1.1).

Following Porter's logic, managers were advised to seek out businesses that had strong bargaining power over buyers and suppliers, low threats of new entry from similar or substitute products, and sustainable competitive advantages that would limit competitive rivalry. It's hard to argue against such a prescription. After all, who wouldn't want to operate in such a business environment? But Porter offered little guidance on how to position one's business, other than suggesting that executing either a lowest-cost or best-product strategy is essential to winning in the marketplace.

In essence, Porter's Five Forces framework—still taught in many MBA programs—gave credence to the notion that there are inherently "good" and "bad" industries, more or less conducive to superior financial results. I disagree and will argue that there are winners in every industry, regardless of the competitive challenges facing incumbents, provided that managers successfully break from industry norms to create meaningfully differentiated products and services. I'll also suggest that choosing between lowest cost and best quality is a false

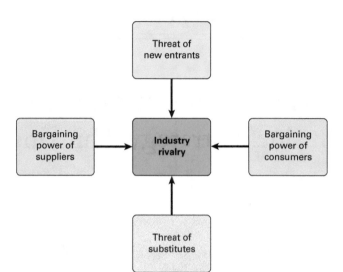

Figure 1.1 Porter's Five Forces framework

dichotomy, as there is a far richer set of performance attributes and differentiated target market positions that companies can exploit to create compelling and profitable consumer value propositions.

Another major contribution to strategic management thinking that gained wide acceptance in the 1970s was introduced by the Boston Consulting Group (BCG), one of the premier management consulting firms. In 1970, BCG founder Bruce Henderson created the growth–share matrix, in which companies were classified in one of four quadrants based on their market share and the overall industry growth rate (figure 1.2).[2] Companies with high market shares in fast-growing industries were designated as "stars," which managers were urged to aggressively pursue. Better yet, BCG suggested that even when stars begin to mature, as evidenced by slowing industry growth rates, their high market shares would likely continue to yield sizeable cash flows that could be harvested as "cash cows" to invest in new star opportunities.

Not surprisingly, BCG counseled companies to avoid getting into businesses in the "dog" quadrant of low market share and slow (or even negative) growth, and to divest any such businesses from their portfolio.

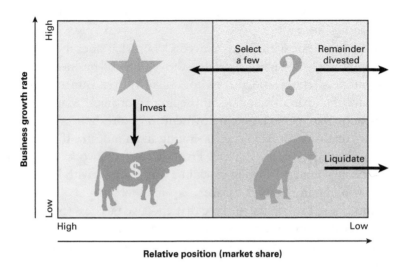

Figure 1.2 BCG growth–share matrix

Both Porter and BCG advanced a somewhat fatalistic view that the inherent structural characteristics of individual business units and industries largely dictated business performance. Echoing this sentiment, Warren Buffett once wittily observed: "With few exceptions, when a manager with a reputation for brilliance tackles a business with a reputation for poor fundamental economics, it is the reputation of the business that remains intact."[3]

This structuralist view of markets and competition was widely accepted at the time and undoubtedly contributed to the popularity of business conglomerates in the 1970s and 1980s. Corporations like ITT, United Technologies, and General Electric (GE) were run as diversified business portfolios, with each unit being evaluated by management on an ongoing basis to determine whether its role was to drive growth, to harvest cash flows, or to be divested. Jack Welch, CEO of General Electric from 1981 to 2001, was an aggressive proponent of this management mindset. Shortly after becoming CEO, Welch publicly declared that any GE business unit that could not achieve a first or second market share position in its industry would have to be immediately fixed, or be sold or closed. During his CEO tenure over the ensuing twenty years, GE divested 117 businesses[4] and acquired nearly a thousand others, increasing GE's market cap by nearly $500 billion along the way.[5]

It's hard to argue with Welch's success,[6] but what does this business philosophy imply for mere mortals—the legions of business managers or business school students—who, unlike Warren Buffett and GE, don't have the luxury of buying and selling companies? Many readers of this book may be seeking employment in or already working for a company that is not a BCG star, operating in an industry that doesn't score particularly well in Porter's Five Forces framework. Does this imply the inevitability of being stuck in a dog business with little prospect of winning in the marketplace?

In this book, I will make the case that effective business strategy and execution can trump industry structure, even in industries that Warren Buffett might think have a bad reputation. I'll provide numerous case studies to highlight companies and brands that achieved outstanding success despite the challenge of operating in mature, brutally competitive industries—e.g., Southwest Airlines and Yellow Tail wine.

Of course, business strategy thinking has evolved considerably since the advent of the Porter and BCG doctrines of the 1970s. In the ensuing forty years, business researchers and academics have advanced theories on management best practices, frameworks to explain disruptive business dynamics, the characteristics of breakthrough product differentiation, and the importance of business alignment to support effective strategy execution. I will explore each of these major developments in the following sections.

The Quixotic Search for Management Best Practices

In the 1980s, attention shifted in some quarters from a focus on industry structure to the search for specific management techniques and behaviors to promote business success. One notable attempt to address this issue—*In Search of Excellence,* by McKinsey consultants Tom Peters and Robert Waterman, Jr.—went on to become the best-selling business book of all time after its publication in 1982.[7]

The premise of *In Search of Excellence* was straightforward and alluring: by studying the business practices of successful companies, the authors argued that it is possible to discern specific management behaviors that can be adopted by any company to promote superior performance.

Peters and Waterman made field trips to forty-three successful companies to observe business operations and to interview senior executives. Based on their analysis, the two McKinsey consultants identified eight basic principles of management effectiveness—for example, having a bias for action, staying close to your customer, promoting productivity through people, and sticking to the knitting that your company knows best. Stated in such broad-brush terms, it seemed reasonable to accept these principles as hallmarks of sound business management.

But as legions of business executives combed through the pages of *In Search of Excellence* for useful tips on how to transform their companies into market leaders, a nagging doubt began to emerge. Several of the companies profiled in the book as exemplars of best practice suffered significant falls from grace: Kodak, Kmart, Delta Air Lines, Wang Laboratories, and Dana Holding Corporation, all of which eventually went bankrupt. This raised troubling questions. Were the companies that Peters and Waterman studied really excellently managed? And were the eight pillars of effective management identified by the authors really necessary, and sufficient to drive superior business performance?

Despite growing concerns with the validity and usefulness of *In Search of Excellence,* the powerful allure of unlocking the management secrets of business success attracted other researchers, most notably Jim Collins. Collins has authored six books over the past twenty-five years similar in concept to *In Search for Excellence,* including *Built to Last, Good to Great,* and *Great by Choice,* which have collectively sold over ten million copies.[8]

Collins distinguished his work by the rigor of his research methodology. For example, Collins applied a matched-pair case method, where each successful company in his sample was paired with a lesser-performing company from the same industry over a common time frame to help isolate the differences in management practices that could account for the observed differences in financial performance. To select his samples, Collins established strict performance criteria that successful companies had to meet over a long period. And finally, Collins used extensive data analysis—reviewing thousands of pages of company reports, books, academic case studies, analyst reports and press coverage—to determine the common best practices of high-performing companies. Looking back at Collins's work from our current perspective of widespread use of "big data" analytics, it is tempting to believe that if one analyzes a sufficiently large sample, statistically significant patterns of best practice behavior can be revealed.

Collins expressed his findings at a high level of abstraction, using clever acronyms, metaphors, and a heavy dose of common sense, which conveyed broad applicability. Examples from his books include:[9]

- Visionary companies set Big Hairy Audacious Goals (BHAGs for short).
- The key ingredient that allows a company to become great is having a Level 5 Leader—an executive in whom genuine personal humility blends with intense professional will.
- First Who, Then What—get the right people on the bus, then figure out where the bus might be going.
- Confront the brutal truth of business situations, yet at the same time, never give up hope.
- Be a hedgehog, not a fox—do one thing and do it well in an endeavor that you are passionate about, that you can be the best at, and with which you can actually make a living.

There is nothing wrong with this advice per se, but to assert a predictive link[10] between the espoused management behaviors and successful business outcomes is profoundly flawed for two reasons: the halo effect and the fact that strategy is context sensitive.

Jim Collins's Management Advice

Have.
Big.
Hairy.
Audacious.
Goals.

The Halo Effect

The *halo effect* describes the human tendency to make specific inferences on the basis of overall impressions.

Earl Weaver, the Hall-of-Fame former manager of the Baltimore Orioles, once offered some sage advice: "You're never as bad as you look when you're losing, nor as good as you seem when you're winning." This is as true in business as it is in baseball.

There is considerable academic research to validate Weaver's observation.[11] For example, when a company is enjoying strong, profitable growth and a surging stock price fueling big management bonuses and career advancement, the tendency is for employees and a fawning business press to heap praise on the CEO for his or her strategic vision, leadership, focus, and decisiveness. After all, these are subjective measures and the top executive is obviously doing *something* right. But if the same company begins to stumble in the marketplace (for any number of reasons), observers are quick to become overly critical of management on the very same subjective terms. In fact, management behaviors may not have changed much, if at all. Rather, company performance, good or bad, creates an overall impression—a halo—that shapes how we perceive its strategy, leaders, employees, and culture.

Look at the accolades heaped on Netflix CEO Reed Hastings, who has been widely considered one of Silicon Valley's best executives and lauded by *Fortune* as their 2010 CEO of the year. In their profile, *Fortune* described Hastings as a visionary, dynamic, and customer-focused leader with amazing foresight.[12] But less than a year later, the very same CEO was widely vilified as out of touch, arrogant, and unprepared every step of the way when the company's financial performance suffered from a misguided business initiative. Some analysts and business pundits called for Hastings's resignation.[13] But Netflix recovered to become one of the top-performing companies on U.S. stock exchanges between 2011 and 2015, restoring Reed Hastings's stature as a highly respected CEO.

Apple CEO Tim Cook provides another example of the halo effect—probably deserving neither his early sanctification nor his subsequent fall from grace in the business press. On June 11, 2012, Tim Cook graced the cover of *Fortune* for a hagiography about the man with perhaps the hardest job in America: to succeed the legendary Steve Jobs, whom *Fortune* had lionized as "the best CEO of the decade" and "the best entrepreneur of our time."[14]

As the *Fortune* piece noted: "Considering the widespread hand-wringing over how rudderless Apple would be without Jobs, it is remarkable how steadily the company has sailed along without him."

Time magazine weighed in with similar praise: "Highly ethical and always thoughtful, he projects calmness but can be tough as nails when necessary. Like the great conductor George Szell, Cook knows that his commitment to excellence is inseparable from the incredible ensemble he leads at Apple."[15]

Such plaudits certainly seemed warranted at the time. When *Fortune*'s story appeared, Apple was trading at $571 per share, 52 percent higher than when Steve Jobs stepped down ten months earlier. Apple's stock crested at over $700 per share in the coming months, prompting *Forbes* and the *New York Times* to speculate that Apple—already the most valuable company in the world—was well on its way to becoming the first trillion-dollar market cap company.[16]

But less than four months later, Apple suffered a few uncharacteristic stumbles in the marketplace. Its stock price dropped by 25 percent and the *Wall Street Journal* ran a story under the headline "Has Apple Lost Its Cool to Samsung?"[17] As for Tim Cook, in mid-February, 2013, *Forbes* weighed in with "The Problem with Tim Cook," raising serious questions about whether Tim Cook was really up to the job as Apple's CEO.[18]

Did Reed Hastings and Tim Cook radically change their fundamental approach to management in a matter of months? Of course not. Rather, these examples illustrate the significance of the halo effect: subjective ratings of managerial performance are inextricably correlated with overall corporate performance.

Therefore the analyses by Jim Collins (and earlier by Peters and Waterman) prove only that the halo effect is alive and well, and not that there is a causal or even a predictive link between subjective impressions of managerial practices and business outcomes. Collins deserves credit for the vast amount of information he examined, but if the underlying subjective data aren't valid, it really doesn't matter how much information was gathered or how sophisticated the analysis appeared to be. As with Peters and Waterman, several of the companies identified by Jim Collins as exemplars of management best practice have suffered serious falls from grace, including Fannie Mae, Circuit City, Motorola, and Sony.[19]

Strategy Is Context Sensitive

Even if some of the management advice set forth in Collins's books is sound, the notion that there are specific prescriptions for success that are universally applicable in companies from different industries and at different stages of development is at best folly and at worst, dangerous. This philosophy tends to promote strategic rigidity. As we will discover throughout this book, effective business strategy needs to constantly adapt to inevitable shifts in technology, the market, and the competitive landscape. Strategic priorities that are effective in one company may be quite harmful if adopted by another company operating in a different business context.

As a case in point—in the context of Jim Collins's advice that visionary leaders should adopt Big Hairy Audacious Goals—consider the approach followed by Lou Gerstner, CEO of IBM in the 1990s, who spearheaded one of the most dramatic corporate turnarounds of all time. When he was asked to share his vision for the company at his first analyst meeting, Gerstner famously replied: "The last thing IBM needs right now is a vision! What it needs right now are tough-minded, market-driven, highly effective strategies."[20] In his first full year on the job, Gerstner cut IBM's headcount in half, shuttered numerous underperforming business units, and engineered an extraordinary $13.6 billion swing in operating profit, from the existential threat of an $8.6 billion loss in 1993 to a $5 billion profit in 1994.

All businesses experience shifts in their competitive landscapes. There are times when an inspiring and audacious vision is highly advantageous and other times when it would distract from the exigencies of more pragmatic imperatives. There are also times when sticking to one's knitting (a Collins recommendation) is entirely appropriate and other times when such advice would hasten the decline of a disrupted business. And so, the notion that sophisticated analysis can uncover timeless and universal truths about management effectiveness is misguided. If there is any timeless advice that executives should embrace, it is that they should continuously adapt business strategy to anticipate and respond to changing circumstances. Effective business strategy is inherently dynamic.

The Need for Continuous Innovation

Shortly after Jim Collins published his first two books about the secrets of enduring business success,[21] Clayton Christensen published his seminal work on disruptive technology. Christensen advanced a theory that strong market forces pose grave and often insurmountable threats to incumbent market leaders across virtually all industries. In *The Innovator's Dilemma,* published in 1997, Christensen argued that widely accepted management best practices advocated by Peters and Waterman and Jim Collins—e.g., stay close to your customers and stick to the knitting of what you do best—were unwittingly sowing the seeds of business failure.[22]

The implications of Christensen's thesis were stark, startling, and notable, for two reasons. First is its broad applicability. Despite its name—disruptive *technology*—Christensen's theory applies to any industry, whether high- or low-tech or whether product- or service-based. Examples covered later in this book will expand on the disruptive forces that have reshaped the competitive balance in industries as diverse as steel, book publishing, computers, travel agencies, and health services. In some cases, industries were disrupted by breakthrough technologies, but in many others, the impetus for industry disruption came from mashups of low-tech components or innovations in business models, not new product technology. For example, Wikipedia's ascendancy at the expense of Encyclopædia Britannica certainly depended on Internet technology, but walk-in medical clinics, now prevalent in Walmart, CVS, and other retail chains are primarily based on a new business model for routine medical services offering more convenience and lower prices than traditional doctor office visits (table 1.1).

The second notable aspect of disruptive technology theory is the elegant simplicity with which Christensen sheds light on the central questions addressed in his book:

- Why do companies have such a difficult time sustaining market leadership?
- Why are newcomers—rather than incumbent market leaders—so often the ones to introduce disruptive technologies and business models?
- What should incumbents do about it?

I'll have a lot more to say about Christensen's work later, but the essence of his argument is that market leaders have strong incentives to prioritize the current needs of their best and most demanding customers. After all, managers are supposed to respond to the

TABLE I.I
Industry Examples of Disruptive Technologies

Disruptive Technology	Incumbent Product
Digital photography	Film
Wikipedia	Traditional encyclopedias
Online booking services	Travel agents
Ultrasound	X-ray imaging
Walk-in medical clinics	Primary care physicians
Minimills	Integrated steel mills
Personal computers	Minicomputers and mainframes

marketplace and to compete aggressively to protect their core business against traditional competitors (who are trying to steal the best customers with even more sophisticated products and services). The net result in many industries is a feature/function arms race where competitors strive to outdo each other with continuous incremental improvements to state-of-the-art products.[23] The resulting product performance trajectory eventually overserves a growing number of consumers who do not value—or want to to pay for—ever-improving best-in-class products.

Overserved markets open the door for disruptive technology players with products that initially are good enough to serve the needs of some customers, often at attractive low prices. For example, the first crude personal computers (e.g., the Apple II) that entered the consumer market in the 1970s were no match for the powerful minicomputers and workstations at the time, but provided an affordable entry point for tech-savvy consumers.

The most demanding customers in the marketplace initially exhibit little interest in such "inferior" products, and incumbent market leaders are generally dismissive of disruptive technologies, for fear of tarnishing their reputation for product excellence or cannibalizing their high-end product margins. But over time, the performance of low-end disruptive technologies steadily improve, making them an increasingly attractive alternative to existing products. In many industries, disruptive technologies eventually render legacy products obsolete, ushering in a completely new set of competitors and product performance norms. This pattern of creative destruction[24] played out repeatedly in each of the product categories noted in table 1.1.

Christensen went on to refine his theory of disruptive technology across a range of industries and more recently extended his framework to explore dynamic changes occurring in education, health care, and even in the performance of national economies.[25] His work is widely considered to be one of the most significant contributions to business strategy theory.[26]

But in many ways, Christensen has become a victim of his own success, as the term *disruption* is now being inappropriately applied in a wide array of business contexts, often bearing little resemblance to the author's original scope or intent. For example, nary an entrepreneur seeking venture capital funding these days fails to hail his or her startup as a disruptive enterprise, regardless of actual business circumstances. And established companies are also staking a claim to disruptive products and services. In launching A.M. Crunchwraps, the chief marketing officer of Taco Bell recently gushed: "We're just getting started with breakfast. Our aim is to boldly disrupt the category."[27] In addition, a whole cottage industry of self-proclaimed disruption experts has emerged offering consulting services, conferences, and seminars to cash in on the popularity of Christensen's disruptive technology framework.[28]

The misuse of the disruptive technology framework has prompted some critics to question the validity of Christensen's work. For example, in one particularly harsh polemic, Harvard historian Jill Lepore recently called Christensen's work "a theory of change founded on panic, anxiety, and shaky evidence."[29]

Ironically, if Christensen's research deserves to be questioned, it is for being too narrowly focused on one particular explanation of industry disruption. For example, in 2007, he told *Business Week* that "the prediction of the [disruptive technology] theory would be that Apple won't succeed with the iPhone," adding, "History speaks pretty loudly on that."[30] Apple's iPhone did not fit Christensen's preoccupation with industry disruption starting at the low end of the market. According to Christensen, high-end, closed-system players like Apple will inevitably be disrupted by lower-cost, open-system entrants like Android.

But in fact, there is a class of highly disruptive products that follows a very different market development trajectory than that advanced by Christensen. Specifically, high-end disruptors aim at underserved customers, initially offering substantially superior product performance at premium prices, before expanding their market reach by lowering prices (and possibly performance). For example, when FedEx launched, it rapidly gained market penetration by offering overnight delivery that was faster and more expensive than competing parcel delivery services. Subsequently, FedEx introduced two-day delivery services at lower prices to expand its market reach. Similarly, Amazon initially marketed the Kindle at $399, with superior performance to existing e-readers (and to hardcover books, as perceived by tech-savvy consumers). But over time, Amazon reduced its e-reader price to as low as $79, while improving performance, which considerably broadened their market reach. Apple followed a similar high-end disruptive technology trajectory with the iPod, from a launch price of $399 to as low as $99 over time.

Christensen's original disruptive technology framework and the high-end disruptive technology examples noted in figure 1.3 have two common characteristics: they represent opposite market entry points—high performance and price, or low performance and price; and it usually takes years for the full impact of either form of disruption to fully play out in transforming an industry.

But what if a disruptive innovation could enter the market offering vastly superior performance *and* lower prices than current products? That's precisely the compelling value proposition of "big bang"

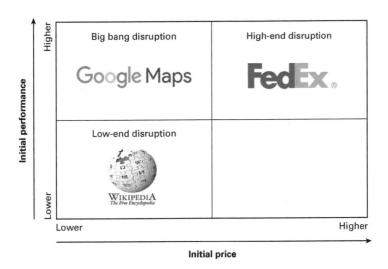

Figure 1.3 Characteristics of disruptive entry relative to best-in-class products. Google logo © Google; Wikipedia logo © Wikipedia; FedEx logo © FedEx. All rights reserved.

disruptors that can overwhelm stable businesses very rapidly, as described in a recent book by Larry Downes and Paul Nunes.[31]

For example, consider the market for portable and in-car GPS navigation devices from Garmin, TomTom, and Magellan Navigation, which thrived in early 2000s. As is usual with sustaining technologies, continuous improvements in these devices enhanced performance and lowered prices. But in 2007, Google Maps for smartphones was released. This was at once cheaper (i.e., free), better (i.e., more accurate and up to date), more convenient (i.e., no need for a specialized additional device), and more personalized (i.e., linked to all the other things on a user's smartphone) all at once. The market for portable GPS devices immediately collapsed, with around a hundred million users downloading Google Maps in the first year. A year later, that number had doubled.[32]

Other examples of products that have suffered big bang disruption include cameras, pagers, wristwatches, maps, books, travel guides, flashlights, home telephones, dictation recorders, cash registers, alarm clocks, answering machines, yellow pages, wallets, keys, phrase books, transistor radios, personal digital assistants, remote controls, newspapers and magazines, directory assistance, travel and insurance agents, restaurant guides, and pocket calculators.

The accelerating pace of big bang disruption is being driven by the increasing role of software rather than hardware in creating product-performance gains and by the substantial decline in software-driven development costs.

Downes and Nunes melodramatically warn: "You can't see big bang disruption coming. You can't stop it. You can't overcome it. Old-style disruption posed the innovator's dilemma. Big bang disruption is the innovator's disaster. And it will be keeping executives in every industry in a cold sweat for a long time to come."[33]

Of course, not all industries are equally prone to big bang disruption. But these evolving theories of disruptive technology dynamics nonetheless suggest that managers should expect continuous upheaval in product lifecycles and industry structure. The important implication is that companies can no longer expect to sustain long-term competitive advantage, unless they are prepared to continuously disrupt themselves. This is precisely the point made by Rita McGrath in her recent book, aptly called *The End of Competitive Advantage: How to Keep Your Strategy Moving as Fast as Your Business*.[34] McGrath notes that for generations of managers schooled and incentivized to achieve long-term competitive advantage, it will be difficult to master a critical new management skill: recognizing when to pull the plug on product and market positions that are still enjoying the rewards of strong market performance.

Thus, the first strategic imperative to learn from the evolution of thinking on business strategy over the past four decades is the relentless and accelerating need for continuous innovation.

The Need for Meaningful Differentiation

In my business strategy course at Columbia, I often share a personal anecdote of a mundane shopping trip I recently made to purchase a bottle of shampoo. Not being the normal consumer of household staples in my home, nor being well schooled in the nuances of hair care, I was immediately overwhelmed by the task at hand when I arrived at the shampoo aisle in my local drugstore. There before me was a dizzying array of shampoo bottles in every imaginable shape, size, and color, each proclaiming to deliver More Body! Extra Sheen! Intense Softness! To my untrained eye, this cornucopia of choice presented an unfathomable challenge, the resolution of which was the selection of a now-forgotten brand in an attractive black plastic bottle adorned with white-and-gold print.

There is nothing notable or remarkable about this vignette other than to note that in too many consumer categories, producers jockey for competitive advantage, endlessly replicating each other's ephemerally distinctive features, yielding a loss of meaningful differentiation across the category as a whole. Sure, there are tangible and intangible distinctions that separate high-priced entries from budget labels in many categories, but in reality, within the consideration set of any given consumer, meaningful differentiation is often missing.

Youngme Moon captured the essence of this pervasive problem in her beautifully written book, *Different: Escaping the Competitive Herd*:[35]

> In so many consumer categories, differentiation has become hard to come by because we have fallen into a pulse of competition that in and of itself has become an impediment to its emergence. . . . Businesses that find themselves locked into this particular pattern of

competitive engagement have become masters at producing product categories filled with heterogeneous homogeneity, or dissimilar clones if you will. Which is to say that they have become masters of a particular form of imitation. Not differentiation, but imitation. Yet because this particular form of imitation is cloaked in the vernacular of differentiation, the myth of competitive separation lives on in the minds of the managers running these firms. Meanwhile, the emperor has no clothes and most consumers know it.[36]

If you have any doubt that this problem is real, ask yourself if you can clearly articulate the compelling differences in consumer value between Mitsubishi and Mazda cars, Crest and Colgate toothpaste, or Huggies and Pampers diapers. Store brands have capitalized on declining brand distinctiveness by gaining share across most categories of consumer packaged goods.

When confronted by this challenge, many of my students question whether it is possible to create meaningful differentiation in consumer packaged goods, household staples, or other products with limited emotional attachment. In their view, it's easy to envy the genius of innovators like Steve Jobs, Jeff Bezos, or Uber CEO Travis Kalanick, who have radically transformed global industries with technological wizardry, but no such opportunity exists in mundane categories like carbonated soft drinks, socks, or table wine.

Or does it? Youngme Moon suggests that the key to creating truly innovative and meaningfully differentiated products is to look for weaknesses in the category as a whole, not in individual products or brands. Take socks, for example. The potential vulnerability of this category is the very characteristic that my students assume makes socks impervious to breakthrough innovation: socks are boring! They come in matched pairs, serving purely functional needs (e.g., athletic socks vs. dress socks) that generate little emotional appeal. As a result, there is low brand awareness and little loyalty or willingness to pay premium prices in this category.

But what if one challenged all the underlying category norms that render socks so boring? What if, for example, socks were sold in threesomes, not pairs? And what if none of the socks in a set matched? Or if they came in exceptionally bright and bold patterns that were constantly updated, generating market buzz around the latest designs? You might think that such ideas are preposterous, but if so, I'm

Figure 1.4 LittleMissMatched Sock designs

guessing that you and your friends are not tweens, who have flocked to LittleMissMatched in droves to purchase just such a product.[37]

LittleMissMatched is not alone in upsetting everyday industries. In each case noted in table 1.2, innovative companies recognized the opportunity to deliver value to poorly served customers by reconstructing category norms and industry conventions to create fundamentally new bases of appeal.

W. Chan Kim and Renée Mauborgne also focused attention on the importance of meaningful differentiation in their widely acclaimed book, *Blue Ocean Strategy,* published in 2005.[38] The title draws on a marine metaphor of red and blue oceans. Red oceans refer to traditional markets, which operate within the boundaries of well-defined category norms (i.e., the third column in table 1.2), in which shark-like competitors bloody each other in an intense battle for a share of existing customers. Companies that swim in red oceans generally face slow growth, low margins and relentless price pressure. Kim and Mauborgne argue that companies can create blue oceans of uncontested market opportunity by meaningfully differentiating their products to serve not only their existing customers but also a potentially large segment of new consumers previously untapped by red ocean players.

When properly executed, blue ocean strategies can create enormous value by tapping into large unserved markets—as Nintendo did with its Wii home video game, which appealed to mass-market

TABLE 1.2
Meaningful Market Differentiation Success Stories

Company	Industry	Industry Norm
LittleMissMatched	Apparel and accessories	Socks are boring.
Swatch	Watches	Watches are functional tools; you only need one.
Cirque du Soleil	Circus/entertainment	Animals are the stars of the circus.
Novo Nordisk	Pharmaceuticals	Insulin is sold to doctors, based primarily on technical merit.
Nintendo	Gaming	The market will always reward more powerful product performance.
Casella Family Brands	Wine	Wine is for special occasions, mostly consumed by aficionados.
CNN	Television news	News is delivered in three defined time slots during the day.
Curves	Fitness	The market will always value more sophisticated equipment and high-intensity fitness classes.

consumers rather than just hard-core game enthusiasts—and rendering competition irrelevant by creating value in a fundamentally different way that is difficult to replicate, as was the case with Cirque du Soleil and CNN.

The breakout success of winners in blue ocean markets eventually attracts competition, turning blue oceans red. For example, many of the exemplars of blue ocean strategy cited in Kim and Mauborgne's book have subsequently encountered stiff competition, reaffirming the need for continuous innovation.

Thus, the second strategic imperative emerging from the evolution of business strategy thinking is the need for meaningful differentiation in the marketplace. But even if companies succeed in the metaphorical feat of becoming a cat in a dogfight, the question isn't whether they'll find themselves in yet another dogfight, but when.

Long-term profitable growth requires an ongoing ability to anticipate and respond to an evolving market.

The Need for Business Alignment

It's one thing to recognize the strategic imperative of continuous innovation aimed at creating meaningfully differentiated, market-transforming products. It's another to get an organization to align its capabilities, business practices, resources, and management incentives to strongly support the execution of this mission. The harsh reality is, in too many companies, there is a serious disconnect between the CEO's stated desire to deliver innovative customer-pleasing products and the actual day-to-day management directives that undermine this objective.

Think about your own business experience. I suspect you may have already witnessed examples of management practices that inhibit continuous innovation and meaningful product differentiation.

Sales

Salesperson compensation is often driven by short-term sales quotas, which are most easily attained by promoting proven products. New products—particularly those that require considerable effort to educate new buyers on new value propositions, or that may damage existing client relationships or cannibalize existing product sales—often get limited salesperson attention. Moreover, internal competition for advertising funds, trade promotions, and other resources often rob new product entries of the critical resources required for success.

Finance

Chief financial officers often have a limited appetite for sustained investment in R&D for breakthrough innovations with delayed paybacks. For example, in one survey of over 400 publicly traded companies, 80 percent of CFOs stated that if it looked like their company would miss earnings expectations, they would cut R&D and other discretionary budgets to meet forecasts.[39] Product R&D teams frequently struggle with uncertain funding, which is tied to annual budget cycles and susceptible to lapses in management interest and leadership changes that wipe out project sponsorship. New product initiatives are often held to unrealistic development deadlines, payback thresholds, and business plans with metrics ill-suited for early-stage ventures, resulting in high mortality rates.[40]

Human Resources

Cross-disciplinary new product development teams are often deprived of critical management skills by business unit general managers who hoard their best talent to focus on established business needs. Project leaders who try valiantly, but ultimately unsuccessfully, to launch risky new businesses are often demoted or fired, sending a strong signal to the rest of the organization about the personal risks of associating with innovative ventures.

Executive Management

Chief executive officers express near unanimous recognition of the importance of continuous innovation to their organization, but few provide effective oversight. According to a 2013 PwC survey of 246 global CEOs, 97 percent cited innovation as a top corporate priority, yet only 37 percent reported that they personally exerted leadership in this area (up from only 12 percent three years earlier).[41] In a 2008 survey, McKinsey reported that while 70 percent of senior executives identified innovation as one of their top three priorities, only 27 percent claimed that innovation was fully integrated into their corporate strategic planning process.[42] As a result, McKinsey found that nearly two-thirds of senior executives admitted being only "somewhat," "a little," or "not at all" confident in their management decisions regarding innovation.[43]

Most CEOs have a sizeable component of their annual executive compensation tied to earnings per share and stock price, which incentivizes short-term results and financial engineering over long-term reinvestment in innovation and growth. While one could argue that such compensation incentives align the interests of the CEO and the shareholders, the reality is that the proportion of corporate earnings going into share buybacks and dividends at the expense of reinvestments in corporate growth has recently reached unprecedentedly high levels. For example, in 2014, spending on buybacks and dividends by publicly traded U.S. corporations surpassed the companies' combined net income.[44] Data analyzed by William Lazonick of the University of Massachusetts confirm that since the early 1980s, when corporate restrictions on open-market buybacks were greatly eased, dividends and stock buybacks have absorbed over 80 percent of S&P 500 net income, limiting capital available for reinvestment in corporate growth.[45]

As one investment fund manager observed: "You can only go so far with financial engineering before you actually have to have a business with real growth. Companies have done about all that they can in terms of maximizing the ability to do those buybacks."[46] Consider IBM, for example. Between 2008 and 2013, it invested 102 percent of cumulative net income on stock buybacks and dividends. Over this time span, IBM's stock price nearly doubled, despite declining revenues and operating cash flows. But after reporting its fourteenth straight quarterly revenue decline in Q3 2015, IBM shares sagged to a five-year low, nearly 40 percent below their 2013 peak.

The bottom line is that there is often a serious disconnect between a company's stated strategic intent for innovation-driven growth and its actual management behaviors. We will explore the reasons for such disconnects later in this book, but suffice it to say here that contributing causes include misaligned incentives, inadequate innovation business practices, and—perhaps at a deeper level—human frailties, including the fear of the unknown, hubris, complacency, and resistance to change, that undermine effective management.

Business researchers have long recognized the need to align corporate capabilities, resources, incentives, and culture to support strategic priorities. For example, early in my career as a strategy consultant for Booz Allen Hamilton,[47] a new theory on management effectiveness emerged under the rubric "capabilities-driven strategy." In their seminal book *Competing for the Future*, C. K. Prahalad and Gary Hamel argued that market leaders owed their success to an identifiable set of core competencies, which allowed them to outperform competitors.[48] These competencies (or capabilities, as they were later called) could be engineering, product design, manufacturing expertise, supply chain optimization, or marketing prowess that enabled those who mastered them to compete in distinctive ways.[49]

For example, through the lens of capabilities-driven strategy, Walmart can be seen to be exploiting their expertise in global sourcing and supply chain optimization to build a formidable competitive advantage: offering wide product selection at everyday low prices. These same capabilities were exploited by IKEA, along with product-design expertise, to create the world's largest furniture enterprise. Nike exploited its expertise in marketing and product development to achieve global market leadership in sports equipment and apparel.

Companies pursuing a capabilities-driven strategy were encouraged to formally recognize the strategic importance of their designated core capabilities, to invest heavily to ensure ongoing competitive superiority, and to exploit market opportunities that could extend their areas of expertise.

This theme was picked up by Bain consultants Chris Zook and James Allen in their 2001 book *Profit from the Core* and the sequel, *Beyond the Core*.[50] Zook and Allen argue that most growth strategies fail to deliver value—or even destroy it—primarily because they wrongly diversify from the core business. The authors contend that building market power in a well-defined core remains the key source of competitive advantage and the most viable platform for successful expansion.

To back up their stick-to-your-knitting prescription, Zook and Allen analyzed the outcomes of hundreds of new business ventures to show that the likelihood of success declined considerably as companies moved farther afield from their proven core competencies. Each new business launch in the analysis was classified in terms of the number of adjacency steps from the core business. For example, targeting a new geography or class of customer was considered to be one adjacency step from the core. A new product technology would add a second step and new distribution channels would add yet another distancing step.

Zook and Allen's analysis showed that business launches involving only one adjacency step achieved a 37 percent success rate, beating the 30 percent success rate overall. A second step reduced the chance of success to 28 percent. And for new businesses that were three adjacency steps removed from the core, the success rate dropped below 10 percent (figure 1.5).

For example, while Walmart was perfecting its core competency of supply chain management, it sought additional growth in adjacent steps—e.g., introducing groceries at existing big-box stores and expanding its everyday low price concept to Sam's Club. In contrast,

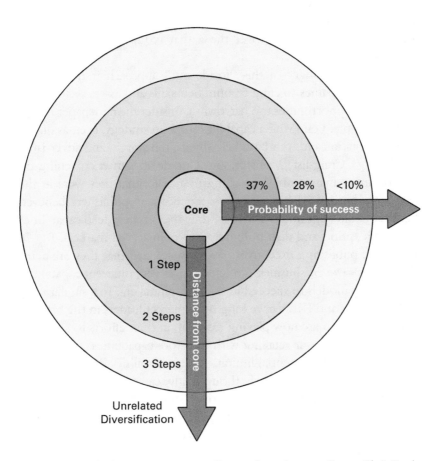

Figure 1.5 New business success rate vs. distance from the core. *Source:* Chris Zook, *Beyond the Core: Expand Your Market Without Abdandoning Your Roots* (Boston, MA: Harvard Business School Press, 2003).

Kmart failed to invest in upgrading its core capabilities, while pursuing distracting acquisitions in new product categories and geographies, including Sports Authority, OfficeMax, Waldenbooks, and Builders Square. Kmart divested many of these acquisitions before ultimately declaring bankruptcy in 2002. In a similar vein, American Express failed in its attempt to diversify into brokerage and insurance services, while its core business has continued to prosper with adjacent expansions into a number of new consumer and business credit categories.

The clear message from proponents of capabilities-driven strategy was that executional considerations—i.e., corporate competence—should guide growth strategy, with a clear bias toward opportunities that draw on existing strengths over those that require the development of new skills.

Of course, a danger of this "inside-out" approach is that it may encourage companies to cling to outdated skills and assets or to define their market opportunities too narrowly. Consider the newspaper industry, for example. Following a capabilities-driven strategy, even as digital news aggregators and web-based classifieds, job search, and advertising players (e.g., Craigslist, Monster, and Google) began encroaching on their business, many publishers clung to a belief that they were in the news*paper* business. From this perspective, many publishers believed that they could continue to thrive by drawing on their deep capabilities to compile, print, and distribute newspapers in served markets. But in retrospect, publishing executives have now learned that they are actually in the *journalism* business, which requires very different capabilities and business models to succeed in the post-digital era. In a similar vein, while Walmart and IKEA have long been market leaders in the big-box retail sector, both are now playing catch-up in their efforts to augment their brick-and-mortar retailing with webstore capabilities.

Recognizing the potential limitations of capabilities-driven strategy, a competing school of strategic thought advocates outside-in thinking for what may be called "customer-driven strategy." In their 2010 book *Strategy from the Outside In,* George Day and Christine Moorman argue that capabilities-driven strategy needs to be turned on its head.[51] In their words,

> Inside-out companies narrowly frame their strategic thinking by asking, "What can the market do for us?" rather than, "What can we do for the market?" The consequences of inside-out thinking can be seen in the way many business-to-business firms approach customer solutions. The inside-out view is that "solutions are bundles of products and services that help us sell more." The outside-in view is that "the purpose of a solution is to help our customers find value and make money—to our mutual benefit."

There is an intuitive appeal to Day and Moorman's perspective, but like any theory, there are limitations to its application. Undisciplined execution of outside-in strategies run the risk of overextending a company's ability to execute and diluting a brand's identity. As we will see repeatedly in this book, the strongest brands are defined as much by what they won't do as by what they do.

Recognizing the importance of operational excellence prompted another influential strand of strategy thinking over the past three decades. In the 1980s, shaken by the rise of the Japanese car industry at their expense, the Big Three U.S. automakers focused considerable attention on understanding the methods of lean product development and lean manufacturing pioneered by Toyota Motor Corporation. This is recounted in James Womack's and Daniel Jones's 1990 book *The Machine That Changed the World.*[52]

Ironically, Toyota developed its storied Toyota Production System by applying the teachings of an American scholar, W. Edwards Deming, who initially found Japanese executives more receptive to his recommendations than their American counterparts.[53] Deming is widely viewed as the father of the Total Quality Management and Six Sigma methods for business process improvement that gained widespread acceptance after being embraced by General Electric CEO Jack Welch in 1995.

The focus on operational excellence took a temporary backseat during dot-com bubble of the late 1990s. In those heady days, the prevailing wisdom was for startups to race for market penetration at whatever cost. Venture capital funding poured into startups that were long on vision, but lacking in executional capability. This mindset was epitomized by the meteoric rise and fall of Webvan, which went from IPO to bankruptcy in sixteen months, after burning through nearly $2 billion in capital by overextending its unproven web-based grocery business in twenty-six cities.

In the humbling wake of the bursting dot-com bubble and a deep global recession at the turn of the millennium, executive attention returned to the blocking and tackling of disciplined operational management as a prerequisite to successful strategy implementation. In *Execution: The Discipline of Getting Things Done,* consultant Ram Charan and then-CEO of Honeywell, Larry Bossidy,[54] write that their thesis "was based on our observation that the discipline of getting things done was what differentiated companies that succeeded from those that just muddled through or failed."[55] In their view, execution trumped strategy as the key driver of success.

Thus, the third strategic imperative advanced as business strategy thinking has evolved over the past four decades is the need for operational excellence and business alignment—i.e., assuring that corporate capabilities, resources, incentives, and business culture and processes are properly aligned to support a company's strategic intent.

Both strategy and execution matter

Summing It Up

Reflecting on the business strategy perspectives shared in this chapter, I believe that each has a contribution to make in answering the overarching questions posed at the beginning of this book:

- Why is it so hard to achieve and sustain long-term profitable growth?
- How can businesses achieve this?

Business strategy books tend to view the business landscape through the lens of a particular theoretical construct, which leads to a normative prescription for more effective management and better performance. When such theories are supported by credible logic, substantiating data, and relevant case studies, they often take on a life of their own; they are applied by acolytes far beyond the authors' original intent or the logical limits of the theory's extensibility.

For example, while Clayton Christensen made profoundly important contributions to our understanding of product life-cycle dynamics, there are other forms of disruptive technologies that are also significantly reshaping the competitive landscape. Executives would be well advised to be on the lookout not only for low-end and new-market disruptions as defined by Christensen but for high-end and big bang disruptions as well.

While researchers have debated the merits of pursuing an inside-out capabilities-driven strategy, or an outside-in customer-driven approach, in reality CEOs need not feel forced to make an unnecessary choice between these two opposing perspectives. A balanced view of both constructs can help guide effective strategy formulation. For example, Apple clearly pursued an outside-in strategy for the creation of the iPod, iPhone, iPad, and Apple Watch by anticipating consumer needs in music and mobile computing. These devices extended Apple far beyond its roots as a computer company, in fact prompting Steve Jobs to change the company's name from Apple Computer to Apple in

2007. But as Apple continues to seek new opportunities for growth, it is also focusing on five adjacencies to apply its core technologies—automotive, home automation, health and fitness, payments, and gaming—each of which could be significant enough to support a future large-cap business of its own.

Deploying capabilities-driven and customer-driven strategies in combination is a more nuanced view than presented by strict advocates of one theoretical construct or the other and can be highly effective.

Finally, while researchers and practitioners have made important contributions in identifying management best practices, it is overreach to say that Jim Collins's recommendations are universally applicable or to accept Charan and Bossidy's assertion that execution trumps strategy in determining business outcomes. Business strategies can be flawed in concept or execution, but both are vitally important in achieving successful outcomes.

It is my intent in this book to integrate key elements of the most influential strategy thinking of the last forty years with my own practical business experience. In the simplest terms, I will make the case that there are three strategic imperatives that drive sustained profitable growth:

---

1. *Continuous innovation*—not for its own sake, but to deliver. . . .
2. *Meaningful differentiation*—recognized and valued by consumers, enabled by. . . .
3. *Business alignment*—where all corporate capabilities, resources, incentives, and business culture and processes are aligned to support a company's strategic intent.

By continuously delivering innovative and meaningfully differentiated products and services, companies can attract and retain customers at favorable prices, while making it difficult for competitors to replicate their products and business practices. These outcomes in turn are the essential drivers of long-term profitable growth (figure 1.6).

While this prescription may seem to draw on a heavy dose of common sense, it turns out to be difficult—and rare—for companies to

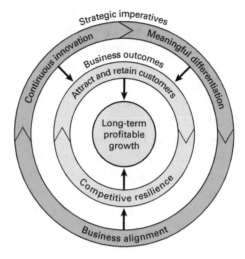

Figure 1.6 Strategic imperatives for long-term profitable growth

actually incorporate these three strategic imperatives as the foundation of their business strategy. The objective of this book is to explore why this is and what to do about it.

The next chapter will begin our journey to explore the application of this prescription by showing how two companies—Casella Family Brands[56] and Southwest Airlines—achieved tremendous success in highly challenged industries.

CHAPTER TWO

There's No Such Thing as a Bad Industry

BY ANY MEASURE, the U.S. wine industry has always been a tough business to make money in.

In 2000, the $20 billion U.S. wine market was slow growing, intensely competitive, fragmented, highly regulated, and subject to global over-supply and growing import competition. Over 6,500 largely undistin-guished brands competed for the attention of distributors, retailers, and consumers in a country that consumed ten times more beer than wine, and where three-fourths of American adults never purchased wine at all. Not surprisingly, few new entries made market headway in this environment, and profitability proved elusive for most vineyards.

And yet despite these challenging conditions, a new product from a small vineyard in southeastern Australia grew to become the top-selling imported wine in the United States within five years of its 2001 market entry.

The story of Casella Family Brands (CFB) and Yellow Tail wine is an inspirational example of how to succeed by becoming a cat in a dogfight. Figure 2.1 provides a vivid picture of what successful growth looks like. How did they manage it?

Industry Norms in the U.S. Wine Market

Americans drank relatively little wine in 2000—on average, about one bottle per adult per month, roughly one-tenth the per capita con-sumption of France or Italy. Furthermore, U.S. wine consumption

Figure 2.1a Casella Family Brands facilities, 1994

Figure 2.1b Casella Family Brands facilities, 2006. Photos courtesy of Deutsch Family Wine & Spirits. All rights reserved.

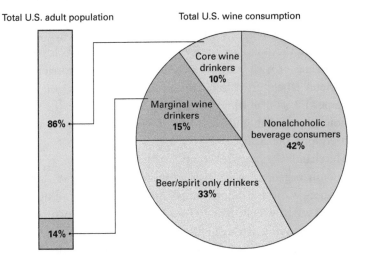

Figure 2.2 Wine consumption by type of consumer. The traditional industry customer focus was on core wine drinkers, the 10 percent of the adult population who accounted for 86 percent of U.S. wine consumption. Yellow Tail targeted 48 percent of the U.S. population who either drank only beer and spirits (33 percent) or who were marginal wine drinkers (15 percent). *Source*: Merrill Research & Associates, Wine Trends and Market Analysis.

was driven primarily by a small segment of committed wine enthusiasts: three-fourths of American adults did not consume any wine, while core wine drinkers, representing only one-tenth of the adult population, accounted for 86 percent of total consumption (see figure 2.2).[1]

While there were cultural and historical reasons for wine's lack of popularity in the United States, widely accepted industry norms passed down through generations also contributed to the uneasiness of U.S. consumers over wine:

- Old world wines offered a sophisticated, complex, and acquired taste that many first-time or casual wine drinkers found unappealing.
- Many premium wines are designed to be aged in the bottle after purchase, rather than sold for everyday casual consumption, and are often reserved for special occasions.

- Brand variety was overwhelming, even for wine connoisseurs. For example, over thirteen thousand distinct wine SKUs were sold in U.S. supermarkets. A well-stocked wine store was likely to carry over one thousand separate brands, many with labels in foreign languages or with confusing enological product descriptors.
- Varietal labels are often confusing, as countries use different names for similar wines (e.g., Burgundy is made with the pinot noir grape; syrah and shiraz are alternative names for the grape used for Côte-Rôtie).
- Merchandising practices compounded the confusion, as stores frequently organized wine displays by country of origin, rather than by grape variety, making comparative shopping more difficult.[2]
- Prices varied widely, from "Two-Buck Chuck" to two-thousand-dollar vintage Château Lafite Rothschild.
- On a dollar-per-drink basis, wine tended to be more expensive than beer or spirits.

It is not surprising that many Americans—including some of the relatively small (25 percent) segment of adults who did consume the product—found wine confusing, if not downright intimidating. According to a 2002 survey, more than 80 percent of U.S. wine drinkers felt their product knowledge was average or below average, 40 percent felt overwhelmed by the selection, and 34 percent did not recognize brand names, leading consumers to hesitate in choosing a wine.[3] About one-third of American adults avoided wine altogether in favor of other alcoholic beverages like beer or spirits. According to one widely recognized wine expert, "Thirty-five percent of the population drinks alcoholic beverages but they don't drink wine. They've tried it; they don't like it. We don't interview them much because they've said they don't like wine so we're not going to find out about wine. Can those people be moved over? Who knows? But probably not."[4]

This is a classic case of the dogfight mentality that pervades most industries. In this case, thousands of producers were clawing for a piece of a relatively small market—the 10 percent of the adult population who were regular wine drinkers—with products that many consumers viewed as undifferentiated, confusing, and off-putting. The industry assumed that nonconsumers were unreachable and saw no reason to question whether their own business practices were in fact limiting consumer interest. And when CFB first entered the U.S. market, it fell into exactly the same trap.

Casella Family Brands's U.S. Market Entry

Casella Family Brands was founded in 1969 by a Sicilian immigrant from an Italian winemaking family who arrived in Australia in the 1950s. Filippo Casella was an itinerant farmhand until he had saved enough to buy a forty-acre plot of land in New South Wales, and he began by selling his wine and grapes in bulk to other name-brand vineyards.

In 1994, the founder's middle son John took over the business after studying enology at Charles Sturt University in Wagga Wagga and working for another Australian winemaker. Seeking to grow his father's operations with the family's own brand of quality wine, Casella hired an experienced executive from an export-oriented competitor to lead an expansion effort. The new export manager coveted new markets, particularly the United States. But as a small and unproven Australian vineyard without an established label seeking to sell in the intensely competitive premium wine segment, the company needed assistance, so Casella turned to the Australian Trade Commission to help him find an American distribution partner.

Around the same time, about twelve thousand miles away in White Plains, New York, Bill Deutsch, founder and CEO of Deutsch Family Wines & Spirits (DFWS), and his son Peter were looking to expand their U.S. wine import business. At the time, Deutsch was importing approximately three hundred thousand cases of wine per year, mostly French, distributed through relationships DFWS had built with dozens of distributors across the United States. Deutsch was interested in diversifying the company's wine portfolio and began exploring potential imports from other countries.

Deutsch saw the opportunity to introduce a fighter brand from Australia and contacted the Australian Trade Commission seeking suggestions for a suitable vineyard partner. Deutsch's inquiry came within days of Casella's similar request, and the connection was soon made. Meeting for the first time at a trade show in San Francisco in 1997, Deutsch and Casella agreed to team up. "It was a perfect match," Deutsch recalled, "two smallish, family-owned businesses looking for growth opportunities; I had a hunch it would work out."[5]

Casella offered access to a new source of lower-priced premium wines, and in turn Deutsch offered coveted access to the U.S. market.

They agreed that in exchange for half-ownership of the brand, DFWS would market CFB's wines in the United States. Shortly thereafter, Casella and Deutsch launched a line of wines in the United States under the Carramar Estate label.

Casella followed conventional wisdom by naming his wine after a local landmark (in this case, an aboriginal vineyard site) to give the brand a sense of terroir and history: Carramar means "by shady tree" and estate conveys a place of stature. The bottle label was adorned with an ornate shield and crown, in stark contrast to the vineyard's humble facilities at the time (figure 2.1 and figure 2.3). Carramar Estate was priced at $9.99, joining thousands of other undistinguished brands in the intensely competitive U.S. premium-wine segment.

Figure 2.3 Casella Family Brands wine labels

Given its "me too" positioning, it is not surprising that Carramar Estate achieved only modest success, selling just twenty thousand cases in its first year. Shortly thereafter, the brand faced a setback as reports began surfacing that consumers were returning purchases to their retailer for a refund, complaining the wine was "corked." Casella discovered that a batch of tainted corks had been supplied for the Carramar Estate wines the company had shipped to the United States. "John Casella was mortified by this incident," recalled Deutsch. "He gave me his assurance to buy back all unsold bottles and offered to withdraw from our partnership. I reminded him that I was committed to a long-term partnership and encouraged Casella to come back with a more interesting wine."

The disappointing Carramar Estate launch proved to be the catalyst that drove Casella and Deutsch to rethink their underlying assumptions of how to compete in the U.S. wine market.

The Birth of Yellow Tail

As Casella contemplated how to produce a wine that would be more distinctive in the crowded U.S. market, he decided to challenge all the conventional wisdoms and industry norms that defined how wines should taste, what they should cost, and how they should be branded, marketed, retailed, and sold in the U.S. market. In other words, instead of rejoining a dogfight, he decided to become a cat.

First was the product. Casella spotted an opportunity to create a wine with a pleasant fruity taste at a lower price—$6 for a 750 ml bottle—to appeal to a broader market than Carramar Estate had. He set out to create an approachable, everyday wine that overdelivered on taste relative to its price, appealing not only to current wine drinkers but also to the larger number of nonconsumers who had previously shunned wine because they didn't like the taste, price, or complexity of traditional offerings.

Both Bill and Peter Deutsch were immediately enthusiastic, noting "it was delicious; an easygoing wine, uncomplicated and fun to drink." Echoing these sentiments, Jon Fredrikson, publisher of an influential California wine industry newsletter, commented that Yellow Tail turned out to be "the perfect wine for a public grown up on soft drinks."[6]

For brand imagery, Casella turned to a graphic artist in Adelaide, who offered a yellow-and-orange rendering of a yellow-footed rock wallaby (a smaller cousin to the kangaroo), evocative of Australian aboriginal art. The yellow-tailed image was seen as friendly and readily identifiable with Australian culture. Casella paid less than five thousand dollars for the design, which served to anchor the development of a marketing campaign for the new wine.

And the brackets used to depict the [yellow tail] brand name? Casella was looking up "kangaroo" in a textbook when he came across the definition of a wallaby. In the margin, alongside the Latin name was the Australian version in brackets: [yellow tail]. Casella decided to keep the brackets to set the wine apart and to use the lowercase spelling to further communicate the brand's lack of pretension.

To reinforce the lack of pretension and the approachability of the wines, Casella decided to shun standard industry practices that had been widely accepted for thousands of years. First, unlike virtually all premium wine competitors, he used the same Bordeaux-style bottle shape for both red and white wines. And second, he avoided enological terminology and ebullient descriptions of terroir on the labels.

For example, a typical premium French wine sold in the United States might carry the following descriptions on its label:

> Château de Fontenille is a splendid property situated in the middle of sixty-five hectares, of which forty hectares are planted with vines, near the ancient abbey of La Sauve Majeure. Aged for eighteen months, 50 percent in oak barrels and 50 percent in a vat. A very harmonious wine with rich red-fruit aromas and silky tannins. Can be kept under good conditions for five to seven years.

In contrast, the far simpler description on the back of a Yellow Tail Shiraz bottle read:

> For three generations, the Casella family has been making wine at their winery in the small town of Yenda in South Eastern Australia. It is here that [yellow tail] is created with a simple purpose in mind: to make a great wine that everyone can enjoy. [yellow tail] is everything a great wine should be. It's approachable, fresh, flavorsome, and has a personality all of its own.[7]

As Casella explained, "We said right from the beginning that we were unpretentious. Heck, we had a kangaroo on the label. We used bright colors. When you turn the bottle around and read the back, the label in no way talks about where the wine comes from, or what the oak barrel maturation was."[8]

Bill Deutsch was somewhat apprehensive about the unusual bottle and label designs at first. Using animals and bright colors on wine labels was just not done at that time, but Peter Deutsch loved the new label. Since he liked the wine, Bill Deutsch agreed to take twenty-five thousand cases for the last seven months of 2001.

The next stage in the birth of Yellow Tail was marketing. Deutsch and Casella continued to break from traditional business practices in how they set out to market and sell the new product in the United States, reinforcing its distinctive brand personality. First, they tapped into Americans' image of Australia as a country of fun and adventure by providing wine-store clerks—many with little wine-selling experience or knowledge of Australia—with indigenous bushman's hats and oilskin jackets to wear at work. Even delivery-truck drivers were adorned with the stylish Australian clothing, to help retailers identify—and perhaps recommend—Yellow Tail. To stimulate impulse purchases, Deutsch and Casella designed colorful endcap displays to set it apart from the competing brands stacked up on wine store and supermarket shelves.

To appeal to nonconsumers intimidated by wine, Deutsch and Casella deliberately kept the Yellow Tail product line simple and attractively priced. At launch, there were only two varietals—Shiraz and Chardonnay—in two bottle sizes. Introductory pricing was highly competitive: five to six dollars for the standard size and ten to eleven dollars for the 1.5 liter bottles, placing Yellow Tail within the popular-premium category, despite a taste that compared favorably with wines costing considerably more. As the widely regarded wine critic Robert M. Parker noted, "In some circles it is fashionable to criticize wine of this genre, but if the truth be known, these are surprisingly well-made offerings."[9]

Yellow Tail wines were an instant hit in the United States. Within six months, sales exceeded 225,000 cases, nearly ten times Deutsch's initial market forecast. The first batches sold out so quickly that an additional supply had to be shipped by plane at considerable expense. Demand quickly outstripped CFB's vineyard capacity and additional grapes had to be bought on the bulk market, temporarily cutting into CFB's thin margins.

By 2002, after only one year on the market, Yellow Tail sales jumped to 1.2 million cases, becoming the number-two Australian wine in the United States. By 2006, sales topped eight million cases, equivalent in volume to Yellow Tail's next five top Australian competitors combined, and exceeding the amount imported from all French producers.

Competitors responded aggressively to Yellow Tail's success. Believing the colorful marsupial was the key, many of the world's wine producers, large and small, responded with hundreds of imitation "critter brands," sporting labels like Porcupine Ridge, Donkey & Goat, Little Penguin, and Smoking Loon. From 2003 to 2006, nearly one in five of the new wines launched in the U.S. market featured an animal on the label, yet none captured widespread consumer interest. Sizing up his competition in 2006, Deutsch noted, "Stores are beginning to look more like zoos than wine retailers." He added, "The wine cemetery is beginning to fill up with animal labels that thought they could emulate Yellow Tail, but they missed it completely in price, positioning and taste and many of these wines are now being closed out or dumped; they will be gone in thirty to sixty days."

Why Did Yellow Tail Succeed?

The story of Yellow Tail reaffirms the prescription for three strategic imperatives to drive profitable growth:

1. *Continuous innovation*—not for its own sake, but to deliver. . . .
2. *Meaningful differentiation*—recognized and valued by consumers, enabled by . . .
3. *Business alignment*—where all corporate capabilities, resources, incentives, and business culture and processes are aligned to support a company's strategic intent.

In this case, no breakthrough technology was required for Yellow Tail's extraordinary success. John Casella is a talented winemaker who created a great-tasting wine at an attractively low price. But there were already thousands of excellent wines on the market. The key innovation was recognizing a unique, untapped opportunity to serve the large number of U.S. consumers that were mostly ignored by thousands of undifferentiated, expensive, and overly complex products on the U.S. wine market. With Yellow Tail, Deutsch and Casella created meaningful differentiation—an approachable, affordable wine for everyday consumption that could be enjoyed by both experienced and new consumers.[10] In the process, they broke a number of industry conventions: Kangaroos on the label! Bushman's hats! Simple language! No barrel aging! Only one bottle shape! As a result, Yellow Tail was dismissed by wine purists, but loved by consumers.

Yellow Tail's contrarian approach also underscores the third key element driving the brand's success—the alignment of all the business practices of CFB and DFWS to support the desired brand positioning. As noted in figure 2.4, a number of interrelated strategic and

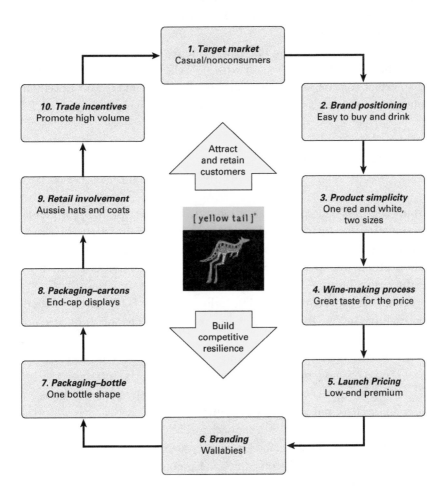

Figure 2.4 Yellow Tail's business alignment

operational decisions went into creating Yellow Tail's brand persona. The collective result was a wine that was appreciated by a large number of new and casual wine consumers and that had competitive resilience against a multitude of imitators.

In 2003, over one-fourth of Yellow Tail consumers were first-time wine drinkers—either category-expansion converts from other alcoholic beverages (mostly beer) or new buyers in the alcoholic-beverage category. Purchase patterns also suggested that wine drinkers who shifted from other brands consumed Yellow Tail wine more frequently.[11] An increasing number of Yellow Tail buyers, including many recent wine converts, bought more wine, more often, than buyers of competing brands. Casella's vision to create a wine for everyday enjoyment rather than as a special-occasion luxury had clearly gained acceptance in the marketplace.

Commenting on Yellow Tail's success in the U.S. market, wine newsletter publisher Jon Fredrikson wrote, "Yellow Tail caught the wave. It's perfect for the newest generation of wine drinkers and potential wine drinkers . . . it's the biggest achievement in the history of wine."[12]

How Southwest Airlines Also Avoided a Dogfight by Becoming a Cat

In my business strategy course at Columbia, I often ask MBA students to suggest an industry cursed with particularly awful structural characteristics, at least as assessed by Michael Porter's Five Forces framework. The sector they most frequently nominate for this dubious distinction is the airline industry.

That's an excellent choice. The airline industry is highly challenged on each of the five forces we saw in the previous chapter (figure 1.1):

1. Bargaining power of consumers: Multiple airlines typically compete on most routes, and with the advent of the Internet, pricing transparency and the ability to rapidly compare and book fares have put the buyer in control.
2. Bargaining power of suppliers: The airlines' two biggest expenses—fuel and labor—are strongly influenced by powerful constituencies—oil companies and unions—which makes it difficult for airlines to exercise direct control over their factor costs.

3. Threat of new entrants: Despite its capital intensity and razor-thin margins, the airline industry has always had an irresistible allure. There have been dozens of new entrants to the U.S. airline industry over the past three decades. As Virgin America founder Richard Branson once waggishly said, "If you want to be a millionaire, start with a billion dollars and launch a new airline."

4. Threat of substitutes: Airline passenger demand in the United States has grown at only 1.1 percent per year over the past two decades,[13] and improvements in virtual meeting technologies pose an ongoing threat, particularly to lucrative business travel.

5. Industry rivalry: To make matters worse, the airline industry is cursed—every day, 100 percent of its product inventory becomes obsolete. In contrast, imagine you are in the business of selling canned peas. If your product doesn't sell on any given day, you can hope to have better luck the following day, perhaps with a promotional offer. But once an airplane departs its gate, the available seats onboard are gone forever. And given the high fixed costs of running an airline, there is a very strong incentive for airlines to place butts in seats on every flight. No wonder there has been intense price competition since the U.S. airline industry was deregulated in 1978.

Given these factors, it is not surprising that the airline industry as a whole failed to meet its cost of capital for decades. According to data from the International Air Transport Association, the airline industry generated an average return on invested capital (ROIC) of 4.1 percent between 2004 and 2011, a small improvement on the 3.8 percent achieved in the 1996 to 2004 cycle. This remains well below the weighted average cost of capital, which falls in a range of 7 percent to 9 percent across the industry.[14]

Michael Porter noticed the travails of airlines in that this industry falls at the very bottom of a long list of U.S. industries ranked by ROIC over the period 1992 to 2006. In a 2008 reprise of his original article on the Five Forces framework, Porter presented the data shown in figure 2.5 to reaffirm his premise that "bad" industries suffer poor returns.[15]

During this era, Wall Street certainly took notice. In figure 2.6, it can be seen that the stock price of American Airlines hardly budged over the sixteen-year period from 1990 to 2006, during which the S&P

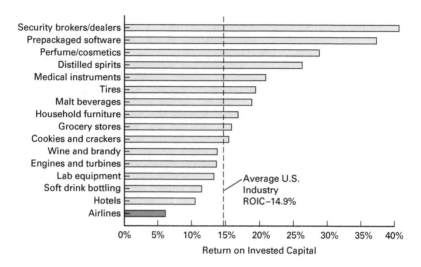

Figure 2.5 Average ROIC in U.S. industries, 1992–2006

500 grew by 237 percent. None of the other major airlines—United, Delta, Continental and U.S. Airways—appear on this chart because they all went bankrupt during this period (as did American Airlines itself in 2011).

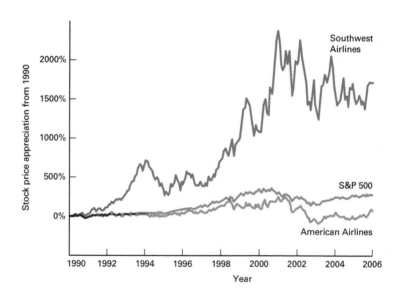

Figure 2.6 Airline industry stock prices

Given all of this evidence, why would anyone want to enter an industry with such dismal performance? The answer with respect to airlines is the same as it was with Yellow Tail wine. If the choice is either to enter a poorly performing industry, playing by the same rules as incumbent market leaders, or to stay out of the business entirely, Michael Porter's and Warren Buffett's cautionary advice is well taken.

But there is a third way, and that is to recognize that the industry as a whole may be missing an attractive opportunity to address an unserved market that can be tapped only by playing by a very different set of rules. One airline that chose to become a cat in a dogfight was Southwest Airlines, which launched as an intrastate Texas carrier in 1971, and has since grown to become the largest domestic passenger-carrying airline in the United States.

Initially, Southwest focused on a segment of the market that was poorly or not at all served by traditional airlines—leisure and budget-conscious business travelers who primarily used personal automobiles (or buses) for relatively short trips. As such, Southwest wasn't just trying to pry market share loose from existing competitors (although like Yellow Tail, they did in fact do so), but also to expand the market by appealing to consumers who previously did not fly.

Prior to Southwest's entry, the legacy airlines like American and Delta primarily focused on the lucrative segment of price-insensitive business travelers, offering an array of amenities that contributed to the high cost of air travel. Herb Kelleher, the co-founder and CEO of Southwest, recognized that the company could expand and capture a bigger market by making airline travel considerably less expensive (initially 60 percent lower than prevailing coach fares), more convenient (by offering more frequent departures from less-congested airports), and more pleasant (with consistently friendly in-flight service) than competing airlines. But to do so he had to break from established industry norms and strategically align Southwest's business practices to support meaningfully differentiated air-travel services.

Less Expensive

At first glance, one might conclude that the key to Southwest's ability to profitably offer lower fares than its competitors reflects its no-frills product offering: one airplane type, relatively short flights, one class of service, no meals, no assigned seats and service from less-congested airports. But an additional consideration was that each of these operational elements also contributed to Southwest's ability to turn around its inbound flights in half the time taken by competing airlines (or less). Over the course of a day, Southwest's sub-twenty-minute turnarounds allowed Kelleher to schedule one or two additional flights with the same aircraft and crew—a significant productivity advantage that remains to this day. Established airlines could not replicate Southwest's productivity advantage, given their route structure, fleet type, labor work rules, multiple-class cabin service, and congested airport locations. Even when legacy carriers tried to mimic Southwest's low-price service model, their cost structures were not competitive, and nearly all shuttered their low-cost carrier subsidiaries after suffering years of significant operating losses. In contrast, 2015 marked the forty-third consecutive year that Southwest reported a positive net income.

More Convenient

Another benefit of Southwest's operating practices was greater passenger convenience. Faster turnarounds meant Southwest could offer more frequent departures than competitors. Its emphasis on point-to-point service rather than hub-and-spoke networks reduced door-to-door travel times for many travelers. And by operating from less-congested secondary airports—e.g., Love Field rather than Dallas/Fort Worth International Airport—airport access and on-time airline performance for most customers was enhanced.

More Pleasant

From Southwest's inception, Kelleher recognized the critical importance of employee satisfaction in delivering a customer-friendly service. Southwest has consistently scored at or near the top of airline rankings for employee and customer satisfaction in an industry better known for sour labor relations and surly customer service.[16] For anecdotal illustrations of Southwest's friendly customer service, try searching for "Southwest Airlines flight attendant" on YouTube for examples recorded by appreciative passengers.

Researchers have studied Southwest for years to understand its hiring, training, and compensation techniques to better understand how the airline has maintained such high levels of employee engagement and customer satisfaction, despite its continued growth.[17] Southwest was one of the first airlines to establish profit sharing for all employees (in 1973) and through its first forty-three years of operations, it has never imposed an employee layoff. More broadly, Kelleher insists that Southwest's positive employee relations primarily reflect a corporate culture that was established and nurtured from day one:

> Years ago, the business schools used to pose it as a conundrum. They would say, "Well, who comes first? Your employees, your shareholders, or your customers?" But it's not a conundrum. Your employees come first. And if you treat your employees right, guess what? Your customers come back, and that makes your shareholders happy. Start with employees and the rest follows.[18]

In summary, Southwest Airlines had the innovative spark to recognize an opportunity to create meaningful differentiation in the airline industry to attract new and existing customers, and strategically aligned all its business practices to effectively capture market share and profitable growth.

As shown earlier in figure 2.6, while historical market leaders like American Airlines were struggling to avoid bankruptcy, Southwest Airlines emerged as one of the highest market cap gainers on the U.S. stock market for decades.

Can the Yellow Tail and Southwest Cases Be Generalized?

These two case studies illustrate that even in "bad" industries, plagued by considerable structural challenges, newcomers who are willing to break from industry norms and play by different rules can achieve considerable success. And while CFB/DFWS and Southwest Airlines were certainly innovative in strategically aligning their resources to deliver meaningful market differentiation, no miraculous technological breakthrough was required in either case to create value in the marketplace.

This raises the important question of how easy it is to generalize these results. Are Yellow Tail and Southwest anomalies, or are there winners (as well as losers) in every industry? Two Booz & Company consultants, Evan Hirsh and Kasturi Rangan, recently published a clear answer to this question by analyzing the total shareholder return

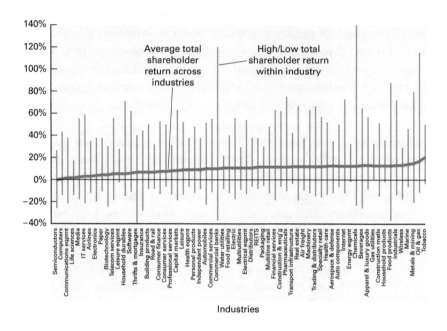

Figure 2.7 Compound annual growth in total shareholder returns, 2001–2011, hi/lo/median by industry

(TSR)[19] from 6,138 companies within sixty-five industries spanning every facet of the global economy between 2001 and 2011.[20] The results in figure 2.7 show that the variance in business performance within a given industry is considerably higher than the variance in the average performance across industries. In other words, there are individual star performers in every industry, regardless of the performance level of an industry as a whole.

Two other insights from figure 2.7 reinforce this important point. Firstly, the average TSR of firms in the top quartile of this distribution (from auto components through tobacco) is 17 percent or higher. Yet the top performer in every industry achieves a TSR of at least 17 percent, and even in the lowest performing quartile, half of the industries listed have at least one company posting a TSR of over 40 percent for the decade.

Secondly, the difference in average TSR between the "best" and "worst" of the sixty-five industries is only 20 percentage points. In contrast, the top companies in each industry have annual TSRs that are on average 72 percent higher than the average TSRs of the companies in a given industry.

The inescapable conclusion from this analysis is that there are exceptionally high performing companies in every industry, regardless of the structural challenges facing the industry as a whole.

In the previous chapter, I quoted Warren Buffett's observation that when a manager with a good reputation meets an industry with a bad reputation, it is normally the industry that leaves with its reputation intact. The analysis presented in this chapter would suggest that an alternative viewpoint is more relevant: Enlightened strategy and effective execution can trump industry structure in driving business success in any industry.

As a corollary to the finding that companies can achieve outstanding performance in any industry, it also should be noted that "good" industries—i.e., those that score well in Porter's Five Forces framework or stand out as stars in BCG's growth–share matrix—can't necessarily count on superior performance over the long term. To illustrate this, consider another analysis from Hirsch and Rangan, who not only looked at the performance of sixty-five industries between 2001 and 2011 (see figure 2.7) but also at how these industries performed over the previous decade. As shown in figure 2.8, of all the industries whose

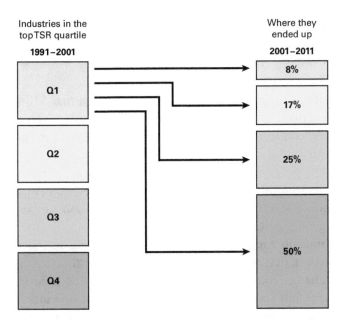

Figure 2.8 Top-performing industries over successive decades

financial performance ranked in the top quartile in the decade 1991–2001, only 8 percent were top performers in the following decade. In fact, three-fourths of the former high flyers actually performed below the median in the following decade.

Implications for Job Seekers and Employees

These results suggest that an industry's past performance is at best an unreliable predictor of future success, and at worst may even suggest the likelihood of a pending fall from grace. This issue is relevant to the legion of MBA graduates and working professionals who aspire to work in "hot" industries. But, as venture capitalist Marc Andreessen cautioned, "MBA graduating classes are actually a reliable contrary indicator: if they all want to go into investment banking, there's going to be a financial crisis. If they want to go into tech, that means a bubble is forming."[21]

Andreessen's assertion has been echoed by others. For example, in his 1989 Wall Street memoir *Liar's Poker,* Michael Lewis observed that "the first thing you learn on the trading floor is that when large numbers of people are after the same commodity, be it a stock, a bond or a job, the commodity quickly becomes overvalued." This argument suggests the likelihood of boom-and-bust cycles when industries are forced to make a correction after hiring too many MBAs at inflated compensation levels.[22]

While there is no statistical validity to the claim that MBA preferences can actually predict future industry performance,[23] it is true that job seekers tend to flock to industries enjoying strong current performance.[24] In the time I've been recruiting from or teaching in business schools, the popularity of individual industries has definitely waxed and waned. In some years, investment banking has been at the top of the list, while in other years MBAs have coveted jobs in consulting, technology, luxury goods, or health services.

But based on the evidence presented in this chapter, job seekers should expect that the competitive landscape in "hot industries" is likely to change considerably over time. It is not the industry per se that ensures job security and strong financial performance, but the enlightened management actions of companies like Casella Family Brands, Southwest Airlines, and the other nameless winners depicted in figure 2.7.

The implication for job seekers is a personalized version of the cat-in-a-dogfight metaphor. When the job-seeking herd is moving strongly towards one particular industry, your best bet may be to move in a different direction: choosing a specific company, regardless of current industry performance, based on three considerations:

- A business that really interests you.
- A management team you truly believe in.
- An opportunity where you can make a difference in driving innovation and meaningful product differentiation.

Coda: Have Yellow Tail and Southwest Airlines Continued to Succeed?

As successful as they have been, Yellow Tail wine and Southwest Airlines provide clear examples of how competitive advantages can shift dramatically over time.

After popularizing a new category of affordable, everyday wines and growing rapidly for five years, Yellow Tail sales plateaued at around eight million cases in the mid-2000s. Casella Family Brands and DFWS struggled with several adverse developments in the U.S. market.

In 2005, E. & J. Gallo Winery, the largest U.S. wine retailer, acquired Barefoot Cellars, a mid-sized California vineyard with its own strong populist brand identity.[25] Under Gallo ownership, Barefoot expanded its range of wine offerings at price points similar to Yellow Tail. Moreover, Gallo heavily promoted Barefoot on a national scale, and used its influence as category captain with major grocery and retail chains to secure favorable merchandising and promotional support. As a result, Barefoot grew at a compound annual growth rate of 47 percent between 2005 and 2013, overtaking Yellow Tail as the sales leader in the six-to-eight-dollar table wine price range (figure 2.9)[26]

The Australian dollar strengthened relative to U.S. currency by 40 percent between 2009 and 2013, putting severe margin pressure on CFB's exports. Given intense price competition in the U.S. wine market and ample supplies of American-grown grapes, Yellow Tail chose not to raise prices to offset adverse currency shifts.

In 2013, Costco, the world's largest wine retailer and Yellow Tail's largest customer, announced that it would stop carrying Yellow Tail in favor of its low-price own-brand label, Kirkland.

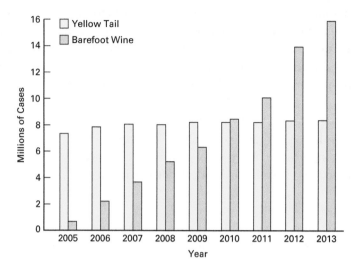

Figure 2.9 Yellow Tail vs. Barefoot wine sales, 2005–2013, in millions of cases

With a strengthening U.S. economy, consumer wine preferences shifted upscale. As shown in figure 2.10, wines in Yellow Tail's six-to-eight-dollar price range exhibited the largest decline in sales in 2014, while wines priced at or above ten dollars per bottle enjoyed double-digit revenue increases between 2013 and 2014.[27]

Casella Family Brands and DFWS have pursued a number of tactics to re-energize growth, including expanding their product range to include more than twenty varietals, blends, and sparkling wines, offering additional bottle sizes, increasing television advertising, and targeting social media. The company has also considered a number of more ambitious strategic brand extensions, including wine-to-go packaging, frozen sangrias, and expansion into additional alcoholic and non-alcoholic beverage categories. Time will tell if lightning can strike twice in creating a new growth platform for Yellow Tail in the United States.

Southwest Airlines has also had to adjust to a very different business environment in recent years. While the airline industry as a whole has benefitted from consolidation-driven capacity rationalization and declining fuel prices, Southwest has faced stiffer competition. After exploiting its low-cost position against weakened legacy airlines through the early 2000s, Southwest now finds itself sandwiched

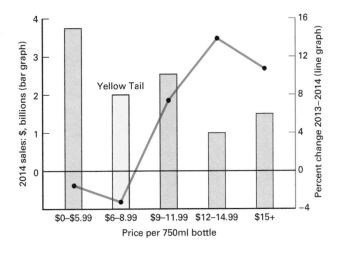

Figure 2.10 U.S. wine sales trends by price range

between increasingly efficient larger airlines like American, Delta, and United at the high end, and no-frills carriers like Allegiant Air and Spirit at the low end (figure 2.11).[28] In addition, relatively recent entrants JetBlue and Virgin America have been gaining share by offering customer-pleasing in-flight amenities like roomier cabins, leather seats, and premium snacks at competitively low fares. With intensifying competition, Southwest's workforce relations—once a significant source of competitive advantage—have grown increasingly contentious, as the airline struggles to control labor costs.

Nonetheless, Southwest has continued to prosper by exploiting the three strategic imperatives for profitable growth. By acquiring AirTran Airways in 2010, Southwest added international service that gives it a strong base for future expansion. Southwest has also maintained its claim for meaningful differentiation by remaining one of the few airlines to not charge fees for checked baggage or reservation changes, and it has improved in-flight amenities, e.g., providing onboard Wi-Fi. Southwest's continued business alignment to support productive operations has allowed it to maintain cost competitiveness despite having some of the highest wages in the U.S. passenger airline business.[29] Between 2012 and 2015, Southwest was one of the most profitable and fastest-growing airlines in the United States, with

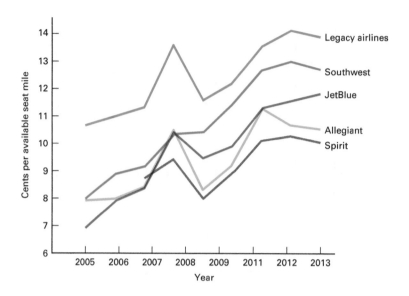

Figure 2.11 Airline Operating Costs, 2005–2013. Competitive cost problems for airlines.

more than double the stock-price appreciation of the rest of the U.S. airline industry.

In summary, there is no such thing as a bad industry. In any industry, companies that can identify and exploit opportunities to offer meaningful differentiation and strategically align their organizations to effectively deliver products and services can enjoy sustained growth and profitability. However, no company can afford to rest on its laurels, and continuous innovation is a prerequisite for superior performance over the long term.

CHAPTER THREE

Why Are We in Business?

THE TITLE OF this chapter sounds like a simple enough question, but in recent years an impassioned debate has raged over very different views of the purpose of a business enterprise. Before spending any more time exploring business strategies, we should probably agree on what business executives should be trying to accomplish in the first place.

In the first class of my business strategy course at Columbia Business School, I often ask my MBA students the following question in intentionally broad terms: "If you were lucky enough to land a job as the CEO of a publicly traded corporation after graduation, what would be your highest priority during the first few years?" I add the caveat that "obviously business circumstances vary, but think about the most generally applicable business purpose that would guide your decision-making."

After basking momentarily in the glory of their hypothetical good fortune, the most common answer from my students is "to maximize shareholder value," followed by "build a strong management team," "achieve market-share leadership," and "drive socially responsible corporate behavior."

The primacy of shareholder returns in shaping the thinking of next-generation business leaders is not surprising. Maximizing shareholder value (MSV) is preached as gospel at business schools, backed by an elegant and compelling theory supported by Nobel Laureates and other luminaries.

The Doctrine of Shareholder Value Maximization

The origin of the MSV doctrine is often attributed to one of the most widely cited academic business articles of all time: "Theory of the Firm: Managerial Behavior, Agency Costs and Ownership Structure," by Harvard economist Michael Jensen and William Meckling, then Dean of Simon Business School at the University of Rochester.[1]

Jensen and Meckling and other MSV supporters note that of all stakeholders in a public corporation, only outside shareholders face the risk of receiving no return on their contributions to the firm, and therefore only they are entitled to profits if and when they materialize. As such, shareholders—the principals who own the enterprise—are entitled to the value created by the organization.

In this view, corporate executives serve as agents of the principals, and their job is to manage the company so as to maximize value that can be extracted by the principals. To avoid conflicts between the objectives of principals and their agents, Jensen and Meckling suggested that firms should turn their executives into major shareholders by offering generous stock-based compensation packages. In this way, both managers and shareholders would share a common MSV goal.

Jensen and Meckling had powerful allies to support their views on MSV, including Nobel Laureate Milton Friedman[2] and two legendary CEOs who created enormous value for their shareholders (and themselves) in the 1980s and 1990s: Roberto Goizueta of Coca-Cola and Jack Welch of General Electric.

In 1970, Friedman wrote an article in the *New York Times* titled "The Social Responsibility of Business Is to Increase Its Profits," in which he fiercely defended the MSV doctrine, asserting that any deviation from managerial adherence to maximizing profits and shareholder value would undermine the bedrock of American capitalism: the efficient allocation of capital to value-maximizing activities for the good of the country as a whole.[3]

Jack Welch also became an outspoken proponent of the MSV doctrine. Shortly after becoming CEO of General Electric in 1981, Welch gave a speech outlining his beliefs in divesting underperforming businesses and aggressively cutting costs in order to deliver consistent profit increases that would outstrip global economic growth.

He told analysts, "GE will be the locomotive pulling the GNP, not the caboose following it."[4]

Over the next twenty years, Jack Welch delivered on his prophecy. Under his leadership, GE's market value grew from $14 billion to $484 billion, making it the highest-valued company in the world. Over one twelve-year stretch, GE met or beat consensus analyst earnings forecasts in forty-six of forty-eight quarters—a 96 percent hit rate, and in 89 percent of those quarters, GE met its earnings-per-share forecasts to the penny! No one in the history of business had ever delivered so much market value, so consistently, and Welch was recognized as "Manager of the Century" by *Fortune* magazine in 1999.[5]

And yet, fast-forward to March 12, 2009, nearly eight years after he retired, and we find that Jack Welch reversed course, renouncing his allegiance to MSV theory: "On the face of it, shareholder value is the dumbest idea in the world. Shareholder value is a result, not a strategy. . . . Your main constituencies are your employees, your customers, and your products."[6] Welch was undoubtedly reacting to the realization that GE's shareholder value in 2009 had fallen to less than 25 percent of its peak under his leadership. But what had happened to make the greatest living disciple of MSV doctrine rethink his views on corporate priorities?

Consider how Jack Welch himself described an incident that occurred about two-thirds of the way through his tenure as CEO:

I was getting ready to leave the office for a long weekend on Thursday night, April 14, 1994, when Mike [Carpenter, head of GE Capital] called with one of those phone calls you never want to get. "We've got a problem, Jack," he said. "We have a $350 million hole in a trader's account that we can't identify, and he's disappeared."

Carpenter told me that [Joseph] Jett, who ran the firm's government bond desk, had made a series of fictitious trades to inflate his own bonus. The phony trades artificially boosted Kidder's reported income. To clean up the mess we would have to take what looked like a $350 million charge against our first-quarter earnings.

The news from Mike made me sick: $350 million, I couldn't believe it. It was overwhelming. I rushed to the bathroom, and my stomach emptied in awful spasms.

That Sunday evening, I called 14 of GE's business leaders to deliver the bad news and apologize to each of them for what had happened. I felt terrible, because this surprise would hit the stock and hurt every GE employee. I blame myself for the disaster.[7]

Notice that Welch's paroxysmal anguish wasn't with the firm's inadequate financial controls or with the possibility that GE had become too reliant on a risky, undercapitalized business unit (GE Capital), but rather that GE would uncharacteristically miss its earnings forecasts. Somewhere along the line, GE, and many other companies who adhered to Welch's management philosophy, had conflated strategy with outcomes. They had focused so heavily on short-term profit and stock price gains, that they lost sight of the key drivers of long-term profitable growth.

Dissenting Views on the MSV Doctrine

Serious concerns about how the doctrine of shareholder value maximization has been practiced by many publicly traded corporations have been raised by a growing chorus of academics, CEOs, and respected business commentators, including Roger Martin, dean of Rotman School of Management, University of Toronto;[8] Clayton Christensen, professor at Harvard Business School;[9] William Lazonick, professor of economics at University of Massachusetts;[10] Jeff Bezos, CEO of Amazon;[11] Howard Schultz, CEO of Starbucks;[12] Martin Wolf, CBE, economics commentator for the Financial Times;[13] and Steve Denning, management commentator at *Forbes* magazine.[14]

Martin Wolf perhaps summarized this group's sentiment best:

Almost nothing in economics is more important than thinking through how companies should be managed and for what ends. Unfortunately, we have made a mess of this. That mess has a name: it is "shareholder value maximization." Operating companies in line with this belief not only leads to misbehavior but may also militate against their true social aim, which is to generate greater prosperity.[15]

Wolf's assessment goes beyond Jack Welch's belated recognition that generating value for shareholders is the result, not the driver, of enlightened business strategy. Wolf and others assert that companies that focus on MSV may actually be systematically destroying shareholder value and undermining societal and economic welfare.

Dissenters of MSV doctrine argue that stock buybacks often reflect a misallocation of corporate capital, diverting capital that might otherwise be reinvested in future growth, resulting in a weakening of corporate capabilities and global competitiveness. They claim that underinvesting in R&D and massive offshoring of product development and manufacturing undermine U.S. capacity to compete long term in global markets, impeding economic recovery. In their view, equity-based management incentives derived from inappropriate metrics skew management priorities toward short-term profit realization, exacerbating income inequality and stunting national growth. These are serious charges against a management doctrine that has been and continues to be broadly accepted. Let's examine each of these criticisms in a bit more detail.

Capital Allocation

There is an inherent tradeoff in the allocation of corporate capital between activities that support value creation—e.g., investing in R&D, fueling market expansion, or for employee development—and activities for value extraction in the form of shareholder dividends and open-market stock buybacks. In the period between World War II and the 1970s, most major corporations emphasized the reinvestment of earnings in business growth.

But as the MSV movement gained momentum in the 1970s, corporate-capital allocation began to shift toward value extraction, and this process accelerated in the 1980s after the SEC removed regulatory restrictions on open-market stock buybacks. The motivation for shareholder buybacks is the belief that by increasing the demand for stock relative to available supply, the price per share is likely to rise, at least in the short term.

As shown in figure 3.1, distributions to shareholders in the form of dividends and open-market buybacks have increased markedly between 1981 and 2012, claiming an average of nearly 80 percent of corporate net income over this period. Stock buybacks have exhibited the greatest growth, particularly over the past decade, with some companies even raising debt capital to fund stock buybacks in excess of their annual net income.

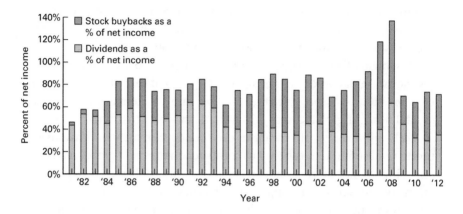

Figure 3.1 Stock buybacks and dividends as a percentage of net income (S&P 500 Companies). *Source*: Lazonick, "Profits Without Prosperity" (*Harvard Business Review*, September, 2014).

What's fueling this trend toward value extraction for shareholders relative to value creation by investment in business growth? I noted earlier that a key tenet of MSV doctrine was the alignment of the interests of principals (shareholders) and agents (executive management). In so doing, most corporate boards have established compensation plans that incentivize senior executives with bonuses for beating earnings-per-share (EPS) targets or with stock options and awards whose value increases with share price.

Companies routinely include EPS in the guidance given to investors about expected profitability for the coming year. Ideally, increasing EPS guidance reflects strong, profitable growth of an enterprise. But what happens if underlying growth or profit prospects dim?

When a corporation repurchases a significant tranche of its own stock on the open market, its EPS increases in direct proportion to the size of the stock buyback. And while there is no guarantee that buybacks per se will increase stock price, the market has generally viewed such activity favorably, at least in the short term. Many investors regard buybacks as a signal that a company believes that the market has undervalued its stock.[16] Moreover, buybacks help offset shareholder dilution from the ongoing issuance of management stock options.

But herein lies a logical disconnect. If a company continuously needs to use stock buybacks to buoy its EPS because underlying earnings are simply not growing, is the company really worthy of such heavy investment? And if such investments come at the expense of R&D and capital expenditures for market-expanding assets, is this a wise allocation of the firm's capital?

Boston Consulting Group studied the impact of capital allocation on stock prices and found that stock buybacks often destroys short-term shareholder value.[17] In one study, BCG examined the share price movements of one hundred publicly traded companies following the announcement of an increase in the size of their share-repurchase program by 25 percent or more. Over the next two quarters, the median change in these companies' valuation multiple was 5 percent lower than the valuation multiple change in the S&P 500 as a whole. The implication is that investors generally do not share management's view that high stock-buyback activity is necessarily a wise use of corporate capital.[18]

The recent experience of IBM illustrates that major stock buybacks may undermine longer-term shareholder value creation as well. As illustrated in figure 3.2, IBM has extracted far more capital to return to shareholders (in the form of buybacks and dividends) than it has reinvested in future growth (in the form of R&D and capital expenditures). Lest there be any doubt that such an allocation reflects a clear tradeoff in management priorities, note that IBM's investment in R&D has

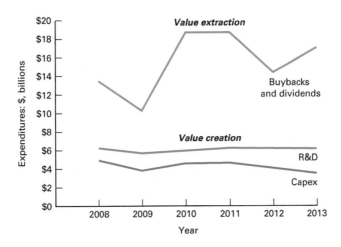

Figure 3.2a IBM Capital allocation and shareholder value: IBM's value extraction and creation spending

SAP	13.6%
Microsoft	13.4%
Google	13.3%
Oracle	13.0%
Cisco	12.2%
Amazon	8.8%
IBM	6.2%
HP	2.8%

Figure 3.2b R&D as percentage of revenue, 2013

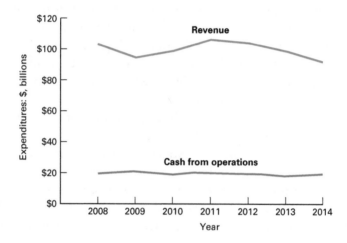

Figure 3.2c IBM's revenue and cash profits

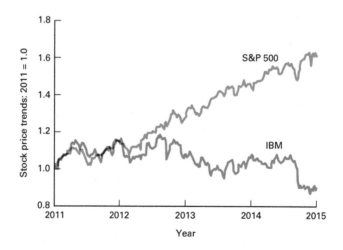

Figure 3.2d IBM vs. S&P 500

been much lower than most other large technology companies. Not surprisingly, IBM's growth has stalled, with revenues declining by more than 15 percent between 2013 and 2015. Investors have taken notice, driving IBM's share price down by 30 percent over the past three years, during which the S&P 500 stock market index grew by more than 40 percent. Despite its massive stock buybacks, IBM has been the poorest performer among all stocks in the Dow Jones Industrial Average index over the past two years.

Weakening Capabilities and International Competitiveness

A second concern with the MSV doctrine is the tendency of many adherents to focus on short-term cost reduction, which shortchanges investments in market-differentiating capabilities to sustain global competitiveness over the long term.

Clayton Christensen has been a strident spokesperson on this point, suggesting that management decision-making is too often guided by financial ratio metrics (e.g., return on assets or benefit–cost measures) whose value can be enhanced by focusing mostly on the denominator.[19] For example, it is argued that firms who aggressively outsource capabilities to reduce assets on their balance sheets or cut R&D to reduce operating costs may achieve short-term gains but weaken long-term competitiveness in ways that are admittedly difficult to measure.[20] The downsides are, for instance, the cost of the knowledge that is being lost (possibly forever), and the missed opportunity for profits that could be made from innovations and capabilities based on this lost knowledge.

Financial theory suggests that the value of a company should reflect the discounted cash flows from all future earnings, yet management decisions are often based predominantly on short-term financial gains.

Inappropriate Management Incentives

The trouble with incentives is that they work. And in that regard, a central tenet of MSV doctrine—the need to align the interests of principals and agents—has undoubtedly contributed to the growing popularity of stock buybacks and other measures to enhance short-term EPS and stock price. With an increasing proportion of CEO compensation shifting toward equity-based rewards, executive pay has flourished. From 1978 to 2013, CEO compensation (adjusted for inflation) increased 937 percent, a rise more than two times higher than overall stock market growth and substantially greater than the 10 percent growth in a typical worker's compensation over the same period.[21]

These trends have sparked questions over whether executive compensation practices exacerbate income inequality, with broader economic and societal consequences. This debate is well beyond my charter in this book. But from the standpoint of effective business strategy, it *is* relevant to question whether executive compensation practices are incentivizing behavior that will promote long-term profitable growth (which benefits all stakeholders) and sustainable increases in shareholder value.

With that concern in mind, William Lazonick studied CEO compensation at the ten companies making the largest stock repurchases over the decade 2003–2012.[22] These companies spent a combined $859 billion on buybacks, representing 68 percent of their combined net income. During the same decade, CEOs of these companies received an average compensation of $168 million, yet only three of these ten companies—Exxon Mobil, IBM, and Procter & Gamble—outperformed the S&P 500 stock price index. Moreover, in the ensuing three years (2013–2015), only one of these companies—Microsoft—was able to grow its revenue at a rate in excess of the overall U.S. GDP. Three of the ten companies (Cisco, Intel, and WalMart) underperformed the GDP on revenue growth, while the remaining six actually shrank between 2013 and 2015 (Exxon-Mobil, General Electric Hewlett-Packard, IBM, Pfizer, and Procter & Gamble).

Thus most companies making the largest stock buybacks have simply stopped growing; they are no longer, in Jack Welch's parlance, locomotives pulling the GNP. It is not clear if executive compensation programs are appropriately incentivizing management to maximize the long-term growth of shareholder value, revenues, profits, or societal welfare.

Let's return this exploration to where I began by asking again, what should be the overarching purpose of a business enterprise? As we've seen, there is a rather significant divide in the arguments for and against the MSV doctrine. Maximizing shareholder value is either the defining bedrock of capitalism and a key driver of corporate value, or a flawed concept that undermines the very values it seeks to nurture.

Resolving the Impasse

In 1954, the venerable Peter Drucker addressed the question of corporate purpose in characteristically clear and insightful terms: "There is only one valid definition of business purpose: to create a customer. Any business enterprise has two—and only two—basic functions: marketing and innovation."[23] Drucker put a stake in the ground by placing customers ahead of other stakeholders served by a business: employees, shareholders, and the broader community in which the business operates.

Sixty years later, Jack Ma, CEO of Alibaba, explained why he subscribes to Peter Drucker's dictate in an open letter to potential investors of what would become the largest IPO in history:[24]

> I have said on numerous occasions that we will put "customers first, employees second, and shareholders third." I can see that investors who hear this for the first time may find it a bit hard to understand.
>
> Let me be clear: as fiduciaries of the company, we believe that the only way for Alibaba to create long-term value for shareholders is to create sustainable value for customers. So customers must come first.
>
> Our company will not make decisions based on short-term revenues or profits. Our strategies will be implemented with mission-driven, long-term development in mind. Our people, capital, technology, and resources will be utilized to safeguard the sustainable development and growth of the Alibaba ecosystem. We welcome investors with the same long-term mindset.[25]

Ma's ordering of stakeholder priorities echoes the philosophy of Jeff Bezos, who shared similar sentiments as CEO of Amazon in his first letter to shareholders in 1997:

> We believe that a fundamental measure of our success will be the shareholder value we create over the long term. This value will be a direct result of our ability to extend and solidify our current market leadership position. The stronger our market leadership, the more powerful our economic model. Market leadership can

translate directly to higher revenue, higher profitability, greater capital velocity, and correspondingly stronger returns on invested capital.

Because of our emphasis on the long term, we may make decisions and weigh tradeoffs differently than some companies. Accordingly, we want to share with you our fundamental management and decision-making approach so that you, our shareholders, may confirm that it is consistent with your investment philosophy. We will continue to focus relentlessly on our customers. We will continue to make investment decisions in light of long-term market leadership considerations rather than short-term profitability considerations or short-term Wall Street reactions. . . .

We aren't so bold as to claim that the above is the "right" investment philosophy, but it's ours, and we would be remiss if we weren't clear in the approach we have taken and will continue to take.[26]

Bezos has faithfully followed these principles, and in fact has included his 1997 missive in every annual report since as a reminder to shareholders of Amazon's corporate purpose. Amazon's "relentless focus on customers" has helped the company consistently set the industry standard for customer value, convenience, and service. Moreover, Bezos's intent to "make investment decisions in light of long-term market leadership" has underscored a rapid escalation in capital expenditures and R&D, essentially wiping out any net income since the company's founding (figure 3.3). As such, the company has never paid a dividend, or invested heavily in buying back company stock.[27]

As he accurately foresaw, Bezos has angered many Wall Street analysts who have been clamoring for more profit realization and disbursements to shareholders. One observer summed up the negative sentiments well by calling Amazon "a charitable organization being run by elements of the investment community for the benefit of consumers."[28]

Is there an inherent tradeoff between the interests of customers and shareholders? Amazon's performance to date demonstrates that a relentless focus on customers and long-term growth can serve customers, employees, *and* shareholders exceptionally well.

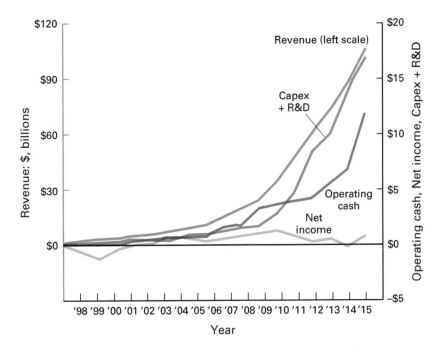

Figure 3.3 Amazon's revenue, profitability, and growth investments, 1998–2015, in billions

Customer Satisfaction

Amazon has consistently achieved the highest customer satisfaction rating among over 230 companies included in the American Customer Satisfaction Index (ACSI), the most comprehensive national cross-industry measure of customer satisfaction in the United States.[29] This is an extraordinary achievement, given the scale of Amazon's business and the breadth of its product range. Other ACSI high performers tend to be upmarket brands (e.g., Mercedes-Benz, Nordstrom) or category-specific providers (e.g., Heinz).

Topline Growth

Amazon exceeded $100 billion in revenue in 2015—becoming the fastest company to reach this threshold.

Shareholder Value

Jeff Bezos ranks as number one in *Harvard Business Review*'s 2015 annual assessment of the 100 best-performing CEOs, based on total shareholder return and market capitalization. During his tenure, Bezos has overseen a nearly $200 billion gain in Amazon's market value, representing a shareholder return on investment of more than 20,000 percent.[30]

Broader Business Purpose: Creating a North Star

Amazon and Alibaba represent successful companies, whose CEOs explicitly anchored their firm's purpose on delivering exceptional customer value. More broadly, the best performing companies in the world—those that dominate the categories in which they compete over the long term—are also guided by clearly articulated corporate missions that are well understood by all stakeholders. Defining a company's purpose, priorities and values provides a North Star to guide how the enterprise will operate. While the pace of change in the market, in technology, and in the competitive landscape seems to be getting ever faster, the foundations of a company's purpose can and should be enduring.

As Jeff Bezos explains:

> When I'm talking with people outside the company, there's a question that comes up very commonly: "What's going to change in the next five to ten years?" But I very rarely get asked, "What's *not* going to change in the next five to ten years?" At Amazon we're always trying to figure that out, because you can really spin up flywheels around those things. All the energy you invest in them today will still be paying you dividends ten years from now. Whereas if you base your strategy first and foremost on more transitory things—who your competitors are, what kind of technologies are available, and so on—those things are going to change so rapidly that you're going to have to change your strategy very rapidly, too.

For our business, most [non-changing business drivers] turn out to be customer insights. Look at what's important to the customers in our consumer-facing business. They want selection, low prices, and fast delivery . . . I can't imagine that ten years from now [customers] are going to say, "I love Amazon, but if only they could deliver my products a little more slowly." And they're not going to, ten years from now, say, "I really love Amazon, but I wish their prices were a little higher." So we know that when we put energy into defect reduction, which reduces our cost structure and thereby allows lower prices, that will be paying us dividends ten years from now. If we keep putting energy into that flywheel, ten years from now, it'll be spinning faster and faster. . . .[31]

Amazon isn't the only successful company that abides by a clearly articulated corporate purpose, defined by deeply held values and beliefs. Take, for instance, Johnson & Johnson, IKEA, and Starbucks.

Johnson & Johnson

By any measure, Johnson & Johnson (J&J) has been an exceptionally successful company. Over the past twenty years, its stock price has grown at a compound annual rate of over 13 percent. Over this span, its operating margins and revenue growth rates have consistently outperformed its competitors in the pharmaceutical and medical equipment sectors in which it operates. Compared to companies of a similar size, J&J currently has by far the highest operating margin (nearly 30 percent) and a growth rate second only to Amazon.

Underscoring J&J's consistently robust performance is a well-defined mission statement.[32] Robert Wood Johnson II, chairman from 1932 to 1963 and a member of the company's founding family, penned the company's credo himself in 1943, just before J&J became a publicly traded company. Like Peter Drucker, but a decade earlier, Johnson singled out customer focus in articulating J&J's corporate purpose:

We believe our first responsibility is to the doctors, nurses and patients, to mothers and fathers and all others who use our products and services. In meeting their needs, everything we do must be of high quality.

Johnson & Johnson's credo goes on to reference the company's obligations to other stakeholders as well, in a prescribed order:

> We are responsible to our employees. Everyone must be considered as an individual. They must have a sense of security in their jobs. Compensation must be fair and adequate, and working conditions clean, orderly, and safe.
>
> We are responsible to the communities in which we live and work and to the world community as well. We must be good citizens [. . .] protecting the environment and natural resources.
>
> Our final responsibility is to our stockholders. Business must make a sound profit. We must experiment with new ideas. When we operate according to these principles, the stockholders should realize a fair return.

Although J&J puts shareholders at the end of their list, the clarity of their overall business mission established an operating environment in which the company and its shareholders could thrive. With the company's credo defining North Star corporate values, J&J management did not have to debate basic strategic direction in responding to changes in market circumstances.

A case in point is how the company handled the Chicago Tylenol murders, a series of poisoning deaths resulting from drug tampering in the Chicago metropolitan area in 1982. The crisis presented J&J with some tough choices. Tylenol represented almost one-fifth of the company's profits, and concerns were raised that declining sales would be difficult to regain in the face of rampant fear and rumor. Yet, rather than attempt to downplay the crisis—it was after all, likely the work of an individual madman in a single metropolitan area—J&J did just the opposite. Chairman James Burke immediately ordered a halt to all Tylenol production and advertising, distributed warnings to hospitals across the country, and within a week of the first death, announced a nationwide recall of every single bottle of Tylenol on the market.[33]

Before relaunching Tylenol in the United States, J&J developed tamper-proof packaging, an innovation that would soon become the industry standard. These actions flowed directly from the company credo, which is engraved in granite at the entry to company headquarters, a North Star goal stating that the company will be guided first and foremost by serving the needs of customers. Yet, in the long run, all stakeholders were well served. Loyalty toward Tylenol soared after the company demonstrated that customer safety came first. Tylenol rapidly regained its pre-crisis market share, and J&J's overall profitability and growth were quickly restored.

Contrast J&J's behavior with how two major corporations lacking customer-centric core values have handled safety crises.

General Motors

General Motors (GM) has been widely criticized for decades for arrogant disregard of customer welfare.[34] In 1965, a little-known congressional aide, Ralph Nader, published a book called *Unsafe at Any Speed*, in which he documented a dangerous design defect with the Chevrolet Corvair. This defect caused several fatal spinout accidents. However, GM disregarded the published evidence and tried to discredit Nader by hiring private detectives to tap his phones, to investigate his past, and to procure prostitutes in attempts to trap him in compromising situations. Nader sued the company for invasion of privacy. Ironically, the press coverage of the lawsuit gave Nader's book the notoriety it never achieved on its own. As a result, a new case law precedent was established for illegal corporate surveillance, and GM was forced to redesign the Corvair suspension system.

Fast-forward four decades to 2004, and GM was once again found to have willfully disregarded internal evidence of a fatal design defect in its ignition switches that caused the deaths of over 100 people.[35]

GM, at one time the largest company in the United States, declared bankruptcy in 2009.

Lumber Liquidators

Lumber Liquidators, a specialty retailer of hardwood flooring, was on a roll as the building sector recovered from the 2009 recession. By 2015, its stock price had soared 476 percent over the prior two years. But if shareholders were happy, some customers were not. Reports began surfacing of consumers becoming sick, and noticing a strong chemical odor originating from their recently installed flooring.

The CBS newsmagazine *60 Minutes* got involved, sending various flooring samples from different lots to independent labs to check the level of formaldehyde—a known carcinogen. Test results found that in the majority of samples, formaldehyde levels were higher than allowed by California law, and in some cases, dangerously so—as high as thirteen times the legal limit.

In a *60 Minutes* segment aired on March 1, 2015, then-CEO Robert M. Lynch said he had no knowledge of the problem and promised an investigation, while steadfastly maintaining that Lumber Liquidators flooring was safe. But *60 Minutes* had already dispatched reporters to Lumber Liquidator's Chinese suppliers, who acknowledged that they had been knowingly using a cheaper manufacturing process with excessive formaldehyde but labeling their shipments as compliant with California law.

Lumber Liquidators responded by offering free testing kits for consumers to test the air quality in their homes, while still continuing shipments of the suspect flooring products. Two months later, the company finally halted all shipments from China, and the CEO unexpectedly resigned. By the end of the year, Lumber Liquidators' stock price had plummeted over 75 percent from its 2015 peak.[36]

The clear takeaway here is that companies like J&J that remain true to a clear, customer-centric mission can survive and prosper through good times and bad. Two other successful companies that have been guided by an exceptionally strong set of core values are IKEA and Starbucks.

IKEA

From its founding by Ingvar Kamprad in 1943, Swedish-based IKEA has been singularly focused on delivering stylish furniture to global customers at competitively low prices as exemplified by the company's two corporate mantras: "Low Price with Meaning" and "A Better Everyday Life."

IKEA articulates its customer-centric corporate purpose as follows:

The IKEA business idea is to offer a wide range of home furnishings with good design and function at prices so low that as many people as possible will be able to afford them.

Most of the time, beautifully designed home furnishings are usually created for the few who can afford them. From the beginning, IKEA has taken a different path. We have decided to side with the many.

That means responding to the home furnishing needs of people around the world: people with many different needs, tastes, dreams, aspirations and wallet sizes; people who want to improve their homes and their everyday lives.

It's not difficult to manufacture expensive fine furniture: just spend the money and let the customers pay. To manufacture beautiful, durable furniture at low prices is not so easy—it requires a different approach. It is all about finding simple solutions and saving on every method, process or approach adopted—but not on ideas.[37]

The company has faithfully executed against this charter for over seventy years, growing to become the largest furniture retailer in the world. As a logical extension of its original charter, IKEA recently announced a "People & Planet Positive" commitment with the objective of creating and selling affordable products and solutions that help customers save money by using less energy and water and by reducing waste. The company also recently upgraded its global employment policies, ensuring better working conditions and compensation for its employees. The company believes that balancing its business and people needs is a wise investment that ultimately will contribute to delivering better service to consumers.

While IKEA is a privately owned enterprise with limited financial disclosure, it has reported consistently profitable operations, achieving 2015 revenues of nearly $36 billion, self-funding the development of over 328 stores in 43 countries.[38]

Starbucks

From its inception, founder and CEO Howard Schultz set out to make Starbucks a different kind of company. In his 2011 memoir, Schultz stated his company's corporate purpose:

At the very heart of being a merchant is a desire to tell a story by making sensory, emotional connections. Once, twice, or sixteen thousand times.

Ideally, every Starbucks store should tell a story about coffee and what we as an organization believe in. That story should unfold via the taste and presentation of our products, and the sights, sounds and smells that surround our customers. Our stores and partners are at their best when they collaborate to provide an oasis, an uplifting feeling of comfort, connection, and a deep respect for the coffee and communities we serve.[39]

Following this North Star, Schultz's strategy emphasized product quality and a superior customer experience, driven by extensive staff training and store layouts that gave customers a sightline to the "theater" of coffee preparation and proximity to barista personnel, many of whom developed a personal relationship with regular patrons.

Starbucks went public in 1992, and under Schultz's leadership the company established a rapidly growing global footprint and powerful brand, supported by intensely loyal customers paying premium prices. By 2000, when Schultz stepped down from his role as CEO, Starbucks had opened nearly four thousand stores worldwide, with revenues in excess of $2 billion and a market capitalization of over $7 billion.

But in the ensuing years, Schultz's successor Jim Roberts strayed from the original corporate vision, pursuing hypergrowth at the expense of customer experience. Wooing Wall Street with aggressive growth targets, Starbucks quadrupled its store count between 2000 and 2007. The company installed faster, larger brewing machines, often blocking the customer view, cut back on barista training, and de-emphasized in-store ambience. McDonald's and Dunkin' Donuts began gaining market share as many Starbucks customers began to question whether declining quality still warranted the premium prices. By the time Howard Schultz returned as CEO in 2008, Starbucks same-store sales were rapidly declining and its market value was in free fall, from a peak of nearly $27 billion in 2006 to just $7.3 billion in 2009.

During Schultz's absence, Starbucks had lost its North Star purpose, with dire consequences in the marketplace. Commenting on his priorities upon his return, Schultz observed, "This has been my life's work, as opposed to a job. I didn't come back to save the company—I hate that description—I came back to rekindle the emotion that built it."[40]

Schultz engineered a turnaround strategy to return Starbucks to its original corporate purpose of delivering premium products and a superior customer experience.[41] In implementing his strategy, Schultz rebuilt his senior management team, united around a clearly articulated corporate vision, and shut down hundreds of stores that were redundant or inconsistent with the company's high standard of customer service. He increased barista training, at one point simultaneously closing over seven thousand U.S. stores for three hours of intensive staff training, which included a video message from the CEO beamed to every store. Schultz also invested in bringing ten thousand store managers to New Orleans in 2008 for a company-wide meeting to reinforce Starbucks's core values. To restore the customer connection with baristas and the coffee-making process, he ordered new store designs with smaller coffee-making machines, and finally, Shultz introduced new products to reaffirm Starbucks as *the* coffee authority.

By restoring the company's core brand values, Schultz's turnaround strategy achieved outstanding results. Between 2008 and 2015, Starbucks reversed year-to-year changes in same-store sales from −9 percent to as high as +9 percent, increased annual sales and net income by 85 percent and 773 percent respectively, and increased market value nearly tenfold.

In summary, Johnson & Johnson, IKEA, and Starbucks all built great companies by creating or restoring a distinctive and well-defined customer-centric corporate purpose—a North Star guiding their management behavior and long-term strategy.

The Purpose of Business: Drucker Revisited

Before leaving this subject, let's revisit Peter Drucker's dictate on business purpose with an amendment to make it more broadly relevant to effective business strategy. Remember what Drucker said: "There is only one valid definition of business purpose: to create a customer."[42]

While Drucker was directionally correct in placing customers ahead of other stakeholders, his singular focus on customer creation is too narrow. After all, any enterprise can attract customers by underpricing (and in the extreme, giving away) their products or services. So first, we need to add a qualifier—to create customers *profitably*.

Secondly, companies are most successful when they can capture lifetime customer value, so customer retention, not just attraction, should be pivotal to business purpose.

And finally, in order to both attract and retain customers over the long term, a business needs to consistently deliver high levels of customer satisfaction. Unfortunately, most of us are personally familiar with industries that have monopoly or oligopoly power, allowing individual companies to profitably attract and retain *dissatisfied* customers for years through coercive or deliberately confusing business practices.[43] But such industries are highly vulnerable to disruption from new entrants that can find a way to provide an equal or superior value proposition to emancipate a legion of dissatisfied customers.

In summary, with a hat-tip to Peter Drucker, we can conclude:

> The only valid definition of business purpose is to profitably create and retain satisfied customers

As I have shown by the examples in this chapter, a customer-centric corporate purpose that also seeks to create value for all stakeholders provides a North Star to guide effective strategy formulation. We can now add the outer ring shown in figure 3.4, reflecting the pivotal role of an appropriate corporate mission in achieving long-term profitable growth.

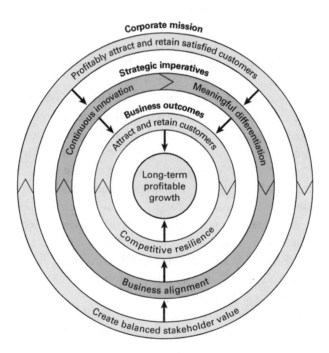

Figure 3.4 Corporate mission guides strategy formulation

Companies that establish and faithfully implement a distinctive version of this foundational definition of business purpose—a North Star that resonates with customers and other stakeholders—are best positioned to build enduringly successful businesses.

Does your current company (or the one you want to build) have a compelling and clearly articulated North Star?

CHAPTER FOUR

The Search for the Holy Grail of Business: Long-Term Profitable Growth

SHAREHOLDER VALUE CREATION is the outcome—not the driver—of effective business strategy, which should be aimed at profitably creating and retaining satisfied customers. But how can a business best do this? In this chapter, I will show how the actions of a firm at all levels can create value for shareholders and other stakeholders.

Drivers of Shareholder Value

Let's start with some definitions of key terms. Market value in a publicly traded firm is best measured by total shareholder return (TSR). This is the return on a shareholder's investment in a company, including accumulated dividend reinvestments, usually over three to five years. For example, if you had invested $1,000 in J&J stock on January 2, 2009, immediately reinvested all dividends in additional J&J shares, and liquidated your J&J stock on December 31, 2013, your initial investment would then be worth $1,810, yielding a five-year TSR of 81 percent.

What determines how and why some firms achieve higher TSRs than others? In simplest terms, TSR largely reflects a firm's performance over time on two key metrics: revenue growth and profitability.[1] Just as shareholder value maximization as a desired outcome is too broad to guide the formulation of specific winning strategies and tactics, so too are revenue growth and profitability. Therefore, we need to further deconstruct the drivers of these high-level business-performance metrics.

Let's start with profit margins. To be more precise, we are examining a firm's return on invested capital (ROIC) relative to its weighted average cost of capital (WACC). Think about it this way: if a company can raise capital by issuing stock or bonds or arranging a bank credit line at a net cost of 7 percent and achieve a return of 15 percent by investing those funds in the business, the profit spread creates considerable value for the owners of the firm. Firms with a consistently positive profit spread can easily attract more capital to generate even more growth.

Under such circumstances, the next logical question is, how can a firm improve its ROIC? Figure 4.1 suggests that the drivers of ROIC include actions that either increase the numerator (by improving operating margins) or decrease the denominator (by reducing the amount of investment required for a given level of business output). These measures themselves can be further deconstructed into a set of management actions that drive higher-level business results.

For example, higher operating margins result from higher prices or lower costs, which can be influenced by product design, advertising, and channel management for price realization, and manufacturing and distribution efficiency for cost control.

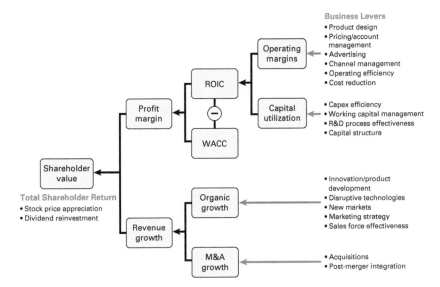

Figure 4.1 Drivers of shareholder value

Firms can also improve their ROIC through a variety of actions that enhance the use of capital—e.g., more efficient deployment of capital expenditures and working capital. Examples of this type of specific action include manufacturing and distribution efficiencies of all types that reduce the need for plant investments and inventories throughout the supply chain.

As for topline growth, shown in the bottom half of figure 4.1, the primary levers to increase revenue are organic growth (through innovative product development, market expansion, or marketing effectiveness) and mergers and acquisitions. The point of this decomposition exercise is to demonstrate that it is the direct result of management actions throughout the firm to improve revenue growth and profitability that ultimately drives the creation of shareholder value.

In this regard, Peter Drucker may be guilty of hyperbole by asserting that "business has two—and only two—basic functions: innovation and marketing. Marketing and innovation produce results; all the rest are costs."[2] As figure 4.1 demonstrates, *every* business function can and should contribute to shareholder value enhancement. Business functions can do this by improving revenue growth, which is the primary domain of marketing and innovation, or through operational and capital efficiency, which is a shared responsibility throughout the organization.

As such, every employee within an organization should clearly understand how the creation and retention of satisfied customers drives overall profits, revenue growth, and shareholder value, and how their actions contribute to this. If employees do not understand the value of their daily activities, they are probably working ineffectively, working for a company with a poorly communicated management strategy, or both.

Is it realistic to expect that every employee should understand and care about how their efforts contribute to overall corporate performance? Consider how JetBlue, a $6 billion airline, communicates the company's strategic intent to over eighteen thousand employees. Every two weeks, all newly hired employees, including baggage handlers, gate agents, pilots, administrative personnel, and senior executives, are required to attend a two-day orientation session at the company's corporate training facility in Orlando, Florida. The first day of this training is devoted to presentations and Q&A sessions conducted by JetBlue's executive leadership team, starting with the CEO. They cover the history and heritage of the airline, the economics of running the company, and the core values that every employee needs to embrace. The CFO provides a candid and eye-opening explanation of the razor-thin margins that airlines run on, driving home the point that *every* employee needs to be on top of their game for the company as a whole to prosper.

While the customer-centric values of JetBlue are easy to translate into the expected daily behaviors of employees in customer-facing positions, the executive team also stresses the importance of employees in administrative positions. For example, as a JetBlue senior operations executive explained at a recent employee orientation session,

> If you are in accounts payable and one of our inflight crewmembers gets frustrated with the difficulty of getting properly reimbursed for travel expenses, he or she may not be in the right frame [of mind] on their next flight. For those of you in administrative positions, your colleagues are your customers. So *every* employee of JetBlue has a role in delivering outstanding customer service.[3]

After these orientation sessions, senior JetBlue executives communicate directly with employees at regularly scheduled company meetings in all their international operational hubs. JetBlue's management practice represents a significant commitment of senior executive time, but it builds business alignment around the airline's founding corporate mission to "bring humanity back to air travel."[4] Therefore, it is no coincidence that JetBlue has ranked first in customer satisfaction for eleven straight years and has outperformed the U.S. airline industry on profit growth and TSR in 2015.[5]

The Relentless Pressure for Profitable Growth

To show the pivotal importance of profitable growth, consider its impact on enterprise value, a broad economic measure of the overall value of a business. In simplified terms, enterprise value (EV) represents the net capital invested in a firm, defined as the market value of all stock *plus* total debt, *minus* cash.[6] In essence, EV reflects the theoretical amount of capital that would be required to acquire a company at its current market value. To illustrate, consider how EV would be calculated for the Coca-Cola Company, using the following formula:

$$EV = (\text{Number of Shares} \times \text{Stock Price}) + \text{Total Debt} - \text{Cash}$$

At the end of 2013, Coca-Cola had around 4.3 billion shares outstanding, selling at $41.60 per share, yielding a market cap of $179 billion. Adding in the company's total debt of $37 billion and subtracting the $10.4 billion in cash on its balance sheet yields an EV of approximately $205 billion.

During 2013, Coca-Cola generated approximately $8 billion in free cash flow (FCF)[7] that theoretically could be extracted by shareholders and debt providers. If the company continued to operate at this level of profitability in perpetuity, the value of Coca-Cola would be $121 billion (as shown in figure 4.2), based on the formula for valuing a fixed annuity

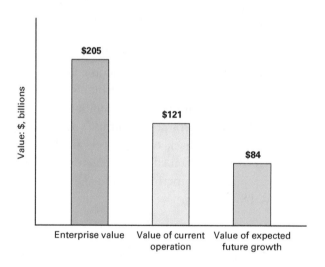

Figure 4.2 Enterprise value for Coca-Cola, 2013

Enterprise value = (Number of shares (4.3) × Price/share ($41.60*)) + Total debt ($38) – Cash ($10.4)

Value of current operations = Free cash flow ($8)/WACC (6.6%*)

Value of expected future growth = EV ($206) – Value of current operations ($121)

*Figures in billions unless marked with an asterisk.

of FCF. But investors were willing to commit capital to the company at a value of $205 billion, nearly 70 percent more than Coca-Cola's current profitability alone would warrant. The reason for this is, of course, market expectations for further growth.

Analyzing all companies in this fashion yields a wide range of market expectations for future growth. For example, at the end of fiscal year 2013, the EV of Staples was 18 percent less than its value based on current FCF, signaling a market expectation for declines in future profitability. In the same year, Starbucks showed an EV 112 percent higher than its value based on current profitability, indicating market expectations for strong future growth.

The common denominator in each of these cases is that the market value of an enterprise is largely determined by its expected future growth. Profitable growth is not only a key determinant of shareholder value, but it also enhances the welfare of other corporate stakeholders:

- *Employees* Growing corporations provide upward mobility and career opportunities at all levels of an enterprise, and possibly, additional profit-sharing rewards.
- *Executives* Equity-based compensation packages richly reward senior executives in profitably growing corporations.
- *Consumers* Companies that consistently do well in the marketplace can reinvest in innovative new products and in delivering superior customer service.
- *Suppliers* Successful corporations provide growth opportunities for suppliers and business partners.
- *Communities* Growing corporations provide jobs, tax revenue, and philanthropic contributions to the communities in which they operate.

No one feels the pressure for sustaining profitable growth more than the CEO, since the consequence of falling short of market expectations is often termination. Over the past few years, approximately one-fourth of all CEO transitions have been involuntary, usually precipitated by disappointing growth or profits. Recent high-profile examples include Bob McDonald (Procter & Gamble), Don Thompson (McDonald's), John Riccitiello (Electronic Arts), Ron Johnson (JCPenney), Tony Vernon (Kraft Foods), and Gregg Steinhafel (Target).[8]

How Well Have Companies Performed
in Sustaining Long-Term Growth?

Given the paramount importance of growth—the sine qua non of corporate performance and CEO job security—it behooves us to ask how well companies have sustained growth over the long term. The short answer is, not very well.

The most definitive study on this question was undertaken by the Corporate Executive Board (CEB), analyzing the long-term revenue growth of approximately five hundred Fortune 100 and comparable international companies over the past half-century.[9] The study defined a revenue "stall" as being a point in time when a company could no longer sustain a real annual revenue growth rate of at least 2 percent over a ten-year period. (In many cases, companies actually experienced a decade or more of declines in revenue.)[10] It should be stressed that the CEB study was explicitly designed to examine long-term performance trends, not the vicissitudes of annual growth rates, which every company experiences from time to time as a result of business cycles or temporary setbacks. Stalled companies identified in the CEB study clearly manifested a serious and sustained decline in business performance, which resulted from structural shifts in business circumstances that management was unable to overcome for at least a decade.

For example, consider the business performance of BFGoodrich (BFG), the first automotive tire maker in the United States. After over a century as a leading industry player, BFG experienced a revenue stall in 1979 (figure 4.3). In the three years prior to stalling, BF Goodrich enjoyed strong growth, with revenues increasing at a compound annual growth rate (CAGR) of over 12 percent. But when Michelin introduced a new, superior product technology—radial-ply tires—BFG's sales stalled, suffering a CAGR of −6.5 percent over the ensuing decade. BFGoodrich never recovered and ultimately sold its tire business at a distressed valuation to a private equity firm in 1989.

BFGoodrich's revenue stall is the norm rather than the exception. The CEB found that 87 percent of the companies in its study hit a stall point at least once over the past half-century. Some, like Apple and 3M, were able to recover. Most others, like RCA, Motorola, and Kodak, however, continued to struggle in ensuing decades, usually

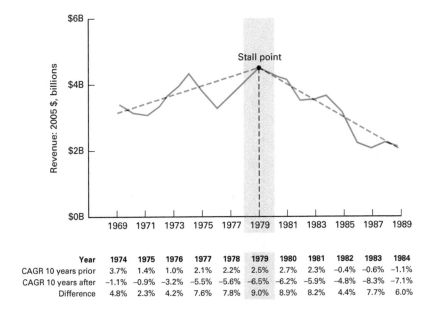

Year	1974	1975	1976	1977	1978	1979	1980	1981	1982	1983	1984
CAGR 10 years prior	3.7%	1.4%	1.0%	2.1%	2.2%	2.5%	2.7%	2.3%	–0.4%	–0.6%	–1.1%
CAGR 10 years after	–1.1%	–0.9%	–3.2%	–5.5%	–5.6%	–6.5%	–6.2%	–5.9%	–4.8%	–8.3%	–7.1%
Difference	4.8%	2.3%	4.2%	7.6%	7.8%	9.0%	8.9%	8.2%	4.4%	7.7%	6.0%

Figure 4.3 Stall point definition: BFGoodrich example

Definition of a revenue stall:
CAGR in real revenues ten years *prior* to stall > 2 percent.
CAGR in real revenues ten years *after* stall ≤ 6 percent.
Stall point has > 4 percent "kink" in ten-year revenue growth.

ending in bankruptcy or forced sale at extremely low valuations relative to their historical peak valuation (figure 4.4).

Additional evidence of the difficulty of sustaining long-term growth can be found in a study that discovered the tenure of companies on the S&P 500 has declined from sixty-one years in 1958 to eighteen years in 2012. Looking forward, this suggests that fifteen years from now, 75 percent of the current S&P 500 will no longer exist, at least as stand-alone entities.[11] This phenomenon is also captured by observing topple rates—the speed with which firms lose their market-share leadership positions. According to a recent study by Deloitte's Center for the Edge, the corporate topple rate has increased by 39 percent since 1965.[12] Clearly, by any measure, it has become increasingly difficult for companies to sustain long-term profitable growth and industry leadership.

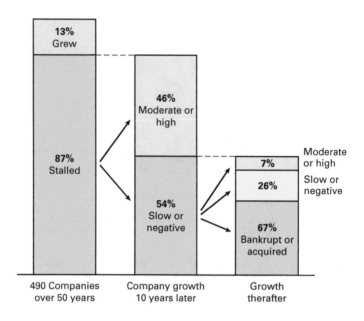

Figure 4.4 Long-term revenue growth among Fortune/Global 100 companies, 1955–2006

The authors of the CEB study went on to characterize the reasons for stalled growth. In 87 percent of the cases, the cause could be traced to factors under management control, like management complacency, failure to maintain product innovation, premature abandonment of a viable core business, or a failed major acquisition. In only 13 percent of the cases was management believed to be the unfortunate victim of external factors outside of its control, like major regulatory reform or geopolitical asset seizure.

There is some degree of subjectivity in the CEB analysis of the root causes of stalled growth. For example, there is a fine line between management complacency and failure to continuously innovate, which in turn might explain an ill-conceived acquisition. Nonetheless, the CEB findings are sobering. Despite the importance of sustained profitable growth, less than one in six large companies in the study were able to achieve it, and most failed for reasons under management control.

Is Sustained Growth Impossible?

Of course, there is the possibility that large corporations are destined to stagnate, decline, or fail in some Darwinian form of the evolution of corporations. In this view, the CEB study simply confirms the inevitable nature of business progress. This warrants further exploration.

We've all been inspired by stories of brilliant entrepreneurs whose game-changing ideas conceived in humble settings—e.g., a garage (Steve Jobs), dorm room (Mark Zuckerberg), or Milanese coffee bar (Howard Schultz)—blossomed into market-leading global enterprises. A new generation of entrepreneurs is building companies that have reached $10 billion in market value in record time (Uber, Airbnb, SnapChat, Xiaomi), posing grave threats to established market leaders. These success stories suggest that the traditional bases of competitive advantage that used to protect incumbent market leaders—scale, operational experience, brand image, customer base, distribution, and financial depth—may no longer be able to withstand the onslaught of upstart entrepreneurs.

This was the theme of Malcolm Gladwell's recent book, *David and Goliath: Underdogs, Misfits and the Art of Battling Giants*.[13] In his retelling of the biblical tale of David and Goliath, Gladwell portrays David as a fearless, agile, and resourceful fighter who defeats the dimwitted, overconfident, and ponderous oaf, Goliath. Gladwell rebuts conventional wisdom that David was an underdog. In this mismatch—and in a surprisingly large number of other situations within business and sports—Gladwell asserts that leaders have liabilities that make them particularly vulnerable to brash upstarts.

As we have seen, history is replete with examples of profitable, market-leading corporations who were felled by smaller, nimbler competitors. For example, when AT&T—the largest company in the United States for much of the twentieth century—failed to adapt to deregulation and the emergence of wireless technologies, it was forced to sell its dwindling assets for a fraction of their historical peak value to one of its former regional divisions. The vulnerability of AT&T as a ponderous, customer-unfriendly monopoly recalls the punch line in a Lily Tomlin skit: "We don't care. We don't have to. We're the phone company!"[14]

General Motors, which held the distinction of being the largest U.S. corporation for decades, declared bankruptcy in 2009 and lives on today in shrunken form as the beneficiary of a taxpayer bailout. The management shortcomings of GM are well documented,[15] becoming fodder for business school case studies on ineffective governance, insular and shortsighted management, and corrosive labor relations.[16]

Or take Kodak. The firm—which enjoyed film industry dominance for over a century, peaking at 90 percent market share in film and cameras in the mid-1970s—declared bankruptcy in 2012. Kodak is a poster child for Clayton Christensen's disruptive technology theory, which explains why large enterprises struggle to adopt innovations like, in Kodak's case, digital imaging.[17]

Are these isolated examples of bad management bringing down venerable institutions? Or are market-leading corporations destined to die by the hands of disruptive upstarts or from aggressive attacks by traditional competitors? Conventional wisdom has increasingly tilted toward the latter belief: market leaders cannot sustain global competitive advantage in the long term.

Apple is a case in point. A gloomy outlook has been predicted for Apple in the post–Steve Jobs era by a Nobel Prize–winning economist (Paul Krugman[18]), an esteemed academic business theorist (Clayton Christensen[19]), a *Wall Street Journal* technology reporter and best-selling author (Yukari Kane[20]), an SAP board member writing for *Der Spiegel* (Stefan Schultz[21]), and the 71 percent of respondents in a 2013 Bloomberg global survey who believe that Apple has lost its way as an industry innovator.[22] The reasoning behind arguments that the mighty must fall is not limited to Apple. This belief stems from a broader conviction that large enterprises inevitably lose their competitive advantages over time.

But this viewpoint is not just flawed; it could even be a self-fulfilling prophecy. If management truly believes that long-term above-market profitable growth is impossible, a logical response would be to harvest and protect current assets and customers for as long as possible. Such an approach only hastens the decline of incumbent market leaders. Business Goliaths can continue to prosper, but only if they maintain the same entrepreneurial spirit and adaptability that led to their success in the first place.

Let's examine Apple.

On September 29, 2012, Apple reported record earnings, capping a remarkable three-year run during which the company increased revenues by 266 percent, profits by 406 percent, and market capitalization by 280 percent. It was implausible that Apple, already the most highly valued company in the world, could continue such a torrid growth rate forever. And indeed, Apple's margins and growth rate began to abate over the next eighteen months. Many pundits declared this was a sign of the erosion of Apple's competitive advantage, dooming them to average financial performance or worse in the future.

For example, one of my esteemed colleagues at the Columbia Business School shared this provocative point of view with MBA students in a schoolwide lecture:

> It's very hard to dominate big, global markets. Nobody has ever dominated electronic devices. Trust me; we've seen it in related industries for Sony, for Motorola, and for Nokia. They've had nothing like the margins of Apple, and the margins of Apple have gone down by at least a third in the last sixteen to eighteen months. You can't dominate a big market. . . . Apple is going straight down the tubes![23]

Why would a company that has repeatedly demonstrated extraordinary customer insight, innovation, design excellence, marketing prowess, high-quality manufacturing, and trendsetting retail practices be so assuredly headed "straight down the tubes"?

I believe there are three misleading arguments that underscore the widespread belief that Apple—or any market leader—must eventually lose its competitive advantage and above-market financial performance over time:

1. The Law of Large Numbers
2. The Law of Competition
3. The Law of Competitive Advantage

The Law of Large Numbers

This law concerns the obvious fact that, as a company grows, the incremental revenue required to maintain above-market growth becomes larger.

For Apple, whose annual revenue is currently over $200 billion, the challenge is daunting.

For example, consider what would be required for Apple to grow its topline by 10 percent over the coming year. (While this is above market average, it's only one-third of the CAGR the company has achieved over the past five years.) Growth of this magnitude in a single year is equivalent to adding the total revenue from companies like Southwest Airlines, General Mills, or U.S. Steel to Apple's current topline.

Another way to grasp the difficulty of Apple's challenge is to consider how much revenue its new product launches must generate to sustain strong sales growth. Apple-watchers eagerly anticipated the April 2015 launch of the Apple Watch, a product in the intriguing "wearable technology" category.[24] Characteristically, Apple was not the first mover in this emerging technology (as was also the case with portable music players, smartphones, and tablets). Smart watches from Samsung, Pebble, and Sony had already been on the market for a year or more.

While Apple does not release official sales figures, industry analysts reported that Apple shipped nearly seven million smart watches in the first six months (more than the combined shipments of all other vendors over the previous five quarters).[25] With strong holiday sales, Apple is believed to have closed 2015 with sales of 12 million units. Assuming an average selling price of $530, this translates into Apple Watch revenues of approximately $6.4 billion in 2015.[26] While we're being generous, let's assume that each consumer also spends an average of $50 on apps each year for their slick, new Apple Watch, of which Apple would claim a 30 percent revenue share. That would add a paltry $180 million in additional revenue, albeit at high margins. The point here is that if Apple's ability to continue to outgrow the market this year requires upward of $20 billion of new revenue (and even more in the years ahead), it will take far more than the hyped Apple Watch to get the job done.

Undoubtedly, it will be difficult for Apple to outgrow the market in the long term. But is it impossible? After all, 13 percent of the five hundred companies in the CEB study cited earlier accomplished this feat for fifty years or longer. Exemplars of long-term growth performance include Johnson & Johnson (130-year-old healthcare products company) and the Ball Corporation (136-year-old provider of food packaging and aerospace products), who have admirably continued to

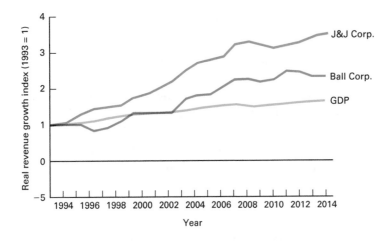

Figure 4.5 Long-term growth stars: J&J and Ball Corporation

outgrow the overall economy over the past two decades (figure 4.5). While outperforming the market long-term is a notably uncommon achievement, it is far from being a mathematical impossibility.

So where might Apple find its next growth wave, if not from their smart watch? There are several major opportunities that Apple could exploit to fuel another round of dramatic growth.

Gaming

The next generation of Apple's iPad is reputed to have processing speeds and video refresh rates equivalent to or better than any high-end gaming console. Combined with further inroads into the television market with streaming technologies, Apple can potentially disrupt the global gaming industry, which currently generates over $90 billion in revenue.[27]

Home Entertainment

Walter Isaacson's 2011 biography quoted Steve Jobs as saying "I finally cracked it"—the it being a uniquely easy-to-use television. Since then, Apple-watchers have been expecting a transformative technology that would put Apple in the forefront of the more than $120 billion global market in home entertainment.

Payments

With a worldwide installed base of over 800 million iTunes customers that have credit cards on file, and a market-leading share of mobile shopping on its iOS devices, Apple is ideally suited to transform the payment-processing industry. With over $4 trillion in credit card transactions in the United States alone, the Apple Pay product built into the iPhone 6 could be a game changer for Apple. Early market reaction from consumers and retailers has been positive.

Retail Services

In the same vein, Apple has been researching a range of in-store retail applications that would enable brick-and-mortar retailers to offer personalized shopping services to customers. Building on an in-store tracking technology called iBeacon, Apple could enable retailers to provide personalized shopping recommendations and cross-sell promotions, loyalty discounts, and automated checkout, all of which would generate transaction fees for Apple.

Mobile Wellness and Health-Care Solutions

Apple is investing heavily in health-and-fitness monitoring applications, to be incorporated in all its mobile computing devices. Industry analysts have forecast that the market for individual and enterprise solutions for mobile wellness is likely to grow to more than $40 billion over the next decade,[28] with Apple expected to be a major provider in its own right and in partnership with IBM.

Enterprise IT Solutions

Following its recently announced partnership with IBM, Apple is poised to significantly expand its presence in the enterprise market. Both partners have complementary objectives to sell integrated mobile business solutions in the iOS environment to IT executives. These solutions include internal management processes (accounts receivable, time-and-expense reporting) and customer-facing apps (customer relationship management, mHealth, order-to-fulfillment processes).

To date, Apple's inroads in the enterprise market has largely been confined to selling smartphones and tablets, sanctioned by IT departments, at corporate discounts. Partnering to move up the value chain to enterprise solutions gives Apple (and IBM) the opportunity to deepen enterprise penetration at attractive value-based margins.

Automotive

Perhaps most intriguingly, Apple is reportedly accelerating efforts to build an electric car, designating it internally as a "committed project" and aiming to deliver by 2020[29] While it's still uncertain how aggressively Apple wants to penetrate the car market, given its past track record and the fact that global automotive industry revenues exceed $1.5 trillion per year, there is obviously considerable growth potential for Apple in this arena.

Over the past two decades, Apple has repeatedly demonstrated an ability to launch market-expanding innovations, offsetting the inevitable sales declines of aging products. Moreover, Apple has been willing to cannibalize its own sales to seek new growth, as shown with the iPhone versus the iPod, and the iPad versus the MacBook. Looking forward, Apple's greatest growth opportunities may now lie in exploiting ecosystem services, supplementing its hardware wizardry with a wide range of solutions in entertainment, mobility, health, finance, and commerce.

Under any circumstances, the assertion that Apple cannot continue to outperform the market because of the law of large numbers is sophistry—a case of simple mathematics posing as immutable business law.

The Law of Competition

A second argument that suggests Apple and other market leaders are destined to decline falls under the rubric of the law of competition. According to this "law," a company's historically sky-high ROIC must inevitably revert to average levels for a number of generalizable reasons:

- The higher a company's ROIC, the more competition it will attract.
- New competitors are attracted to attack the market leader even if their cash returns are slightly lower than the market leaders. As long as the opportunity to generate above-average returns by

attacking the market leader is deemed higher than alternative uses of capital, direct competitors will flood the market.

- As more competitors enter the market, the market leader's product differentiation will weaken, pricing pressures will mount, and ROIC for all players will inevitably decline.
- This process will continue until profit spreads (ROIC less the cost of capital) approach zero, at which point a new industry equilibrium will be established with market leaders reduced to operating at or near industry-average net returns.

This theory is elegant and underlying data appear to be supportive. For example, figure 4.6 displays the distribution of ROIC versus market cap for all publicly traded U.S. companies in 2013. Adherents of the law of competition would claim their theory is validated by the observed decline in Apple's ROIC and market cap between 2012 and 2013. Presumably, this is a timid first step toward Apple "going down the tubes" in the wake of growing competition.

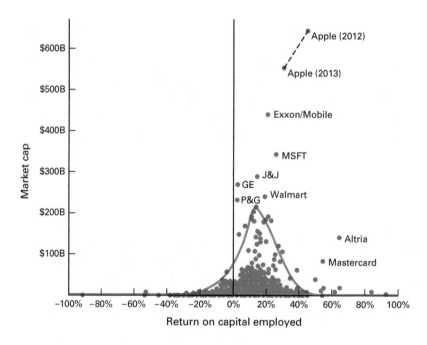

Figure 4.6 Financial performance of U.S. companies, 2013. *Source*: Osiris Financial Database

Many industry observers have also pointed to Apple's loss of technological leadership in the smartphone and tablet market[30] and the four-year lag since its last game-changing product (the iPad) as further evidence of its inability to maintain the competitive advantage required to sustain high margins.

The inexorability of this interpretation of the law of competition as applied to Apple and other highly profitable corporations is fundamentally flawed on two grounds.

First, this "law" applies only if the market leader stands pat, opening opportunities for competitors to catch up with or surpass the technical merits of current product offerings. If the market leader continuously adapts its strategy, renewing its bases of competitive advantage, competitors may be put in a position of perennially playing catch-up. Take Amazon, for example. If Amazon had been content to sit on and defend its market-leading e-commerce book business, it would be a declining business worth no more than $3 billion today. Instead, Amazon, currently a $100 billion company growing at more than 20 percent per year, chose to disrupt itself in the book market and dramatically expand the scale and scope of its enterprise. It put competitors on the run, rather than exposing itself to the law of competition. True, most companies struggle to maintain a perennial industry-leading pace of product innovation, but there is no immutable law preventing such an achievement. Apple's track record over the past two decades in this regard has been extraordinary. As noted earlier, Apple faces no shortage of future growth opportunities. In 2015, Apple reversed its temporary decline in financial performance in 2013, achieving a market cap of over $700 million and an ROIC in excess of 48 percent.

Second, as applied to Apple, many critics of its current products apparently misunderstand the basis of the company's competitive advantage. Apple has never billed itself as a first mover or laid claim to leadership on technical specifications, such as the "speeds and feeds" of its products. Rather, Apple has created competitive advantage by consistently providing a superior customer experience across an expanding array of hardware devices and consumer services. This source of competitive advantage has as much to do with Apple's integrated software-development prowess as with its hardware wizardry. Apple's product-design superiority is another intangible but highly significant differentiator. Lest one doubt that these sources of Apple's competitive advantage can continue to nullify the law of competition, consider the latest consumer electronics battlefield: smart watches. More than three dozen manufacturers have rushed products to market in this space, led by Samsung, Pebble, and Sony. But as *New York Times* fashion writer Vanessa Friedman noted in her "On the Runway" column, reviewing Samsung's initial smart watch entries,

> Neither [smart watch model] does what the best design does, which is make you rethink all your old assumptions about the form . . . In fact, the watches do the opposite: they re-enforce all our old assumptions about the form, which is that you take your phone screen, make it small and stick it on your wrist. All I can think when I see them is "Beam me up, Scotty!" And where's the joy—or the desire—in that? . . . Admittedly, this has entirely to do with aesthetics, not functionality or engineering. But a smart watch is an accessory, so aesthetics matters.[31]

Tech writers have been largely negative as well, noting the lack of useful functionality and confusing user interfaces of the current offerings.[32] Given these reviews, it's not surprising that early sales in the smart watch category have been disappointing. But after the Apple Watch's first six months on the market, history appears to be repeating itself. Apple is expanding the size of the category and selling more than twice as many smart watches as the rest of the industry combined, once again setting a new standard for style, form factor, capability, usability, and market leadership.

Critics who bemoan Apple's late entry in this category as proof that Apple has lost its innovative edge in the post-Jobs era should remember that Apple's unprecedented success with the iPod, iPhone, and iPad came at least a decade after competitors pioneered products in these categories, as noted in figure 4.7.

The few times Apple has stumbled in launching a new product is when it has rushed a new product to market without taking the time to refine the user experience. Examples of this include the Newton personal digital assistant and the Rokr, Apple's first mobile phone (in a joint venture with Motorola). More recently, and characteristically, Apple waited to launch its electronic wallet service, Apple Pay, in conjunction with the introduction of the iPhone 6 product line. In doing so, Apple took the time to learn from the earlier unsuccessful mobile

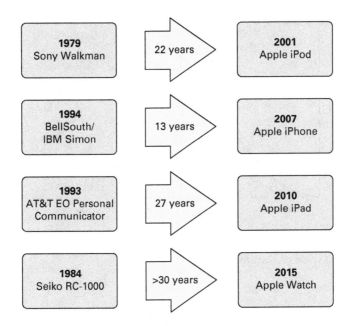

Figure 4.7 Time between first mover and Apple's first entry

wallet entries from Google, PayPal, and others to perfect its industry-leading user experience.[33]

The bottom line is that companies can overcome the law of competition, provided they continue to innovate with superior—if not first-to-market—product technologies.

The Law of Competitive Advantage

At the heart of the notion that large companies cannot sustain long-term profitable growth is the belief that the basis of a company's competitive advantage inevitably erodes over time. This argument rightfully recognizes that all products and services experience a life cycle. The familiar bell-shaped curve shown in figure 4.8 traces the typical sales trajectory of a new product through early adoption, rapid growth, maturity, and eventual decline, all driven by advances in competing technologies and shifts in customer preferences.[34] Joseph Schumpeter described this process as "creative destruction" over fifty years ago.[35]

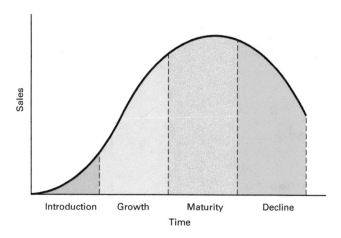

Figure 4.8 Typical product life cycle

While the underlying dynamics are still true today, Downes and Nunes have argued that product life cycles have dramatically shortened due to a number of emerging information technologies.[36]

Whatever one assumes about the duration of a product lifecycle, it is undeniable that to sustain long-term market leadership, companies must consistently renew their product lineup with the next new thing in each of the categories in which they compete. This does not mean simply adding incremental improvements, which, notes Christensen, propels most companies into a no-win, feature–function arms race. Instead, successful companies must rethink their consumer value proposition and consider entirely new product concepts aimed at not only current customers but also at those poorly served by current offerings.

Herein lies the challenge. Most established market leaders are extremely reluctant to disrupt themselves and, as a result, are eventually overtaken by newcomers bringing radically different solutions to market that are better and/or cheaper than existing products.

The reason incumbents usually fail to disrupt themselves often boils down to the strong tendency of large companies to focus on their bigger, more demanding customers, who typically push for incremental improvements in current products, and on traditional competitors, who behave similarly. They tend to dismiss non-traditional entrants, whose initial product entries may be relatively crude and unsophisticated, and lack interest in nascent or underserved segments that seem to offer limited short-term revenue opportunities. Incumbents often lack internal processes and management mindsets that promote corporate entrepreneurship, and establish incentives that reinforce short-term profit-taking while dissuading risky or long-term business development. As a result, most companies wind up riding the tail end of their product life cycles to stalled growth or worse.

Is it possible to overcome these barriers to innovation, allowing a company to renew its basis of competitive advantage and sustain market leadership?

The answer is *yes*, provided that a company faithfully executes the three pillars of the strategy for long-term growth that I identified earlier: *continuous innovation* to generate an ongoing stream of *meaningfully differentiated products and services* valued by consumers, enabled by *business alignment* of all corporate capabilities, resources, incentives, and business culture and processes to support a company's strategic intent.

Such an approach yields a succession of new product launches whose growth trajectories more than offset declining sales of aging products. This is shown in figure 4.9, where total company sales at any given time is equal to the sum of sales from each product at the respective stage of its product life cycle.

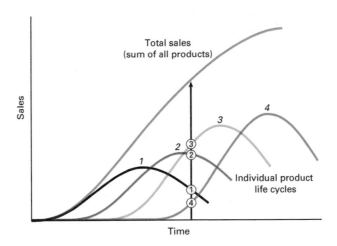

Figure 4.9 Long-term growth over successive product life cycles

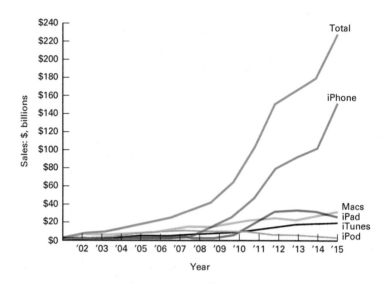

Figure 4.10 Apple sales by product line

This is precisely what two of the most rapidly growing large companies—Apple and Amazon—have done over the past two decades. For example, Apple has sustained rapid growth by repeatedly launching innovative and meaningfully differentiated products, sometimes at the expense of cannibalizing its older product lines (figure 4.10). Similarly, Amazon's exceptionally strong sustained topline growth (if not profitability) has been driven by relentless scope expansion and product innovation. This also often comes from initiatives with long-term payoffs that cannibalize existing product lines (as was the case with Kindle e-books versus print books and Amazon's new streaming music service versus CD sales).

Summing It Up

In summary, the belief that business Goliaths will eventually lose their basis of competitive advantage and suffer declining business performance stems from an implicit assumption that large enterprises exhibit strategic inertia. It is true that if a company, whether small or large, focuses more on defending current market positions than on renewing its basis of competitive advantage with meaningfully differentiated innovative products and services, it *will* fail, for a number of reasons.

First, the law of large numbers will catch up with the company as its products saturate maturing markets. For example, Apple's iPhone sales are already more reliant on repeat purchases than new-to-category customers.

Second, competitors will relentlessly attack current products with comparable (or better) features, often at lower cost, eroding margins and enterprise value. For example, Xiaomi became the top-selling smartphone in China after only three years on the market by aggressively matching iPhone functionality at half the price but has since lost ground itself to other low-cost smartphone competitors.

Third, the historical basis of a company's competitive advantage will be weakened or possibly destroyed by emerging disruptive technologies. For example, Apple's industry-leading music download business (iTunes) has already stalled as a result of aggressive expansion by streaming music services from Spotify, Pandora, and Amazon.[37]

While inevitable, product life cycle effects are not inescapable. Unlike scientific laws, which describe intrinsic, immutable characteristics of our physical world, supposed business laws like the law of large numbers can be broken by strong leaders that continuously adapt their business strategy to sustain long-term profitable growth. As I pointed out earlier in this chapter, 13 percent of large corporations have been able to sustain above-market growth for a half-century or more despite relentless external competition and internal barriers to corporate entrepreneurship. Exceptional CEOs such as Howard Schultz (Starbucks), Craig Jelinek (Costco), Fred Smith (FedEx), and Tim Cook (Apple) are able to achieve long-term profitable growth, defying the chorus of naysayers who insist that the mighty must eventually fall.

CHAPTER FIVE

Do You Know
What Your Strategy Is?

CHAPTER 3 CLOSED with a question: Does your company (or the one you want to build) have a compelling and clearly articulated North Star? This refers to a company's stated purpose, values, and priorities. The logical extension of this question is explored here: Do you know what your strategy is?

As I will explain in this chapter, in far too many companies the answer is no. Corporate executives often struggle with strategy formulation and communication. In such cases, the problem often starts with an inability to define genuine North Star corporate goals that can be translated into specific, measurable, achievable, relevant, and time-dependent objectives. This often leads to strategic inertia, undermining the ability to effectively respond to the accelerating pace of marketplace shifts.

Ask any CEO, and you'll undoubtedly hear this: "Of course we know our strategy!" If this were the case, one should also get the same response from each of the company's key constituencies: the board of directors, employees, business partners, customers, and investors. But the reality is, far too often, companies can't or don't express their strategy in terms that are clearly understood and embraced by their stakeholders. Or there is a serious disconnect between what senior executives *say* their business strategy and priorities are, and how employees are actually managed and incentivized.

According to research recently cited in the *Harvard Business Review*, only 29 percent of employees of high-performing companies with publicly stated strategies could correctly identify their company's strategy out of six choices. As such, a majority of employees are not in a position to link their personal work initiatives and decision-making to the desired direction of the firm.[1] Think of it like this: a racing scull with rowers each choosing their own pace or direction would not win many races.

Discouragingly, this problem exists between senior executives and their boards as well. Of the 772 directors surveyed by McKinsey in 2013, a mere 34 percent agreed that the boards on which they served fully comprehended their companies' strategies. Only 22 percent said their boards were completely aware of the ways their firms created value, and just 16 percent claimed that their boards had a strong understanding of the dynamics of their firms' industries.[2]

A company's stated strategic intent is also often misunderstood—or worse, not believed—by consumers or employees. For example, take the two companies with the lowest ranking among 230 companies surveyed in 2014 by the American Customer Satisfaction Index organization: Comcast and Time Warner Cable.[3] Consumers have consistently reviled these companies for poor customer service and deliberately confusing business practices, belying corporate pronouncements to the contrary:

> The way we interact with our customers on the phone, online, in their homes, is just as important to our success as any other products that we provide. Put simply, customer service should be our best product.
>
> —BRIAN ROBERTS, CEO, COMCAST[4]

> We're telling our customers how we've made profound changes over the last two years to better respect their time, provide more value for what they pay us, and deliver the kind of experience anyone would expect from a leading entertainment and technology company. The many changes we've made are just the beginning of the new TWC service experience.
>
> —ROB MARCUS, CEO, TIME WARNER CABLE[5]

In a similar vein, consider that nearly three-fourths of senior executives proclaim that innovation is among their top three corporate priorities according to a recent BCG survey.[6] But in my experience, corporations often fail to translate such intent into meaningful action to make innovation a natural and ongoing component of an organization's operations.[7] For example, if you work for an organization ostensibly committed to innovation, are your answers to the following questions consistent with what you would expect?

- How have you been trained and encouraged as a business innovator?
- If you have a new idea, how easily can you get seed capital and the time to experiment?
- Does your company have a culture that rewards new initiative and tolerates false starts?
- Are all levels of management responsible for innovation, and do results contribute to compensation and career advancement?
- Are innovation initiatives supported even in tough market conditions?

Negative responses to these questions are indicative of situations where a lack of strategic clarity or ineffective or disingenuous intent frustrates customers, confuses employees, and undermines long-term business performance.[8]

Sometimes, the problem isn't simply poor communications, but the inherent confusion arising from a poorly conceived or ever-changing strategy. For example, prior to his resignation in 2015, Dick Costolo, the CEO of Twitter, struggled to define a strategy to translate the company's outsized societal impact into meaningful business results, frustrating employees and investors alike. On his first post-IPO analyst call in early 2014, Costolo stressed that his sole focus would be on expanding the size of Twitter's core user base to "reach every person on the planet." Yet, just six months later, Costolo confusingly stated that "we think about everything we do in the context of [a] set of geometrically eccentric circles."[9]

The *Wall Street Journal* noted that "the strategy shift reflected Mr. Costolo's management style. Interviews with current and former Twitter employees and others close to Mr. Costolo and his company describe the former improv comedian as a reactive thinker who bounces from one idea to the next."[10]

Twitter's dearth of strategic clarity has been costly. In 2014 and 2015, Twitter's active user growth slowed dramatically, executive turnover was rampant, and its market cap declined by 67 percent.

Management Hierarchy

To put the issue of strategic clarity in context, let's start by defining terms. Figure 5.1 illustrates the four hierarchical elements required to formulate and execute effective business strategy. The starting point is a set of overarching *goals* that establish a company's long-run intent and management priorities. We've already noted several examples in the North Star mission statements of Johnson & Johnson, Amazon, and Starbucks. A company's stated goals identify the broad boundaries of business scope and the areas of business activity and performance of greatest concern to management, e.g., consumer satisfaction, employee safety and welfare, shareholder value, and sustainable business practices.

Objectives are more concrete and provide specific targets to guide an organization's strategy in prioritizing initiatives, making tradeoffs, and measuring progress against defined metrics. To serve their intended purpose, objectives should be SMART:

SPECIFIC. Defined in precise terms that reflect strategic priorities, like customer retention or earnings.

MEASURABLE. Remember the saying, "You can't manage what you can't measure"? Objectives should be stated in terms of metrics that can be quantitatively tracked, like customer loyalty rates and total shareholder returns.

ACHIEVABLE. While objectives should ideally stretch and motivate the organization, they should be realistically achievable within a specified time frame.

RELEVANT. Objectives should focus the company's energies on making progress towards achieving stated goals and supporting corporate values.

TIME DEPENDENT. Explicit deadlines should be established to signify whether or not objectives have been met within a prescribed time frame.

To illustrate these concepts, let's say a firm has established the goals of providing innovative products and superior customer service to foster growth, employee opportunity, and shareholder value.

Figure 5.1 Management hierarchy

SMART objectives to measure how well these aspirations have been met by the end of the current fiscal year could include: launching at least three new products in categories that show signs of reaching maturation in the market; increasing overall revenue by at least 15 percent while improving operating margins by 1.2 percentage points; achieving top-rated customer satisfaction as measured by a specified, nationally recognized market research organization; improving employee engagement scores by at least 5 percent as tracked by company-wide surveys; and growing earnings and total shareholder returns by at least 18 percent.

A company's *strategy* describes how it plans to meet its stated objectives. Strategy is all about making choices, and a company's strategy guides which market opportunities to pursue, which products to create, which distribution channels to exploit, and which business partnerships to form. Strategic choices to ignore certain opportunities are just as important as actionable commitments. For this reason, unrealistically broad targets like Costolo's "reaching every person on the planet" provide little meaningful guidance on the focus and tradeoffs that must be made in the *tactics* required to implement a clearly articulated strategy.

Can You Reduce Your Strategy to a Sound Bite?

Taken together, the four elements depicted in figure 5.1 provide the basis for strategic clarity, where all stakeholders should clearly understand a company's strategy with respect to the target customers it is intending to serve, the products and services it will provide (and *not* provide) in serving the needs of these customers, the basis of competitive advantage that will allow it to provide more value to the target market than competing alternatives, and the business and financial objectives that should be achieved over a specified time period if the strategy is successfully implemented.

It sounds pretty straightforward, doesn't it? Most of my MBA students think so, until they put strategy formulation to a test suggested by a recent *Harvard Business Review* article titled "Can You Say What Your Strategy Is?"[11] In this provocative article, David J. Collis and Michael G. Rukstad challenge executives to summarize their business strategy, scope, and advantage in thirty-five words or less. Scope refers to the boundaries defining the business in terms of geography covered, customers targeted, and products and services to be offered. Advantage describes how management intends to create competitive advantage.

Why reduce business strategy to a sound bite? We've already seen that many companies struggle to articulate their strategy in simple terms that can be easily understood (and, it is hoped, embraced) by shareholders, employees, and customers. Forcing a company to describe its approach in thirty-five words or less stress tests strategic clarity. If the CEO can't explain the company's strategy in concise terms, how can he or she expect the marketplace to fill in the blanks? Companies routinely market their products in thirty-second spots, pop-up online ads, and one-line mobile banners. Short and clear messages are an everyday reality. Collis and Rukstad assert that the inability of most companies to effectively articulate their strategy in short form is proof that they lack strategic clarity.

In my class, after reading a detailed case study on the Colorado-based Coors Brewing Company, students are asked to describe the company's business strategy in the 1970s in thirty-five words or less, and contrast it with Coors's apparent strategy today. Two lessons learned emerge from this exercise. First, it is not nearly as easy as students expect to crystallize a company's strategy. Despite being presented with all the relevant facts describing Coors's market environment and the approach the company took to achieve considerable success in the 1970s, most students struggle to synthesize the essence of the company's strategy in simple terms. Second, as the case study discussion unfolds, it becomes clear that even companies with a clear and winning strategy need to adapt their strategy over time. What worked well for Coors in the 1970s would not be effective or relevant today.

The text box below shows a "school solution" for Coors's mid-1970s strategy expressed in thirty-five words, and how it addresses three key questions defining strategic scope and advantage.[12] Despite its brevity, this sound bite strategy conveys the tradeoffs the company made in formulating a strategy to differentiate itself from market leader Anheuser-Busch. As noted in table 5.1, Coors earned a reputation for superior taste (from clearly stated product advantages) despite its lower price (supported by economy of scale and lower regional distribution costs), allowing the company to outperform Anheuser-Busch in the western states on market share, revenue growth, plant utilization, and both gross and operating profit margins throughout the 1970s. Coors is an excellent example of how a clearly articulated and well-executed strategy can drive superior business results.[13]

But market circumstances inevitably change, as success provokes competitive response. In the 1980s, the two largest U.S. beer companies, Anheuser-Busch and Miller, aggressively increased brewery capacity in Coors's western market territory and engaged in an unprecedentedly intense advertising war that increased marketing expenditures on a per-barrel basis by an order of magnitude. Moreover, the growing

---

Strategic Clarity: Coors Brewing Company—1970s

[Serve discriminating beer drinkers in western states][1] [with affordable, superior quality premium beer][2] [from Rocky Mountain waters, natural ingredients, and a unique brewing and aging process in the highest scale, lowest cost vertically integrated brewery].[3]

1. Who is Coors trying to serve?
2. With what product?
3. With what basis of differentiation and competitive advantage?

TABLE 5.1

Comparison of the Strategies of Coors and Anheuser-Busch—1970s

Strategy Element	Coors	Anheuser-Busch
Market coverage	Western states	National
Customer focus	Sophisticated beer drinkers	Mass market
Brand message focus	Product superiority/ authenticity	Lifestyle
Product differentiation	Rocky mountain waters, no pasteurization, premium ingredients	Nothing specific; asserted to be "King of Beers"
Operations	Single large-scale brewery	Distributed small-scale breweries
Price point	Lower	Higher

popularity of light beers pioneered by Miller began to erode sales of full-bodied lagers, notably the company's only product, Coors Banquet. In response, Coors radically altered its strategy by expanding to national distribution, adding a light beer and switching to less distinctive lifestyle advertising themes. As a result, virtually every element of Coors's competitive advantage dissipated in the 1980s, leaving the company with weaker distribution, higher transportation costs, lower aggregate share of advertising voice, and less perceived product distinctiveness. Coors consequently experienced a significant decline in market share, profit margins, and market capitalization, reinforcing the imperative for strategic clarity *and* effective responses to shifts in the market and competitive environment.

To generalize the importance of achieving strategic clarity, responsive to current market needs, consider this thought exercise: What companies come to mind when you think of the best- and worst-managed companies? You might include Apple, Costco, or Nike in the first category and Sears, Yahoo, or Hewlett-Packard in the second. Now ask yourself which of these companies appear to have a clearer, more concise business strategy. If you can more clearly articulate the strategies of companies in the first category than those in the second, you've likely identified the starting point for explaining the differences in observed business performance.

Checklist for Effective Strategy Formulation

An effective strategy is one that creates, captures, and sustains value.

As shown in the left-most panel of figure 5.2, *value* is created whenever a company can create a product where a consumer's willingness to pay (WTP) exceeds the company's cost to serve (CTS).[14] The difference between WTP and CTS defines the magnitude of value created, to be split in some fashion between the consumer and provider.

A company achieves *competitive advantage* when it can deliver products to the market with either a lower cost, a higher consumer WTP, or both, compared to competitors. In this case, the advantaged company creates more value in the marketplace, as shown by the height of the highlighted bars in figure 5.2. We already saw such an example when Coors enjoyed a higher consumer WTP along with a lower CTS than Anheuser-Busch's competing Budweiser brand in the 1970s.

Where does price fit in? As shown in the right-hand panel of figure 5.2, companies can choose to price their products anywhere between WTP and CTS. This is a strategic decision that reflects how a company wants to divide the product value between itself and its customers. Consumers benefit from lower prices by enjoying a higher *consumer surplus,* the difference between what a consumer is willing to pay for a product and the actual price charged. High consumer surpluses spur sales, increasing growth and customer satisfaction.

Producer surplus is an equivalent concept from the opposite perspective—the difference between the price a company charges and

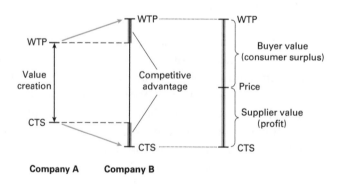

Figure 5.2 Value, competitive advantage, and consumer surplus

its unit cost. Obviously, companies that enjoy a competitive advantage in the marketplace have more pricing flexibility when choosing how to allocate value between the company and consumers. In the beer industry example, Coors chose to price its Banquet lager beer below Budweiser, which helped it achieve higher sales, growth rates, market share and plant utilization. Despite lower pricing, Coors's lower cost structure allowed it to achieve higher profit margins than Anheuser-Busch. Competitive advantage, while it lasts, is a wonderful thing.

External Alignment

The starting point for an effective strategy is the development of appealing, differentiated products with compelling value propositions, for which targeted consumers are willing to pay considerably more than the company's unit costs. Unless the company is committed to be *the* low-cost provider for products in the markets it serves, meaningful product differentiation driving high WTP is the critical requirement to achieve competitive advantage. The challenge of course is that customer preferences, product technology, and the competitive landscape are highly dynamic, requiring continuous innovation to respond to ever-changing market circumstances.

Just look to the airline industry for an example of the challenges of achieving and sustaining competitive advantage.

For many years, JetBlue Airways competed on the basis of delivering a distinctive, premium coach class service at moderate (albeit not the lowest) fares, with perks not normally found on competing carriers: roomier leather seats, satellite TV service, premium snacks, free non-alcoholic beverages, and free baggage check. In contrast, many of JetBlue's competitors chose to compete for coach class passengers on the basis of lowest baseline cost, stripping out basic amenities (e.g., seat room) while charging fees (often hidden) for every imaginable service: rebooking, baggage check, priority boarding, roomier seats, drinks, snacks, blankets, etc.[15]

JetBlue's customer-friendly services have been recognized and appreciated by passengers, who have given the airline the highest rating for customer satisfaction among low-cost airlines for eleven consecutive years.[16] But customer satisfaction doesn't necessarily translate into a willingness to pay higher fares for all passengers, and competitive pricing pressures have constrained JetBlue's pricing ability to offset its higher costs and self-imposed lack of revenue from ancillary fees. The net result has taken a toll on JetBlue's financial performance relative to competing low-cost carriers; in 2014, its operating income as a percentage of revenue was roughly half that of Spirit Airlines, two-thirds of Allegiant Air, and three-fourths of Southwest.

In response, starting in 2015, JetBlue revised its pricing and product strategy to create and capture additional value, adding more seats to its aircraft, reducing baseline fares, charging additional service fees and adding new coach fare classes. The new strategy better matched JetBlue's product offerings and prices to segmented consumer preferences. Customers who preferred *and were willing to pay for* superior perks (e.g. faster check-in, extra legroom, no baggage fees) could opt for a higher-priced service, while budget-conscious flyers could buy a no-frills ticket at a low fare.

The market response has been quite positive. In 2015, JetBlue's operating income more than doubled relative to the prior year, while its stock price increased by 43 percent, the highest percentage gain in the U.S. airline industry. JetBlue's example illustrates that companies need to continuously innovate to create meaningfully differentiated products and services that not only are recognized and appreciated by consumers but drive a higher willingness to pay.

Internal Alignment

The second requirement for an effective strategy is for a company to capture the value it creates in the marketplace by appropriately deciding where and how to compete, and aligning its capabilities— its core business processes, operations, management systems, and culture—to support its intended value proposition. Effective internal alignment positions a company to deliver differentiated products at a cost structure that allows it to capture most of the value created (table 5.2).

For example, consider IBM, who enjoyed market dominance in the personal computer market in the 1980s. The IBM Personal Computer, introduced in 1981, achieved immediate market success—generating more revenue within three years than that of IBM's four largest competitors combined.[17] But IBM made what turned out to be a pivotal mistake: it outsourced the development of the operating system to Microsoft and the microprocessor design and fabrication to Intel.

TABLE 5.2
Strategy Objectives

Strategy Objectives	Strategic Focus	Requisites for Success
1. Create value	Who to serve? Which products? What price? Deliver compelling consumer value proposition Create value-added Price relative to WTP	External Alignment: Develop products which meet differentiated consumer needs
2. Capture value	Where and how to compete? – Where in the market? – Where in the value chain? – Achieve competitive advantage	Internal Alignment: Develop capabilities to support strategy and intended value proposition
3. Sustain value	When to adapt? – How to erect barriers to entry? a. Patents b. Customer lock-in (e.g., ecosystem) c. Scale/experience d. High brand equity – When to adapt current strategies?	Dynamic Alignment: Revise strategy to respond to changes in market and competitive environment

This decision opened the door to low-cost imitators, who could now access the same core technologies as IBM and flood the market with PC clones. IBM relegated itself to compete on the basis of its relatively high-cost, nonproprietary computer design and assembly. Eventually, intense price competition eroded IBM's operating margins to unsustainably low levels, prompting the company to divest its PC division to Lenovo in 2004. At the same time, "Wintel" providers— using Microsoft's Windows operating system and Intel's microprocessors—were able to capture most of the profits in the PC value chain (figure 5.3).[18]

In this example, IBM did not align its internal capabilities to support sustained product superiority and capture significant value in the PC industry. In contrast, Apple has retained vertically integrated control

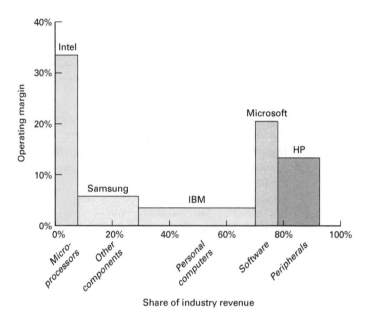

Figure 5.3 PC value chain—1998

over the design of proprietary operating systems, microprocessors, and its mobile apps platform, enabling it to design consistently superior computers and mobile devices and to capture industry-leading profit margins.

Let's compare these two companies: while IBM struggled to maintain a 5 percent operating margin on its stalled PC business in the late 1990s, over the past five years, Apple has sustained an operating margin of over 30 percent, while growing at a compound annual growth rate of almost 40 percent.

Across all industries, successful companies ensure that their strategies are *externally aligned* with the needs of their targeted customers and *internally aligned* to nurture the capabilities required to deliver superior products and to capture value. Just look at Southwest Airlines, BMW, or Intuit.

Southwest strives to deliver frequent, friendly, reliable airline service to price-sensitive leisure and business travelers at a price others can't profitably match. To do so, Southwest maintains standardized and simplified flight operations (e.g., one plane type, one class of service, no meals), strong labor relations (to enhance morale and foster a service-oriented culture), and highly disciplined growth (to avoid overextending in the cyclical, competitive airline industry). As a result, Southwest has enjoyed decades of extraordinary shareholder value growth, with highly satisfied customers and a loyal and engaged workforce.[19]

BMW offers premium-priced "ultimate driving machines" that are valued by a select segment of automotive enthusiasts. To support its strategic mission, BMW has built an organization that stresses R&D, state-of-the-art engineering, and disciplined product development processes, while nurturing a corporate culture committed to best-in-class motor vehicles. These are expensive capabilities to maintain, but BMW recognizes the imperative for external and internal alignment to serve a class of customer that is able and willing to pay for superior products. As a result, BMW has been among the top-selling global luxury automobile brands over the past decade, despite intense competition from Mercedes-Benz, Audi, Lexus, and others.[20]

When Intuit entered the U.S. market in 1983, it was the forty-seventh company to offer software to help people track their finances, yet it quickly became a top seller by excelling in the creation of intuitive, easy-to-use products. To maintain market leadership, Intuit has invested heavily to instill design thinking throughout its organization, increased its design staff nearly sevenfold over the past six years, and acquired companies bringing innovative new functionality and approaches to its core product suite. Intuit's commitment to "design for delight" has allowed it to increase its market share, revenues, and operating profit margins over the past five years in a category where fierce price competition and high topple rates—a measure of the change in market leadership— are more the industry norm.[21]

Companies that tightly link their internally and externally aligned strategies make it difficult for competitors to copy them. For example, it would be easy for a competing airline to temporarily slash fares to match Southwest or to provide bare-bones service at lower prices, but unless competitors can develop an equivalent operational focus, organizational culture, and management discipline, they won't duplicate Southwest's bundle of appealing service *and* low fares over an extensive route network. Similarly, automotive competitors have tried to claim for years that their products compare favorably with BMW at a far lower price. But automotive aficionados have generally continued to discern, recognize, and reward BMW's product superiority, despite premium pricing. Intuit has also faced intense competition, including many new entrants offering "freemium" products promising consumers basic functionality at no cost. But Intuit's continued Design for Delight emphasis has kept customers coming back, and allowed it to increase market share and profits over the past five years.

Dynamic Alignment

The pace of change in the underlying drivers of business performance keeps accelerating. Instantaneous global communications, big bang disruption, big data analytics, cloud-based software services, the Internet of Things, design thinking, Lean LaunchPad, global sourcing, crowdsourcing product reviews and funding, and other technology-driven forces are challenging companies across all industries to rethink their traditional business practices. *Dynamic alignment* is the third essential element of an effective strategy: the need to continuously revise a company's bases of competitive advantage. Strategy renewal needs to be as dynamic as the market, technology, and competitive forces influencing business.

To put this issue in historical perspective, I fondly recall one of my first corporate strategy clients who retained my consulting firm to help them prepare their annually updated five-year strategic plan, which in retrospect reinforced incremental thinking and management rigidity. The process was a top-down, tightly orchestrated exercise in which each business unit was required to fill out a tortuously detailed questionnaire on market and competitive trends, investment requirements, and pro forma financial projections. Each division knew that other business units would be padding their investment requests, so the name of the game was to add a significant cushion to actual corporate funding needs.

When all submissions were complete, the corporate staff and consultants analyzed the data, allocated scarce investment capital, and set preliminary divisional financial targets for the coming five years. After a final round of heated divisional negotiations, the five-year plan was set in stone—or rather, in leather. The finalized five-year plan was printed on heavy stock paper and encased in a gold-embossed leather cover, lending gravitas to the guesstimates masquerading as reliable business forecasts and to the questionable relevance of the long-term strategic plans.

Despite the ensuing market dynamism and the widely recognized gamesmanship underscoring this strategic planning process, the resulting financial targets took on a life of their own. Executives strove to "make their numbers," because underperformance carried financial and career penalties, while dramatic overdelivery would undoubtedly raise the bar for future years, increasing the risk of future shortfalls. Such rigid strategic planning processes put a premium on predictability and orderly execution, belying considerable marketplace uncertainties and relentless change.

It would be tempting to conclude that this anecdote represents a quaint and extreme historical example. Surely no modern enterprise would willfully disregard the ever-changing market and competitive environment, the increasingly frequent need to reallocate corporate capital to preempt disruptive industry forces, or the need to strategically respond to new market insights. Or would they?

Some sobering observations suggest that *strategic inertia*—the tendency for organizations to remain mired in the status quo and to resist strategic renewal outside the frame of current business operations—is still prevalent in corporate strategy processes.[22]

First of all, too many companies still conflate their annual budgeting process with enlightened strategic planning, which unwittingly contributes to strategic inertia. The need for major strategic renewal doesn't neatly fit into traditional annual budget cycles or processes. Traditional annual budgeting processes tend to perpetuate incremental adjustments to existing divisional budgets rather than effectively reallocating corporate capital to support major new strategic initiatives. Many of my EMBA and MBA students confirm that the budget planning process described above (and its attendant consequences) still largely persist in the firms they have worked for. As Rita McGrath writes in *The End of Competitive Advantage* "If you dropped into a boardroom discussion or an executive team meeting, chances are you'd hear a lot of strategic thinking based on ideas and frameworks designed in, and for, a different era."[23]

The consequence is that incumbent market leaders too often tend to prop up existing products long after they have begun to show signs of commoditization or worse, near-term obsolescence. Companies like Blockbuster, Sears, Kodak, Nokia, and Borders certainly were aware of disruptive technologies threatening their industries and had the resources to reposition their businesses. But each pursued a tepid strategic response, which ultimately contributed to their severe decline or liquidation.

Strategic inertia should not be confused with doing nothing. Each of these companies continued to actively plan and manage their businesses through the decline, investing in incremental product improvements, cutting costs and prices, and marketing existing products. This is a common response from leaders of declining businesses, whose first priority is often to protect their threatened organizations and business franchises, rather than reconceptualizing the basis of value creation in the marketplace.

McKinsey has analyzed the prevalence and consequences of corporate strategic inertia as measured by a tendency to invest the same level of capital in existing business units over long periods of time. The results of this analysis of business unit capital allocation for more than sixteen hundred companies over a fifteen-year period (1991–2005) were striking.[24]

For one-third of the companies in the sample encompassing a diverse range of industries, the amount of capital allocated to business units in a given year was almost identical to the amount received in the prior year, despite widespread changes in their marketplaces.

Companies that did respond more dynamically to market threats and opportunities—the top third of McKinsey's sample that shifted an average of 56 percent of capital across business units over the fifteen-year observation period—made on average 30 percent higher total returns to shareholders than the companies in the bottom third of the sample. Companies with more dynamic capital reallocation were also less likely to declare bankruptcy or to be acquired and showed increased CEO job tenure.

Why is there such a disconnect between the widespread recognition that marketplace forces are becoming more dynamic and corporate willingness to accelerate and broaden their strategic response?

There are several root causes of strategic inertia: short-term risk aversion, cognitive biases, corporate culture, bureaucratic constraints, and ineffective governance.

Short-Term Risk Aversion

In the previous chapter, I noted that in pursuit of maximizing shareholder value, too many companies adopt an overly short time horizon—one that favors cost-cutting and quick fixes over long-term investments in strategic repositioning for value creation. Managers are well aware that reallocating capital to new ventures is risky, as it entails operating in uncharted territories with respect to market acceptance, technology feasibility, and organizational execution. But such risks must be assessed against the almost certain decline in financial performance associated with sticking to aging products in the existing business portfolio. The greatest risk a company faces is often failing to respond to emerging market opportunities and threats.

Cognitive Biases

There are also significant cognitive biases that unwittingly reinforce strategic inertia: loss aversion and anchoring. Loss aversion refers to an individual's behavioral tendency to seek to minimize losses rather than to maximize gains. This cognitive bias steers managers away from pursuing new ventures, which often require trading short-term losses for the promise of long-term value creation.[25]

For example, in the McKinsey study,[26] the companies that reallocated higher levels of resources over time spans of less than three years delivered lower shareholder returns than their more static peers. But, over the long term, these dynamically managed companies significantly outperformed companies manifesting strategic inertia.[27]

Anchoring refers to an individual's tendency to over-rely—or to anchor—on one salient piece of information when making decisions. For example, a business unit general manager's budget allocation for the previous year often serves as an anchor during strategic and budget planning deliberations, even if market circumstances suggest the need for a radical shift in investment focus.[28]

Corporate Culture

Given the prevalence of gamesmanship underscoring corporate budget planning I described earlier in this chapter, cultural norms often dictate that executives "go to the mats" on behalf of their business unit. No business unit general manager wants to be seen to be losing funding relative to other divisions. Moreover, executive bonuses, self-esteem, and career progression prospects are often tied to short-term business performance. There is often no incentive for a business unit general manager to voluntarily play Robin Hood—cede a portion of his or her divisional budget—to help fund a promising venture in need of corporate investment capital.

Another form of short-term thinking may also be at play in this regard. If an executive expects to spend no more than a few years leading any given business unit, he or she will be motivated to maximize short-term results. If the business unit ultimately fails to position itself for long-term success, the consequences are likely to fall on an unfortunate successor.

Bureaucratic Constraints

Even if an enlightened senior executive within an enterprise seeks to radically rethink his or her business unit strategy, he or she is likely to be constrained by corporate management processes that influence the way a company allocates resources, evaluates employees, negotiates contracts, and communicates with internal and external stakeholders. After all, corporate strategists like to conduct elegant analytical reviews, HR likes to standardize performance management systems, lawyers like to write bulletproof contracts, and PR wants to control message content.

Moreover, these business processes are interdependent, creating a tightly woven management structure that cannot easily be pulled apart (e.g., legal reviews of HR procedures and PR press releases). For example, imagine a dynamic business leader attempting to create a new business unit requiring a distinctly different approach, requiring new skill sets, compensation schemes, and fast-paced marketing communications associated with social media. He or she is likely to find that in trying to end run one process, two or three others become upset, and pretty soon, the intrepid entrepreneur is taking on the entire corporate bureaucracy.

Ineffective Governance

As noted earlier, too often boards of directors lack sufficient understanding of their company's strategic imperatives, sources of business unit value creation, or market and industry dynamics to provide adequate oversight. As such, there are insufficient checks and balances to offset the pervasive forces promoting strategic inertia in many organizations.

Strategy Flaws in Concept and Execution

This chapter opened with the question, do you know what your strategy is? Regrettably, we concluded that the answer is often no. Too many companies are hampered by ineffective strategy formulation, communication, or both. In such cases, the problem often starts with an inability to clearly articulate genuine North Star corporate goals, which can be translated into specific, measurable, achievable, relevant, and time-dependent objectives. Moreover, we stipulated that effective strategy needs to be externally, internally, and dynamically aligned with evolving marketplace needs. And finally, we concluded that a number of factors contribute to strategic inertia, undermining the ability to effectively respond to the accelerating pace of marketplace shifts. The next chapter will identify corrective actions.

CHAPTER SIX

Getting Strategy Right

ABOUT TWENTY-FIVE YEARS ago, Audi of America hired a new president to turn around its sagging fortunes. For Markus Huber (not his real name),[1] this was a career highlight. Markus had worked his way up the marketing ranks to become VP of a competing German carmaker before finally getting tapped to head Audi.[2]

This anecdote illustrates the challenges and payoffs of getting strategy right.

While Markus knew he was joining a troubled company, the depths of Audi's problems did not become fully apparent until he settled into his new job. Audi's sales in the U.S. market had plummeted six years earlier when *60 Minutes* aired a segment detailing the alleged tendency of Audi's flagship model to exhibit unintended acceleration. The results were frightening and sometimes tragic, particularly as told by a devastated mother sharing the nightmare of running over and killing her six-year-old son. The segment included footage of the accelerator pedal of an Audi 5000 model moving on its own, propelling the driverless car forward, as graphic evidence of the car's fatal design flaw.

However, an exhaustive investigation by the U.S. National Highway Traffic Safety Administration subsequently concluded that Audi's uncontrolled acceleration resulted from driver error, not a design flaw.[3] In the tragic accident cases, drivers mistakenly pressed the accelerator rather than the brake pedal when trying to stop. Eventually, *60 Minutes* was forced to acknowledge that an air pump had been concealed in the test car to mechanically move the accelerator for a dramatic camera effect.[4]

But despite its total exoneration, Audi's image had been tarnished and sales remained deeply depressed. By the time Markus assumed his leadership role in 1993, Audi was selling about twelve thousand cars annually in the United States, nearly 85 percent below its sales rate prior to the damning *60 Minutes* broadcast. The company was losing over $60 million per year, with no realistic prospects for a near-term turnaround.

Playing the Hand You've Been Dealt

Having worked with Markus earlier in his career, I arranged a meeting to brainstorm how to improve Audi's business performance. Markus agreed to fund a short consulting assignment, in which my team would evaluate Audi's market and competitive situation and recommend a way forward. While we were focusing on Audi's strategic response, Markus had his hands full with tactical and cost-cutting priorities.

In order to understand our findings and recommendations, a brief review of Audi's background is in order.

Audi, a subsidiary of Volkswagen AG, is one of the German "Big Three," along with BMW and Mercedes-Benz, representing the best-selling luxury automakers in the world. In the 1980s, Audi competed in the shadow of its more prestigious brethren, selling compact and midsize front-wheel-drive (FWD) sedans in the United States at lower prices than the luxury rear-wheel-drive models from BMW and Mercedes-Benz. Audi's cars at the time were generally considered as somewhat undistinguished: they suffered spotty quality, conservative styling, and spartan interiors and appealed primarily to budget-conscious customers seeking the prestige of German automotive engineering at a relatively low price.

The exceptions in Audi's lineup were its Quattro models, incorporating a unique all-wheel-drive (AWD) design that had achieved remarkable success on the European rally racing circuit since its introduction in 1980. Quattro models featured a unique technology, which continuously adjusted the amount of power delivered to both front and back wheels, depending on the optimal traction required for varying driving conditions.

Audi first launched Quattro technology in the United States in 1983, bundled with luxury features that carried a considerably higher price tag than its higher-volume FWD models. Quattro models sold in limited numbers to automotive enthusiasts, inspired by the superior performance and road handling.[5] Through the early 1990s, the Quattro continued to build a stellar technology reputation, untarnished by Audi's broader image woes in the U.S. market. Quattro models remained unchallenged by BMW and Mercedes-Benz, neither of whom would introduce comparable technology for another seven years (and even then, in extremely small numbers). With Quattro, Audi truly had a crown jewel in its midst.

Even though Audi's overall U.S. sales collapsed following the *60 Minutes* report in 1986, Quattro sales continued to grow, reaching 18 percent of Audi's twelve thousand unit sales total in 1993. But Audi could not stem the decline in its FWD car sales, despite steep discounts that reduced prices well below the company's costs. In essence, while Audi's traditional sedans had always been considered a notch below the prestige of BMW and Mercedes-Benz models, its FWD cars had become virtually sale-proof by the early 1990s.

In the fall of 1993, my consulting team completed its extensive analysis of market data, reaffirming that Audi was holding a losing hand in the United States. At Markus's request, I delivered a summary of our findings and recommendations at a private meeting in his office.

The report was short and to the point. The opening page, reproduced in the text box below, starkly concluded that the company would probably not survive another year, barring sweeping changes in its U.S. market strategy. This was followed by numerous market analyses characterizing Audi's untenable market position. Every measure—brand awareness, consideration, purchase intent, customer satisfaction, owner loyalty, image strength, product quality, dealer profitability, advertising share of voice, price realization and financial performance—pointed to a continued exodus of current Audi owners trading for competing makes, coupled with an inability to attract enough new customers (even with financially ruinous discounts) to reverse sales declines.

The presentation concluded with the recommendation that Audi should rebuild its entire brand persona around Quattro models, while discontinuing its money-losing FWD model range. By focusing entirely on Quattro, I argued that Audi could successfully penetrate a defensible segment of the market with uniquely appealing products that could command profit-generating prices. I predicted that, over

Audi Situational Assessment—1993

Audi's deteriorating U.S. market and competitive position has brought the company to a strategic crossroads.

- Audi suffers from untenably weak consumer awareness and its ill-defined image has been further weakened by the lingering effects of the unintended acceleration crisis.
- Aggressive and strengthening competition from traditional and new players in Audi's price segment is eroding Audi's market share.
- As a result, sales have declined over 80 percent in the past five years to around twelve thousand units, despite heavy discounting . . . below critical mass to sustain a national brand.
- Neither Audi nor most of its dealers are profitable, and prospects to reach breakeven on the current course are remote.
- **Barring a fundamental shift in its current strategy, Audi is unlikely to survive in the U.S. market beyond the next year.**

time, Quattro's technology advantages would fuel growth that would restore Audi as a legitimate Big Three contender in the U.S. luxury car market.

Through much of this presentation, Markus listened quietly and attentively, interjecting only to clarify a few points. But when I was done, he became more agitated: "Did I understand correctly that you are suggesting I stop selling FWD models? Are you crazy?! This company has lost 80 percent of its sales over the last five years and here you are suggesting I walk away from products accounting for 80 percent of what little sales I have left. That's ridiculous!"

"Well," I responded, "you can phase out your FWD models over a couple of years as you ramp up the Quattro line. And with increased emphasis on Quattro at more competitive prices than you currently charge, we expect rapid growth will make up for lost FWD sales. By implementing this strategy, you can rebuild around Audi's strength, rather than letting crippling weaknesses kill the brand. So, yes, that is exactly what I am suggesting."

After a long silence, Markus concluded our meeting with a disingenuous promise to give some more thought to our conversation. No follow-up action was discussed or planned.

I have shared this anecdote with several of my MBA classes at Columbia Business School over the years to stimulate class discussion about strategy formulation and consulting practice protocols. At this juncture of the story, I typically ask my students which of the following actions Markus should have taken after receiving my consulting report, that in essence had delivered a death sentence to his company.

Management Next Steps

If you were president of Audi of America presented with such a consultant report, what would be your next step(s)?

1. Request additional data to substantiate conclusions and recommendations.
2. Convene a follow-up meeting with direct reports to review and debate findings.
3. Brief superiors at German HQ and seek their involvement in next steps.
4. All of the above.
5. None of the above . . . go to lunch and forget this meeting ever happened.

Most of my students opt for the prudent fourth response. But last semester, one bold MBA student voted for number five, suggesting that Markus should go to lunch and forget our meeting had ever happened! When I asked this student to share her reasoning with the class, she said

> It's not that I think Markus *should* blow off your meeting, but I think that's what he probably did. The strategy you recommended would likely face strong resistance from his staff and probably from his superiors in [the] German headquarters as well. It's not clear to me that Markus would have the conviction, political capital, or courage to press forward with such a bold plan. Better to lay low for a while and hope for a miracle.

This student's assessment was spot on, as Markus did indeed pick the last option, willfully disregarding my stark conclusions and my recommendations for a turnaround strategy. In the weeks that followed,

I tried to arrange a follow-up meeting to discuss next steps but received no response to repeated correspondence and phone calls. During our last encounter, Markus had not rebutted any of the facts or conclusions presented, nor shared any reasons why the recommended strategy was incorrect or impractical. But from his final outburst and subsequent silence, the message was clear: as far as Markus was concerned, our conversation was over.

This turn of events often precipitates another active debate in my class in response to the question, "What would you do next if you were in *my* shoes?" Many of my MBA students plan to pursue a career in consulting, so this question has particular relevance. It is not at all unusual for consultants to reach conclusions that push beyond their client's comfort zone. What *is* unusual is to be precipitously shut off from any meaningful dialogue on an appropriate strategic response when the client's near-term survival is so clearly at risk.

Each semester, some of my students with a non-confrontational bent suggest that I should have licked my wounds, accepted the dead-end outcome, and moved on to the next consulting assignment. Others suggest that I should have looked for a more open-minded subordinate on Markus's staff who might be enlisted to press their boss for another meeting with me.

As it turned out, I decided against both these options, the first because I couldn't ignore my fervent conviction that Audi could be saved, and the second because I didn't want to put a subordinate employee in an awkward position with his recalcitrant boss. Instead, I wrote to the CEO of Audi AG in Ingolstadt, Germany, recounting the substance of my findings, conclusions, and recommendations and the resulting tacit rejection by the president of his U.S. division. I recognized that I was unilaterally end-running my client but justified the action given the urgency of the situation and Markus's lack of professional courtesy responding to it.

To my surprise, I was immediately invited to fly to Ingolstadt to present my consulting report to Audi AG's management board. When I was ushered into the boardroom, I found myself facing fourteen unknown Audi senior executives sitting around a large conference table, and one familiar face—Markus Huber—sitting alone in a chair against the back wall.

After being introduced by the CEO, I launched into the presentation. There were several polite questions and generally supportive comments, before the CEO concluded the meeting by expressing his support for the substance of my recommendations. At this point, Markus leapt to his feet, proclaiming, "I would like to personally thank the board for its support. Dr. Sherman and I have been working closely on this initiative for the past three months and I will follow up shortly with more detailed proposals to move our recommendation forward!"

Coda and Lessons Learned

The Audi story represents a classic case of "shrink-to-grow" strategy. When a company finds itself in severe distress, often the best corrective course of action is to strip away the broken core to rebuild around an initially smaller but more defensible and profitable business segment. By analogy, if a large, old building is teetering on a shaky foundation, it makes little sense to continue renovating the top floors. Better to demolish the building and rebuild on a new solid foundation.

Several large companies have successfully pursued a shrink-to-grow strategy over the years, including Thomson Corporation, General Motors, and Apple.

Thomson Corporation, once one of the largest newspaper chains in the world, presciently foresaw the declining business outlook for print journalism and the promising growth of specialized information services. Starting in the 1970s, Thomson began divesting most of its newspaper holdings, including the London *Times*, the *Scotsman*, and over fifty others and invested the proceeds in a number of specialized (and eventually digital) information services, including *First Call*, *Westlaw*, and *Physician's Desk Reference*. During its thirty-year shrink-to-grow transition, Thomson grew in value from $500 million to over $29 billion.[6]

General Motors, after resisting a shrink-to-grow strategy for years, emerged from bankruptcy in 2009 with five fewer brands than it had owned five years earlier. Although GM is now a smaller company than it was prior to declaring Chapter 11, the company has restored profitable growth from a stronger and more focused brand portfolio.[7]

Perhaps the most dramatic shrink-to-grow strategy was engineered by Steve Jobs when he returned as CEO of Apple in February 1997. At the time, most industry observers believed that Apple was just a few months away from bankruptcy. Apple's dwindling share of the personal computer market had dropped below 4 percent and annual losses exceeded one billion dollars. Three CEOs had come and gone in a decade, and board members had tried to sell the company but found no takers. At a tech industry symposium in October 1997, Michael Dell opined that if he ran Apple, he'd "shut it down and give the money back to shareholders."[8]

But Steve Jobs was determined to deliver on his founding vision of creating transformative consumer technologies. Upon his return, Jobs's first priority was to discontinue underperforming product lines that weakened Apple's brand image and management focus. At the annual Macworld Expo in August 1997, Jobs told Apple software developers and corporate partners, "If we want to move forward and see Apple healthy and prospering again, we have to let go of a few things."[9]

By the end of that year, Apple discontinued several products, including the Apple Newton personal digital assistant, the Pippin game console, the QuickTake digital camera, the Color LaserWriter and the eMate schoolroom touchpad. Jobs then focused the freed-up engineering resources on developing a series of transformative products. Starting in 1999, Apple launched the products— the iMac, iPod, MacBook, iPhone, and iPad—that reversed the company's fortunes. Shareholders should be gratified that Steve Jobs was at Apple's helm, not Michael Dell. Apple's market capitalization went from $3 billion at the start of 1997 to over $600 billion by the end of 2015.

In Audi's case, within three years of my meeting at corporate headquarters, Audi had converted its entire U.S. product range to Quattro models. With its new focus, Audi reconfigured its standard and optional feature mix to improve price competitiveness and completely realigned its marketing and distribution strategy to emphasize Quattro's unique performance advantages over the competition. Audi's image, sales, price realization, and profitability rapidly improved, allowing the company to extend its Quattro product range to new models, including roadsters, SUVs, coupes, and convertibles. By 2015, Audi sales in the United States had grown to nearly two hundred thousand vehicles and the company enjoyed strong profitability, customer satisfaction, and luxury cachet.

There are six lessons learned from Audi's strategic turnaround that can be more generally applied to effective strategy formulation.

1. Strategy is context sensitive.
2. The CEO must own the strategy.

3. Meaningful differentiation lies at the heart of successful strategy.
4. Leading strategic change takes courage.
5. The company must go all-in to completely support its strategy.
6. Continuous innovation is essential in sustaining superior performance.

Strategy Is Context Sensitive

Formulating the right strategy depends on the hand you've been dealt. For example, the appropriate focus for a profitable market leader should differ from the strategic imperatives of a weaker competitor struggling to survive.

One way to quickly establish a company's current business context in order to guide strategic priorities is to evaluate competitive performance characteristics. Figure 6.1 depicts a simple framework to accomplish this.[10] In this exercise, the horizontal axis measures market share relative to the market leader.

The vertical axis depicts a measure of profits relative to resources employed, which could be total assets, invested capital, or equity. This information is admittedly difficult to find for privately held companies, but rough estimates will suit the purpose.

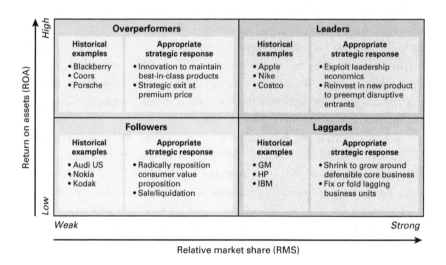

Figure 6.1 Business context and strategic priorities

After placing each of the competitors within a given industry on this business-performance map, an individual company will find itself in one of four quadrants, each with clear implications for the appropriate strategic focus.

Industry leaders are arrayed in the upper right-hand quadrant. These players enjoy the largest market share and profit levels, often with distinct advantages in image strength, distribution breadth, and economies of scale. Current examples include Apple, Nike, and Costco. The strategic priority for industry leaders should be to exploit their current marketplace advantages, while reinvesting in new products and technologies to preempt disruptive competition.

At the opposite extreme, industry followers have low market shares and returns, and often this disadvantaged position is a sign of weak products, poor image, or high costs. Audi was clearly in this position when I had my first meeting with Markus Huber, as was Nokia prior to its sale to Microsoft and Kodak prior to its bankruptcy. For such companies, the only logical strategic response is radical repositioning in pursuit of a significantly different consumer value proposition. Incremental tweaks to a follower's extant strategy are unlikely to close the gap against industry leaders and will further consume what little time a follower may have left to survive.

In the upper left quadrant of figure 6.1, some competitors are in the overperformer category, with relatively low market share, but high levels of profitability. This is a characteristic of niche specialists whose well-designed products appeal to a distinct consumer segment. Examples include Porsche, Blackberry prior to the introduction of Apple's iPhone, and Coors before the 1980s. Because of their extremely attractive returns, overperformers need to anticipate aggressive attacks from traditional and new competitors. Overperformers should commit to continuous product innovation to retain best-in-class performance or to a strategic exit for the benefit of shareholders. For example, Porsche has been able to retain its overperformer position in the automotive industry, whereas Blackberry failed to innovate and suffered disastrous consequences. Some overperformers may perceive ahead of the market that their product category will face inevitable commoditization, and choose to exit at a high acquisition premium for the benefit of shareholders.

Companies in the lower right quadrant are profit laggards, who suffer low profitability despite relatively high market share. The root causes can often be traced to high costs, weak products requiring steep discounts, poor product mix focused on inherently unprofitable market segments, or a combination of all of the above. Recent examples of laggards include General Motors, IBM, Hewlett-Packard, and Yahoo. The appropriate strategic response is often to shrink to grow, refocusing the company around defensible and profitable product categories. For example, IBM has done so by selling its high-cost personal computer, server, and printer businesses to concentrate on future growth opportunities in software, analytics, consulting, and cloud services.

Laggards and followers often replace their CEOs in search of a new winning strategy. While the appointment of a new top executive represents an obvious checkpoint to reassess a company's basic strategic direction, all companies should continuously monitor whether changes in their competitive environment warrant rethinking strategic priorities. In Audi's case, Markus ultimately had no choice other than radically repositioning the business to save it. Now, Audi can focus its U.S. strategy on maintaining a luxury segment leadership position, with continuous investment in innovative new technologies and ongoing initiatives to strengthen customer and dealer satisfaction.

The CEO Needs to Own the Strategy

Shortly after arriving as the new president of Audi of America, Markus solicited input from each of his business-unit heads on business priorities. Predictably, he received conflicting advice, shaped by the tactical focus of each business unit. His sales director and dealers wanted a new round of price discounts to stimulate customer demand, which was opposed by his finance director, already struggling to cope with below-cost pricing. The marketing department was clamoring for increases in their advertising budget to launch a new seasonal campaign, while the manufacturing liaison pushed for higher production runs with lower product complexity. These are legitimate inputs from executives dutifully doing their defined job. What about Markus?

In reflecting on the role of a CEO, Peter Drucker has identified four key tasks that *only* the top executive can perform:[11]

1. Define the meaningful outside, that is, a realistic, accurate, and evolving understanding of the market and competitive environment.
2. Decisively decide what business you are (and are not) in.
3. Balance the present and future in allocating human and financial capital.

4. Shape corporate values and standards to establish and nurture a culture strongly aligned with strategic priorities.

With a persistent push from his consulting advisors and strong support from his parent organization, Markus ultimately met the challenge of becoming an effective leader and succeeded in turning Audi of America around.

Chief executive officers can choose to get more or less involved in a variety of corporate activities, be it hands-on oversight of engineering, design, marketing, or partner development, reflecting their personal interests. Some CEOs are reflexively micromanagers; others are motivational delegators. But at the end of the day, it is the CEO's job alone to take ownership of each of the four tasks noted above to establish and guide a winning strategy.

Meaningful Differentiation Lies at the Heart of Successful Strategy

In the first chapter, I referred to the ongoing debate between two schools of thought, one advocating a customer-focused, outside-in perspective driving effective business strategy, and the other arguing that effective strategy should build on a company's advantaged internal capabilities. Either approach (or more likely, a hybrid of the two) can be the basis of a winning strategy, provided they end up in the same place: continuously delivering meaningfully differentiated products that are recognized and valued by consumers in the marketplace.

Meaningful differentiation should be a company's consummate strategic objective. No business can succeed long-term unless it maintains a compelling consumer value proposition. In Audi's case, the ability to deliver meaningful product differentiation was readily at hand: in its AWD technology. All companies need to find the crown jewels in their product portfolio.

Leading Strategic Change Takes Courage

In retrospect, the critical decision driving Audi's turnaround in the U.S. market—to focus exclusively on AWD vehicles—seems fairly self-evident. So what held Markus back?

The simple answer is fear. Leading a strategic transformation that significantly departs from company tradition and industry norms may fail, perhaps even catastrophically. And once a CEO puts a strategic change initiative in motion, he or she owns it. By definition, putting meaningful differentiation at the center of your company's strategy means you've committed to a path less traveled.

That's not to say there aren't business tools and tactics to help mitigate business risks. Companies can and do rely on reams of market research and consumer feedback in designing, beta testing, and piloting new product launches. New businesses can often be implemented in manageable phases. Software and web-based products have the added advantage of shorter time frames to build, pilot, and refine designs with the help of A/B testing.[12] But the reality is, strategies committed to continuous product innovation and clear market differentiation are inherently risky, requiring a resource that is often in short supply: CEO courage.

A Company Must Go All-In to Support Its Strategy

To succeed, it's not enough for companies to clearly articulate a market-differentiating strategy; they must go all-in to ensure corporate capabilities are properly aligned. In Audi's case, not only did the company change its product lineup to achieve market differentiation, but it also fundamentally changed every aspect of its supporting business operations: marketing, pricing, sales, and customer support.

Consider Swatch as an exemplar of CEO vision and courage. When low-price Asian imports and new digital technologies threatened to decimate SMH,[13] one of Switzerland's largest watchmakers in the 1980s, CEO Nicolas Hayek committed to launch a new division—Swatch—that would not only compete with low-cost entrants but would also fundamentally change how its products would be perceived in the market. Implementing Swatch's business strategy required a number of bold and unconventional steps that significantly repositioned its product range as more of a fashion accessory than a watch:

- Bold, bright-colored designs with plastic casings—a first for the normally staid Swiss watch industry.
- Frequent new entries from noted designers to create market buzz, stimulating fashion-conscious consumers to buy multiple versions for their wardrobe.

- Simple pricing—initially $40 per watch—which remained unchanged for a decade even for the most popular models. At these attractive price levels, many consumers acquired Swatches as an impulse purchase.
- Dedicated, exclusive retail outlets to clearly differentiate Swatch from other watch brands.
- Brash, highly theatrical product launches, often using guerilla-marketing tactics to spike consumer interest. For example, to announce its entry into the German market, Swatch erected a five-hundred-foot working model of a Swatch on Frankfurt's tallest building.
- Ambitious global expansion, even when market receptivity was uncertain. For example, after a successful European launch, Hayek pushed forward with Swatch's U.S. market entry despite weak pilot results, arguing that the planned bold launch tactics could not be properly assessed in a limited market trial. Hayek proved to be right, as the United States emerged as Swatch's largest national market.

The bottom line is that successful strategy requires decisive action in both concept and execution. The CEO must ensure that the entire organization is motivated and incentivized to support the company's strategic direction.

Continuous Innovation Is Essential to Sustain Superior Performance

Successfully defining and implementing a market-differentiating business strategy earns a company the ephemeral right to reap financial rewards while preparing to respond to the inevitable changes in the market.

All of the companies profiled in the business cases I have been using in my strategy course at Columbia Business School have experienced significant changes in their market and competitive environment in recent years. For example, Swatch's parent corporation, which initially survived an existential threat with its brilliant Swatch strategy, now faces a decrease in demand as a result of widespread smartphone ownership, and an onslaught of smart watches, which may once again profoundly redefine marketplace dynamics. Delta Airlines, initially an example of a high-cost, poorly managed company under siege from low-cost carriers, has since emerged from bankruptcy, a major acquisition, and with new management to become a strong performer in the airline industry. Starbucks lost its way in the mid 2000s with an ill-considered expansion binge that undermined the company's brand character and eroded profitability, before the founder returned as CEO to restore brand cachet and profitable growth. Every business case seems to require a new chapter every year. Every company must constantly write its own next chapter.

What Can *You* Do if Your Company's Strategy Is Broken?

In this chapter, I have highlighted the challenges and payoffs of getting strategy right. Most of my commentary has been oriented toward the CEO, as he or she is uniquely positioned to define and guide successful business strategy implementation.

Many of the cited cases provide inspirational examples of creative and courageous leadership, driven by CEOs who live by the credo "no guts, no glory" in personally driving winning business strategies. But what are the implications for MBA graduates, or mid-career, mid-level executives? They are generally not in a position to exert courageous leadership. Or are they?

A recent guest speaker in my class—entrepreneur, author, and blogger Seth Godin—urged my students to approach their first (and every) job with the mindset to "make a ruckus" and "not be afraid to be fired."[14] Godin was channeling themes from my course in very personal terms. Customer centricity and playing to win (as opposed to playing not to lose) are not just mantras for corporate leaders but should be a code for every manager to live by.

Of course, it's easy for financially secure elders like Godin or me to proselytize a message of personal leadership that involves rocking the boat. But what if you're just feeling your way around a new job in a company whose paycheck is critical for repairing your post-MBA balance sheet or supporting a growing family on a tight budget? How and where do you draw the line between pushing for constructive strategic change and being a solid team player in support of your company's current business direction?

My short answer to this question is there is no hard line; the extent to which an employee chooses to proactively offer feedback on management policies is a decidedly personal decision. But I do advise my students that under no circumstances should they be dishonest with themselves about what they choose to do and why.

It's quite natural for MBA graduates to approach their first job with a combination of optimism and excitement. But once on board, what would you do if you were concerned your company was headed in the wrong direction? Arguably, you have three choices:

1. Persistently push (as hard as you feel comfortable) to make the case for constructive change.
2. Leave and find a more enlightened employer or start up your own company.
3. Ignore your misgivings and embrace the corporate doctrine in the hope of kudos, bonuses, and promotion down the road.

If you're inclined toward option three, you might want to rethink whether an environment that may not respect or address your concerns—or in any event appears headed in the wrong direction—is a place you want to work over the long term. Ignoring your instincts or being dishonest with yourself may be a Faustian bargain.

Consider this hypothetical situation. Suppose you believe in the premise that strategy should be formulated from an "outside-in" perspective—that is, the highest priority is to create and consistently deliver compelling consumer value. Logically, you also believe that internal capabilities, incentives, and corporate policies should be aligned and managed to this end.

That all sounds reasonable, but the reality is that companies vary widely in their genuine commitment to operate in such a fashion. The key is to watch what companies do, not what they say. Every company *says* that they value their customers, but there is a wide variance in perceived customer satisfaction across industries that suggests otherwise.

For example, figure 6.2 displays 2015 results from ACSI, a spinout from the University of Michigan, for customer satisfaction by industry on a 0–100 index.[15]

It shouldn't come as a surprise to see that companies at the bottom of the list—Internet service providers (like Comcast), subscription

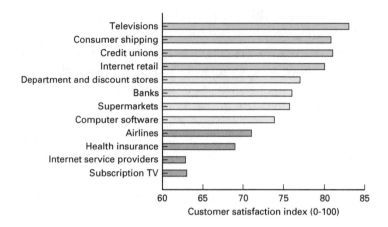

Figure 6.2 Customer satisfaction scores by industry

television services (like Time Warner), health insurance providers (like Cigna), and airlines (like United) score quite poorly in delivering an appealing customer experience. There are a few bright spots among these industry groups (like JetBlue), but by and large, companies in these industries have knowingly implemented business practices to extract revenue in ways that aggravate customers.

Now suppose that you, with your freshly minted MBA degree, were hired to manage strategy and policy assessment for the customer service group of one of the poorer-performing companies in this group. After a few months on the job, with due diligence under your belt from proprietary company surveys, audits of customer service calls, and interviews with colleagues, you are asked to report your initial findings to your boss.

To begin, you confidently summarize what you believe to be the root causes of your company's chronically poor customer satisfaction performance:

- Multiple, hidden fees and penalties.
- Deliberately confusing prices, rate plans, and ever-changing promotions.
- Inflexible service plans designed to lock consumers into long-term contracts.

- Bundled offerings forcing consumers to buy services they don't want or value.
- Unresponsive and inflexible customer service, handled by representatives with limited authority to deviate from restrictive scripts and incentives to shorten customer contact time at the expense of effective problem resolution.

Before you go any further, your boss interrupts to suggest limiting your discussion to the last item on the list. "We have no control over the business policies of the company," she says, "so let's just focus on what we can control in this department regarding the customer contact center."

With MBA case studies on the business practices of truly customer-centric companies still fresh in your mind, you object, noting that focusing only on post-transaction customer complaints is inherently self-limiting and will ultimately reduce lifetime customer value. But your boss stands her ground, noting that "corporate management is well aware of the frequency and cause of customer complaints, and they've done their homework to determine our profit-maximizing business model."

You're tempted to press further—questioning the time frame of the company's analysis and whether the impact of customer churn has been considered—but your boss's stern look signals that this conversation is over, at least for now.

Figure 6.3 Personal choices

Now what? You recognize that you've essentially been asked to put lipstick on a pig whose behavior is largely outside your control.

Perhaps you will get the opportunity to revisit your company's broader business strategy after having had more time to gather evidence and get savvier about internal politics. But the possibility—and likelihood, given your current position in the company—is that you will not be able to instigate a personally satisfying course correction. Let's say you've been at it for sixteen months, and it's time to revisit the options depicted in figure 6.3.

Which door will you choose?

CHAPTER SEVEN

Creating Strong Brands

IN THE PRECEDING chapters, I have focused on the requirements for effective business strategy, a key element of which is meaningful product differentiation. But any consideration of the positioning of products in the marketplace must also include the impact of branding on consumer choice. I will discuss the role of branding in business strategy in the next two chapters.

Strong brands are the physical and emotional embodiments of successful business strategy. Customers reward strong brands with enduring loyalty, often at premium prices, and by serving as brand evangelists, which can bolster a company's financial performance for years. Strong brands are perceived to not only deliver superior product performance or value but also evoke a deeper emotional response, underscoring how consumers feel about their experience with the brand.

At the other end of the spectrum, ask any group of consumers to identify their least favorite brands and the conversation is likely to turn lively and salty. Brands are powerful forces in the marketplace.

To introduce this topic, in my first class each semester, I often ask my MBA students to identify their favorite brand and to explain the reasons for its appeal. The responses span a wide range of products, from quotidian consumables to aspirational luxuries. Figure 7.1 displays a sample from a recent class, organized by category.

What this diverse array of favored brands has in common is a deep customer connection, described in the adulatory comments shown in the box (see page 141). Competitors would be hard-pressed to gain favor among my students, whose favorite brands evoke fond memories of childhood (Nutella), provide a conduit to express personal feelings (Papyrus), or go

Figure 7.1 MBA student favorite brands. Does not represent endorsement by pictured companies. Logos © Nike, Inc.; Unilever; Equinox Fitness; Clinique Laboratories, LLC; SoulCycle; Veuve Clicquot Ponsardin; Rent the Runway; Fresh Direct, LLC; Papyrus, Schurman Retail Group; Kayak.com, The Priceline Group; Louis Vuitton Malletier; BMW AG; Trader Joe's; Zara, Inditex Group; Inter IKEA Systems BV; Apple, Inc.; The Emirates Group; Toyota Motor Sales, Inc.

beyond mere utility and into the realm of desire (Louis Vuitton). Such consumer sentiments are the hallmarks of exceptionally strong brands.

The Meaning of a Brand

A logical starting point for the exploration of brand dynamics is to identify the critical characteristics required to build and maintain a strong affinity with consumers. Strong brands deliver a *promise*, convey *mutual trust*, and reinforce a consumer's *symbolic identity*.

Brand Promise

A brand promise clearly communicates what a company's products stand for. Every brand identified in figure 7.1 delivers a strong brand

Representative Reasons for Brand Affinity

Nutella

"I have been eating Nutella since I was a very young child. It has always meant to me both a memory of my childhood and a fundamental component of my breakfast before doing sports activities. Despite having tried many other chocolate spreads, both commercial and artisan/homemade, I would always choose Nutella above all of them."

SoulCycle

"I have become habituated to logging on to the website on Mondays at noon when the class schedule opens for the week to be among the first to book. Even though every week the website freezes at that time and I feel frustrated, I continue to sign up and go to the classes because I do not think there is another workout, or even cycling class, that delivers that same mix of challenge and fun."

Rogue Fitness

"Rogue's equipment is perfectly suited to the type of workout I do and their brand is aggressive and in-your-face, which appeals to my personality. The colors on their equipment, website, and marketing are suited to people of like sensibilities and reinforce their aggressive branding (black and red). Rogue has stayed consistent with this branding and continually released more and more desirable equipment to keep my engagement with my hobby fresh and exciting."

Emirates

"Emirates provides an in-flight experience that is very different to any other airline. The food is amazing, the planes are always new and clean, and the staff attentive and thoughtful. I will always pay a premium for this service. My experience with Emirates is also associated with traveling to fun holidays and exciting new adventures, which adds to the brand's appeal."

Papyrus

"Papyrus is my favorite place to buy greeting cards. They are in convenient locations around the city and I am always able to find the perfect card for a special occasion. Though cards are more expensive than a typical greeting card, often twice as much, I think cards are a really great way to express my feelings and add a personal touch to make something more memorable. The thoughtfulness that can be expressed in the perfect card is worth paying extra for."

Louis Vuitton

"One of my favorite brands is Louis Vuitton. I truly admire brands that are able to tell a story and deliver a transporting, emotional experience to their audience, and Louis Vuitton does this masterfully on its website, in its 'maisons' and through runway shows, museum exhibitions, and creative collaborations that celebrate the art of travel and of living, eliciting in the consumer a need that goes beyond mere utility and into the realm of desire."

promise, whether it is "ultimate driving machines" from BMW, adventurous, great-tasting, and affordable foods from Trader Joe's, or exquisitely designed lifestyle-enhancing technologies from Apple. A brand's promise is defined not only by how a product is expected to perform but also by how it makes a user feel.

From a consumer's perspective, a strong brand promise reduces the cognitive strain to understand the detailed attributes of complex products or the need to analyze competing and confusing advertising claims. For example, BMW loyalists need not concern themselves (unless they want to) with the technical wizardry underlying BMW's full-color heads-up displays, Valvetronic engines, or aluminum crankshaft designs, provided that they perceive overall that the brand continues to deliver an "ultimate driving experience." From a company's perspective, a strong brand promise represents a critically important corporate asset, contributing lasting value beyond the lifespan of any given product. Several respected independent assessments have estimated the value of top-performing global brands to be in excess of $100 billion.[1] Strong brands serve customers and companies extremely well.

Maintaining a strong brand promise requires creative and disciplined product development coupled with effective marketing communications to reinforce a clear consumer value proposition. In this regard, it is illustrative to contrast Apple's approach to archrival Samsung in the consumer electronics space.

Neither Apple nor Samsung use a signature tagline like BMW's "The Ultimate Driving Machine" to define their brand promise.

So consumers have to form their own impressions from the timing and types of products released, and how each company chooses to communicate its brand story.

Apple is widely considered to be among the most valuable brands in the world.[2] How would you articulate Apple's brand promise? When I've asked my MBA students this question, their responses can be synthesized as follows.

> Apple creates beautiful, technologically advanced, easy-to-use products that enrich my life and help me express myself.

Students are a bit less certain about Samsung's brand character. What emerges from class discussion is as much shaped by the negative feelings some students harbor toward Apple as it is by distinguishing positive attributes of Samsung's brand per se. The following statement best captures how my students describe Samsung's brand promise.

> Samsung creates first-to-market, cutting-edge products at competitive prices that allow me to organize my life around Google apps.

Apple clearly evokes a deeper, more emotive bond with its brand enthusiasts than Samsung, whose customers tend to express more technical respect than love for the brand. Broader market research from a Harris Interactive consumer survey confirms that Apple enjoys a considerable advantage over Samsung in image strength (figure 7.2).[3]

As a testament to how clearly a strong brand promise can be understood in the marketplace, consider the print advertisements depicted in figure 7.3, which reinforce the value propositions of Axe body sprays and Federal Express *without the need for any explanatory text*.[4] You may not be a hormonal male teenager or in need of shipping a package from London to Barcelona, but there should be little doubt about the brand promise of either of these companies. A clear, consistent, and relevant value proposition lies at the heart of companies that succeed in delivering a strong brand promise over the long term.

Mutual Trust

Brands that build a strong bond with customers enjoy a symbiotic relationship of mutual trust. Consumers trust their favored brands

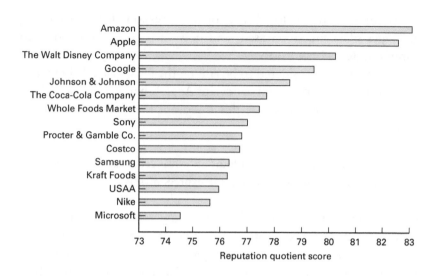

Figure 7.2 Brand image strength

to consistently deliver appealing products and are likely to maintain loyalty—as long as their expectations are met. On the other hand, companies need to trust that their targeted customers will remain loyal as long as they continue to deliver on their brand promise. This implies the need for strong brand discipline to avoid racing to market with immature products of dubious value, getting caught in a "feature–function arms race" against competing brands, which overshoots the real needs of market, or introducing dissonant product-line extensions that dilute brand equity.

As an illustrative example, perhaps the most celebrated case of a company breaking its mutual trust with customers was the 1985 launch of New Coke.[5] Coca-Cola's iconic brand had long dominated the U.S. market for carbonated soft drinks, peaking at over 60 percent of the market shortly after World War II. However, archrival PepsiCo began gaining share with its pleasingly sweeter-tasting cola, promoted heavily to younger consumers in the long-running "Pepsi Generation" advertising campaign.[6] By the early 1980s, Coca-Cola's market share had shrunk to 24 percent and Pepsi was actually outselling Coke in supermarket chains.[7]

Alarmed by Pepsi's market gains, and by its own blind-taste tests that showed that a majority of consumers preferred the taste of Pepsi,

Figure 7.3 Wordless print ads for Axe (*top*) and FedEx (*bottom*). © Axe Body Spray, Unilever, and © FedEx Corporation. All rights reserved.

Coca-Cola CEO Roberto Goizueta ordered a product development team to develop an improved version of Coke's century-old secret formula. The team eventually settled on a sweeter-tasting cola that consistently beat both regular Coke and Pepsi in blind-taste tests. Extensive market research confirmed consumer preference for what came to be known as New Coke, although the company did detect a vocal minority (10–15 percent) of focus group participants who viscerally opposed the prospect of tampering with Coca-Cola's trusted brand.

Coca-Cola announced the launch of New Coke with great fanfare on April 19, 1985, and ceased production of its original formulation the same week. Despite encouraging initial sales of the new product, hundreds of thousands of angry letters and phone calls poured into Coca-Cola's Atlanta headquarters, amplified by widespread press coverage of public protests in southern U.S. cities depicting dissatisfied consumers emptying cans of New Coke into the streets. Company executives became concerned as the sales of New Coke slowed, and U.S. bottlers and overseas divisions began expressing growing anxiety over adverse market reactions.

After just seventy-nine days, Coca-Cola altered course, and re-introduced its original product, now called Coke Classic, alongside New Coke. The company promoted the return of Coke Classic with advertisements touting the brand's heritage and traditional values, accompanied by nostalgic images reminiscent of Norman Rockwell paintings. Consumers responded by flooding corporate headquarters with thankful letters and calls, prompting one executive to remark "you would have thought we'd cured cancer."[8]

Coca-Cola sales immediately soared, and by the end of the 1985, Coke Classic was substantially outselling both New Coke and Pepsi. By the following spring, the market share of New Coke had slipped to only 3 percent, despite having outspent Coke Classic on advertising since its launch.[9] Coke Classic continued to build on its market leadership, and in 2002, Coca-Cola quietly discontinued New Coke (then called Coke II) and dropped "Classic" from the name of its iconic soda.

In retrospect, Coca-Cola concluded that it had profoundly underestimated the backlash from a vocal segment of its customer base whose trust in the company was broken by the new product substitution. Ironically, years after its failed launch, blind-taste tests continued to confirm that New Coke was preferred over Pepsi and Coke Classic.

But as Coca-Cola found, it had built an exceptionally strong bond with its customers, rooted in intangible brand associations with tradition, legacy, and trust.

When Coca-Cola broke its mutual trust with consumers, abandoning its proud heritage in search of new customers, it triggered a rebellion that resonated with a large segment of the market. As it turned out, by quickly learning from its mistake and responding to consumer sentiment, Coca-Cola emerged stronger than ever in the ongoing cola wars with PepsiCo. This infamous case clearly illustrates the importance of mutual trust in building and nurturing a strong brand.

To illustrate a more recent example of how mutual trust can strengthen consumer affinity to a brand, let's return to the competition between Apple and Samsung. By most objective measures, Samsung should be faring better in the consumer electronics market. After all, true to its brand promise, Samsung did beat Apple to market with larger smartphones, higher-resolution cameras and screens, and high-tech features like bump-to-share file transfer, all at lower average selling prices than Apple. Samsung also launched its first Galaxy Gear smart watch more than eighteen months before Apple's initial entry into this category. To tout these achievements, Samsung has heavily marketed its technical prowess and speed, considerably outspending Apple on global advertising and promotion. For example, figure 7.4 displays a 2012 Samsung Galaxy S III smartphone print advertisement touting its far longer list of technical features than Apple's comparable (and, at the time, yet to be introduced) iPhone 5.[10]

Nonetheless, Samsung has been losing global market share over the past three years (at the time of this writing), and Apple outsold Samsung's smartphones in the two largest markets—the United States and China— in the first quarter of 2015.[11] Moreover, in 2015, Apple's mobile devices earned more than seven times the operating income of Samsung, accounting for a market-dominating 91 percent of total industry profits.[12]

The reason is that Apple's brand promise delivers more *meaningfully differentiated* value to a large class of customers who are willing to wait for—and have a far higher willingness to pay for—what is perceived to be the most elegant and sophisticated product designs on the market. Rather than promote a long list of technical product features, Apple's marketing communications consistently reinforce how its iPhones enrich the lives of its customers.

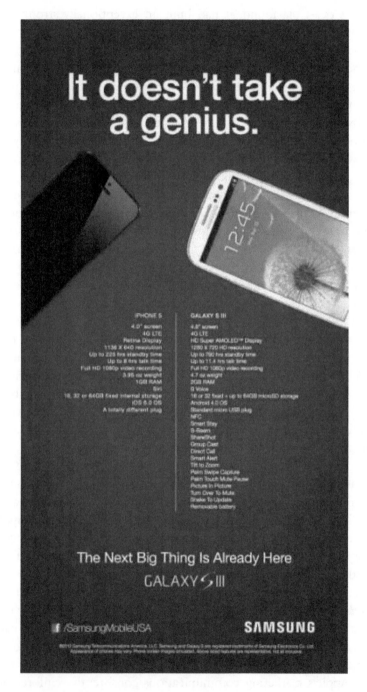

Figure 7.4 Samsung "It Doesn't Take a Genius," print advertisement, 2012.
© Samsung Electronics. All rights reserved.

To be sure, there are customers who will always want to be the first to own the latest high-tech products. But Apple is not interested in serving the early-adopter segment, or, for that matter, budget-conscious consumers, focusing instead on the far more lucrative segment of consumers with patience and the willingness to pay for highly sophisticated and refined product designs.

Despite its reputation for innovation, Apple actually has a long history of not being the first mover in any of the consumer electronics categories it has entered and dominated over the past two decades (see figure 4.6). As such, Apple has demonstrated admirable discipline as a brand leader, building mutual trust in two important respects.

First, strong brands define themselves as much by what they won't do as by what they will do. Apple has resisted the temptation to rush new products to market to match competitors on new technical features. Rather, the company takes the time required to refine the overall user experience and perceived value before releasing a new product.

Second, strong brands define themselves as much by the consumers they *don't* target as those they do. Apple has ignored critics who have strongly urged the company to launch budget-priced models to extend its penetration in rapidly growing Asian markets. Instead, Apple has remained true to its historical practice of exclusively serving the premium end of the consumer electronics market

As a result, Apple and its customers have developed a strong mutual trust that has served both sides exceptionally well.

Symbolic Identity

For many consumers, the purchase or ownership of a brand signals membership in a desired social grouping. This is particularly true in categories where tangible product differences are difficult to discern, yet consumers still express fierce loyalty to brands perceived to reinforce their values and social standing. In short, many consumers strongly prefer brands that appeal to "people just like me."

Brand managers recognize the importance of symbolic identity and often focus advertising themes on lifestyle images rather than tangible product attributes. Some of the most successful and iconic advertising campaigns of all time—including the "Marlboro Man," the "Pepsi Generation," and L'Oréal's "Because You're Worth It"—are rooted in the exploitation of symbolic identity.

To illustrate the importance of symbolic identity in brand development, consider the extraordinary case of Pabst Blue Ribbon (PBR) beer. The beer category presents an interesting challenge to marketers because most consumers are unable to identify their preferred brand in blind-taste tastes. Thus, symbolic identity associated with beer brands plays a pivotal role in consumer choice.[13]

Pabst Blue Ribbon is a 125-year-old brand that peaked in the late 1970s as the third-best-selling beer in the United States, with sales of over twenty million barrels. But adverse U.S. beer consumption trends and internal management turmoil took its toll on PBR, and sales declined for twenty-three consecutive years to less than one million barrels in 2001.[14]

Customers of PBR skewed toward lower-income, older men clinging to a venerable beer brand sold at a budget price. Pabst sought to harvest what remained of its dwindling market by cutting costs, contracting out production, and eliminating brand advertising.

But then a curious thing happened. For reasons that are murky at best, PBR sales began taking off in northwestern states. The company sent a marketing team to investigate and discovered that PBR had become the brand of choice for young hipsters—e.g., bike messengers in Portland and snowboarders in Idaho. These countercultural consumers preferred the least pretentious, most unglamorous beer they could find, expressing their rebellious symbolic identity. The fact that Pabst could not afford to advertise proved to be a blessing in disguise for these unanticipated new fans.

It is important to note that PBR's new brand image and popularity was created by consumers, not company marketers. Countercultural consumers self-identified with a decidedly non-mainstream brand.

Once Pabst understood the basis of PBR's growing appeal, the company worked in the background to fuel the flames of symbolic identity, sponsoring small, local tournaments that would be popular with young hipsters (e.g., for skateboarding and bike polo), but never "going corporate" with TV commercials or major event sponsorships like the X Games. Pabst also paid for product placements to associate the brand with offbeat, tough guys like Clint Eastwood in the movie *Gran Torino* and Dennis Hopper in *Blue Velvet*.

With word-of-mouth referrals going viral, PBR sales grew by double-digit percentages through the 2000s, exceeding six million barrels by 2008. While PBR's case is perhaps an extreme example of the importance of symbolic identity to a brand's persona, all companies should be conscious of the opportunity to nurture an emotional bond with their core consumers.

A more recent example of a company that built a powerful brand by focusing on symbolic identity is Dove—a personal-care products division of Unilever. While Dove has long enjoyed market-share leadership in bar soap, the signature product that launched the brand in 1957, Dove struggled to achieve similar success with its subsequent entries in the personal-care category, including deodorants, lotions, and hair-care products.

Rather than try to take on industry leader Procter & Gamble and other leading personal-care brands in an expensive marketing campaign focused on product attributes, Dove recognized the opportunity to create a strong bond with consumers by initiating a global dialogue on a healthier and more holistic view of the meaning of female beauty.

The Dove Campaign for Real Beauty was conceived in 2004 after market research revealed that only 4 percent of women consider themselves beautiful. The mission of Dove's Real Beauty campaign was "to create a world where beauty is a source of confidence and not anxiety."[15]

To implement the campaign, Dove used billboards, print advertising, social media, YouTube videos, and television commercials, all with the unifying theme of celebrating the beauty of women of all ages, shapes, and sizes (figure 7.5).[16]

In 2013, Dove produced a six-minute video posted on its YouTube channel to extend its Real Beauty campaign.[17] In the video, several women portray themselves to a hidden forensic artist, who sketches their face to match their self-image. The same artist then sketches the women again, this time using the descriptions provided by strangers who met the subjects the previous day (figure 7.6).

The sketches are then compared, with the stranger's image invariably being both more flattering and more accurate, evoking a visceral and highly emotional reaction when shown to the subjects of the experiment. The "Sketches" campaign created a viral sensation, and went on to become the most-watched YouTube advertisement in history, reaching more than 200 million global viewers.[18]

Dove's Real Beauty campaign succeeded in tapping into an issue of widespread concern to women. What made the campaign successful is that women of all ages and cultural backgrounds could symbolically identify with the message that Dove was promoting. As such, Dove's products became associated with a positive brand image, which has

☐ grey?
☐ gorgeous?

Why can't more women feel glad to be grey? Join the beauty debate.

campaignforrealbeauty.co.uk 🕊 | *Dove*

☐ flawed?
☐ flawless?

Is beautiful skin only ever spotless? Join the beauty debate.

campaignforrealbeauty.co.uk 🕊 | *Dove*

Figure 7.5 Print ads for Dove's Real Beauty campaign. © Dove Beauty, Unilever. All rights reserved.

helped the company increase its global market share.[19] For example, between 2008 and 2014, while Procter & Gamble's personal-care product sales were flat, Unilever's sales over the same period grew by 56 percent.[20]

Connecting the Dots: Business Strategy Drives Brand Strategy

As all the examples in this chapter illustrate, strong brands rest on a foundation of a clear brand promise, mutual trust, and a symbolic

Figure 7.6 Still from Dove's "Sketches" commercial. © Dove Beauty, Unilever. All rights reserved.

identity that resonates strongly with consumers. Companies that nurture and strengthen their brands over time can earn attractive returns on a valuable asset and achieve enduring competitive resilience. Companies should focus on building and nurturing strong brands as if their corporate lives depended on it, because it often does.

In chapter 1, I made the case that there are three strategic imperatives to drive sustained profitable corporate growth:

1. Continuous innovation—not for its own sake, but to deliver. . . .
2. Meaningful differentiation—recognized and valued by consumers, enabled by . . .
3. Business alignment—where all corporate capabilities, resources, incentives, and business culture and processes are aligned to support a company's strategic intent.

We now are in a position to make the logical connection between the requirements for effective business strategy and brand strategy.

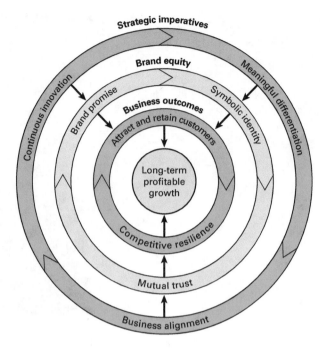

Figure 7.7 Link between business and brand strategy

As shown in figure 7.7, companies that continuously innovate to deliver meaningfully differentiated products and services can reinforce their brand promise, sustain mutual trust, and strengthen the symbolic identity that consumers associate with the brand. These mutually reinforcing elements of effective business and brand strategy provide the basis to attract and retain customers and create competitive resilience. If all of these strategy elements are in place, companies are well positioned to achieve the holy grail of business: long-term profitable growth.

CHAPTER EIGHT

Brand Builders and Killers

OVER THE PAST decade, brand managers have recognized the need to build deeper and more meaningful relationships with customers in an environment where product lifecycles are shortening, new technologies are enabling product personalization, and social media platforms are changing how consumers engage with brands. Recent research by the public-relations firm Edelman confirms that there is the sizable need and opportunity for companies to close the gap between how they are currently serving customers and what consumers expect from preferred brands.[1]

Brand Builders

As shown in figure 8.1, while 87 percent of consumers would like to experience a more meaningful relationship with their favored brands, only 17 percent believe companies are currently meeting their expectations.[2] Three particularly promising opportunities to enhance brand strength and business performance warrant further exploration: personalization, community-based marketing, and customer dialogue.

Personalization

We've come a long way since Henry Ford's Model T became the best-selling car in the world—a record it held for nearly five decades. The Model T's rigidly standardized product design fostered assembly line efficiencies that gave Ford Motor Company a sizeable cost advantage.

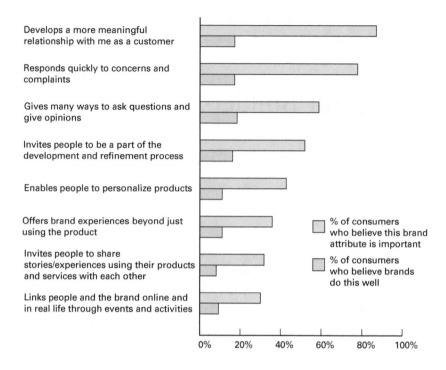

Figure 8.1 Gap between desired and delivered brand attributes

As the company's founder quipped at the time, customers could have the Model T in any color—so long as it was black.

The Model T was an example of a *one-to-many* product strategy, where a single product is intended to serve multiple consumer segments, or the market as a whole. The drawback of such an approach, of course, is that consumer preferences vary considerably across market segments. And in fact, General Motors overtook Ford as the largest car company in the world in the 1930s by executing CEO Alfred Sloan's strategy of producing "a car for every purse and purpose." Sloan set up multiple brands—e.g., Chevrolet, Oldsmobile, Buick, Cadillac—to create distinctive car designs at differing price points to appeal to a broad range of consumers.[3]

The success of General Motors under Sloan was an early example of the most common product strategy, *many-to-many*, where a company creates multiple product offerings to appeal to multiple market segments.

As we've moved from the industrial to the information age, the basis of competitive advantage in many product categories has moved from standardized mass production to personalized product design enabled by digital customization. New production technologies have enabled *one-to-one* product strategies, where products can be uniquely configured to serve individual customers.

Personalized products can strengthen brands in three ways:

1. Personalized product-line extensions to expand market reach and profits.
2. Personalized services to strengthen consumer value and brand loyalty.
3. Personalized product configuration to extend a brand's value proposition.

Personalized Product-Line Extensions

Personalized product-line extensions allow a company to move beyond the many-to-many strategy to attract new customers. Consider, for example, one of the world's bestselling candies, M&M's. Traditionally, the Mars company marketed hundreds of varieties of its candy treats, in multiple flavors (e.g., milk and dark chocolate, peanut, almond, peanut butter), package sizes (from two to fifty-two ounces), and product types (e.g., candies, baking bits, ice creams). Mars's many-to-many product strategy addressed a wide range of consumer preferences, uses, and needs, helping to drive global sales of over $3 billion.

But beyond its traditional range of product offerings, Mars identified an opportunity to further strengthen its brand and capture additional profits by *personalizing* its signature product. On the "Personalized M&M's" website, customers can select their own imprinted messages, images, and colors to individualize their order of M&M's. Personalization has allowed Mars to tap new consumer markets with special packaging available for weddings, birthdays, baby showers, corporate events, and other special occasions. The price for personalized M&M's is ten times higher than traditional product variants (on an equivalent dollars-per-pound basis), demonstrating the high value consumers place on customization.

The opportunity to exploit personalization to tap high-margin new markets is gaining acceptance across a number of product categories. For example, Hasbro has been using 3-D printer technology to allow customers to put a realistic rendering of their own head atop their favorite action figure. Personalized action figures carry a price premium three times higher than standardized equivalents and appear to be generating an enthusiastic market response.[4]

Similarly, Nike offers customers the option to personalize their sneaker designs. Visitors to the NIKEiD website can choose their own color preferences from among more than two billion combinations and can emboss their initials on their personalized design. Personalization adds $45 to the price of the base sneaker.

Personalized Services

Customer information can be exploited to tailor products and services, driving increased customer value, purchase frequency, and brand loyalty. For example, Amazon has enhanced consumer value by personalizing product recommendations and streamlining its one-click checkout process by drawing on a consumers' past purchase history, demographics, and stored payment information. These personalized enhancements give Amazon a significant competitive advantage over other online retailers selling similar goods at comparable or lower prices.

Similarly, Sephora, an omnichannel cosmetics retailer with nearly two thousand stores in twenty-nine countries, offers a variety of benefits for consumers who opt in for personalized beauty services. To begin with, consumers can visit their local Sephora store to receive a free color consultation, using a patented device to determine a "Color IQ" rating that matches skin color and physiology to one of 110 unique cosmetic shades. This personalized color rating can then be used to identify Sephora's products best suited to individual appearance, which can be accessed on demand in any Sephora store or company website. Sephora also provides a range of additional services to enhance value for loyal customers, including online beauty clinics, priority access to new products, birthday gifts, loyalty rewards, and free shipping for online purchases.[5]

These examples of personalized services create the potential to significantly enhance consumer value, changing the basis of competition from generic comparisons of product attributes and prices to a consumers' assessment of what's best and most convenient *for them.*

Personalized Product Configuration

Many native-digital products were designed to promote personalized product configuration as the foundation of their business value proposition. For example, Pandora and Spotify allow consumers to personalize their streaming music selections to suit individual tastes and preferences. In their own words, Pandora has "a single mission: to play only music you'll love,"[6] while on Spotify "the right music is always at your fingertips; choose what you want to listen to, or let Spotify surprise you."[7]

Other examples abound; personalized services including health and wellness, newsfeeds and all forms of social media, and customized products in categories spanning eyewear to lighting systems are indicative of the growing importance of personalizing products and services to strengthen brand value.[8]

Community-Based Marketing

While personalization provides a powerful mechanism to enhance the value of specific products and services to individual consumers, there are also opportunities for companies to develop strong customer *communities*, which strengthen brand appeal by reinforcing the symbolic identities of consumers. Community-based marketing strategies are intended to engage a company's target customer audience in interactive dialogues to promote and extend a brand's reach, appeal, and authenticity, and to provide ongoing feedback to adapt and improve products and services.

Companies use a variety of tools to execute community-based marketing strategies, including corporate websites, social-networking platforms, community-of-interest blogs, and sponsored owner groups.

For example, consider Procter & Gamble's challenge in convincing shoppers that their Pampers diaper brand is better than Kimberly-Clark's Huggies, strictly on traditional product performance attributes (e.g., absorbency, ease of use, comfort, price). Both companies are locked in a stalemate of making similar and often confusing claims of product superiority. As a result, Procter & Gamble and Kimberly-Clark have sought to supplement traditional product-based marketing efforts with initiatives to build brand-sponsored customer communities.

As a case in point, expectant and current mothers who go to the Pampers website will find a well-executed two-way communication portal which features informative video clips, timely and useful parenting tips, customized newsletters to match their baby's stage of development, loyalty rewards, and links to Twitter streams and Facebook forums.

These resources are intended to develop a strong bond between target customers and the company, which enhances the perceived image of the Pampers brand as a trusted and valued partner. And while customers can shop for diaper products on the company website, the primary purpose of Pampers.com and related company social media is to strengthen brand appeal, ideally providing a tiebreaker in the choice between competing products with similar features.

In some cases, the perceived value of a product may be largely driven by the membership it conveys in a community of like-minded consumers. An excellent example of a company that exploited community-based marketing to strengthen its brand appeal is Harley-Davidson.[9]

Harley-Davidson, currently one of the largest and most profitable motorcycle companies in the world, was on the ropes in the early 1980s. Japanese competitors had launched an all-out assault on the U.S. motorcycle market, and Harley was hemorrhaging market share with poor-quality, outdated, and expensive products. The corporate owner at the time lost patience and sold the company to an investor group which included the founder's grandson. Considerable credit for Harley's post-acquisition turnaround has been attributed to the improvements the company made in manufacturing quality and product design.[10] But arguably far more important was the new owners' commitment to community-based marketing, spearheaded by the creation of Harley Owners Group (H.O.G.) chapters across the country.

Harley-Davidson had always attracted a fiercely loyal following among free-spirited "bad boy" riders, as captured in the 1969 movie *Easy Rider* (figure 8.2). As Richard Teerlink, the CEO who guided Harley's turnaround noted, "there are very few products that are so exciting that people will tattoo [your company's] logo on their body."

But the new management team realized that once the company addressed nagging quality and product design deficiencies, the essence of the brand could appeal to a far wider audience. Teerlink reenergized the company's brand promise in terms that would attract new customers beyond its bad-boy roots (figure 8.3).

Figure 8.2 A still from the 1969 movie *Easy Rider*, starring Peter Fonda and Dennis Hopper. This movie captured the ideal of the Harley-Davidson motorcycle and its rider.

EXPRESS YOURSELF
IN THE COMPANY OF OTHERS.

Figure 8.3 Harley-Davidson succeeded through a broader brand promise that its consumers were not just buying a motorcycle, but becoming members of a community that shared a love of personal freedom, nonconformity, and endless possibilities. Photo © Harley-Davidson, Inc. All rights reserved.

Corporate communications heavily promoted the ownership *experience*, not just the product, and company-sponsored H.O.G. chapters became local forums to spread the mystique of Harley ownership to new customers from many walks of life.

Community-building efforts included a number of initiatives:

- Harley stores were reconfigured to serve as hangouts for customers to share stories and experiences.
- Boot camps were organized to train new riders.
- Garage parties were organized for women to learn about life with their own Harley-Davidson motorcycle.
- The company organized national rallies every five years to celebrate the company's founding. The 100th anniversary was attended by well over one hundred thousand riders in Milwaukee.
- The company sponsored factory tours at all its facilities.
- The H.O.G. website served as an information source and community forum for local events throughout the country.

The genius of Harley-Davidson's emphasis on community-building efforts was that while many competing Japanese motorcycles were more technically sophisticated, faster, and more fuel efficient, Harley's uniquely American patriotic marketing themes made product-based comparisons irrelevant to their target audience. Harley's message wasn't about the machine; it was about the individual and shared experiences among the community of freedom-loving Harley owners.

Two final examples— the United Services Automobile Association (USAA) and GoPro—provide additional insight into the use of community-based marketing to strengthen corporate brands. The USAA, a member-owned insurance provider to over ten million customers, restricts its services to members of the armed forces and their families, explicitly aligning its corporate mission with the values of its military customer community. As the company notes on its corporate website, "USAA began in 1922, when twenty-five Army officers agreed to insure each other's vehicles when no one else would. Today we follow the same military values our founders prized: service, loyalty, honesty, and integrity. When you join USAA, you become part of a family that's there for you during every stage of your life."[11]

The Fortune 500 insurance provider has built an exceptionally strong bond with its self-selected community of consumers. As a testament to its brand strength, USAA consistently achieved the highest customer satisfaction rating (Net Promoter Score) of 220 companies surveyed by Satmetrix across twenty-two industries between 2009 and 2014,[12] and was ranked among the world's most admired companies in 2015 by *Fortune* magazine.[13]

GoPro, which makes small and rugged cameras used to capture riveting video of action sports and other adventures, tries to distinguish itself from growing competition through its community-building media endeavors. To increase brand awareness and user appeal, the company displays GoPro-produced and user-submitted content on its own website and social media channels, and on YouTube, Virgin America's in-flight television channel, and Roku's streaming media service. GoPro's action-packed and melodramatic videos often evoke a viral viewer response, which has helped build an audience of over four million YouTube subscribers and over one billion video views.[14]

Professionally produced extreme sports are a recurring theme, featuring jaw-dropping views of mountain bikers, snowboarders, and wingsuit flyers. But some of the most popular videos on GoPro's distribution channels are shot by independent GoPro users. One of its biggest hits, with nearly thirty million views, is a tear-jerking video of a California firefighter rescuing an unconscious kitten from a burned-out home and then reviving the pet with an oxygen mask and splashes of cold water. GoPro received permission from the firefighter before professionally editing the video and publishing it on the company's YouTube channel.[15]

To further engage with its current and prospective customer community, GoPro maintains an active dialogue with viewers on its social media and YouTube channels, often responding directly to consumer questions regarding camera techniques or appropriate equipment. By the end of 2015, GoPro had attracted over sixteen million followers on its Facebook, Twitter, YouTube, and Instagram accounts. These community-building efforts have helped GoPro build exceptionally high consumer awareness, sector-leading market share, and a brand name synonymous with the product itself.[16]

Customer Dialogue

GoPro is not alone is maintaining an ongoing dialogue with customers to enhance loyalty and strengthen its brand image. As was shown in figure 8.1, customers value companies that recognize and respond to their individual questions and concerns but are often disappointed with corporate inattention. Social media affords the opportunity for companies to build strong rapport with their consumers in a forum that also reaches a broader audience. JetBlue Airways provides an excellent example of best practice in this regard.

JetBlue's social media journey began serendipitously, as an outgrowth of a corporate crisis. Following a freak ice storm on Valentine's Day, 2007, JetBlue suffered a catastrophic operational breakdown that left one thousand passengers trapped on aircraft on the JFK airport tarmac for as long as nine hours. Needless to say, passengers were outraged, and JetBlue's reputation for customer-friendly service took a serious hit from widespread media coverage.

While JetBlue executives immediately apologized on televised interviews, news coverage continued to focus on the lingering human drama of the ice storm, further damaging the airline's image.

Five days after the incident, then CEO David Neeleman delivered a heartfelt apology on YouTube,[17] which at the time was a nascent and relatively unknown website acquired by Google just three months earlier. As it turned out, Neeleman's three-minute video apologia (and call to action) generated considerably more supportive and constructive customer feedback from the four hundred thousand viewers than JetBlue ever imagined.

Out of adversity, JetBlue recognized the power of social media to effectively communicate with customers and the public at large. The airline set up a Twitter account a few months later, which now has over two million followers. JetBlue currently employs more than two dozen full- and part-time employees responsible for social media interactions, resolving problems for individual travelers, identifying policy issues requiring quick attention, and communicating with JetBlue social media followers at large.

For example, in a typical exchange, JetBlue communicated with two of its passengers as follows:

JetBlue Twitter Dialog with Passengers

Passenger1: @jetblue In Denver and want to check my bag but there is no one at the counter. What's wrong with this picture?

Passenger2: @passenger1 the JetBlue crew in Denver's usually only there ~2 hrs before the flight. You'll probably have to wait 30–45 minutes.

JetBlue: @passenger2 is a step ahead of me, but sending a note to the GM and Supes as a heads up anyway. Are there many waiting?

Passenger1: There are probably 5 or 6 waiting. Not too bad.

JetBlue: Sent a note to Theresa, our General Manager out there.

JetBlue: You should see some crewmembers showing up shortly— our offices in Denver are away from the ticket counter.

Passenger1: @jetblue @passenger2 Thanks for the team action.

This entire exchange took place within a few minutes, and shows the power of social media for passengers to communicate effectively not only with JetBlue but with other members of the JetBlue customer community to jointly solve problems.

In another instance, a JetBlue customer in Portland, Oregon, was charged $100 to check a folding portable bicycle on a JetBlue flight, even though it was packed in a travel case that was within the size and weight limits of JetBlue's guidelines for free checked baggage. The ticket agent explained that JetBlue corporate policy mandated that all checked bicycles, regardless of type, had to be assessed a special baggage charge. Just before boarding his flight, the passenger tweeted and blogged his frustration with what he considered to be an illogical policy. A JetBlue social media representative quickly contacted the gate agent to verify the circumstances and alerted a senior JetBlue executive in headquarters about the situation. While the passenger was still airborne, JetBlue made a quick decision to change its policy, allowing qualifying portable bicycles to be checked for free. JetBlue then arranged to have a gate agent meet the arriving flight to personally deliver an apology and refund to the surprised passenger. JetBlue also publicized their quick response on the passenger's Twitter account and blog, which virally spread through his network of fellow bicycle enthusiasts.

Having learned of the power of social media from its ice-storm crisis in 2007, JetBlue was also well equipped to deal with another public relations challenge five years later when a JetBlue pilot experienced a mental breakdown and ran through the cabin of a cross-country flight ranting in a frightening manner. JetBlue immediately began tweeting real-time updates and created a live blog to keep its customers and stakeholders aware, informed, and comforted.

These examples show that social media can serve as a powerful customer-communication and brand-building tool, provided that a company is prepared to engage in real-time meaningful dialog and problem-solving with its customers. JetBlue has been an industry leader in the use of social media, attracting more followers than any other airline, despite being only the fifth-largest carrier in the United States by passenger numbers.

It is interesting to note that although American Airlines has been the most active tweeter among U.S. airlines (figure 8.4), its use of social media has not been effective in enhancing customer satisfaction.[18] In a recently released survey of customer satisfaction with U.S. airlines, American ranked sixth, while JetBlue was ranked number one.[19]

A review of the use of Twitter by American Airlines suggests two counterproductive flaws. First, a failure to consistently follow up or to meaningfully respond to customer complaints and inquiries. Unlike JetBlue, American has often failed to follow up customer inquiries, or, even more gallingly, has provided disingenuous apologies or unhelpful responses. For example, in one recent exchange, a customer tweeted the airline with a concern about the price of her ticket. American

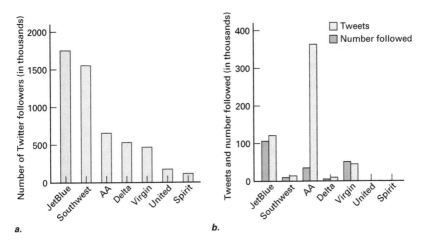

Figure 8.4 Airline activity on Twitter. *a*, Number of Twitter followers, in thousands; *b*, Tweets and number followed

responded with a request for more information. The customer tweeted back that American had lowered the fares for her flight after she had purchased her ticket but refused to let her take advantage of the lower fare without a $200 change fee. After American failed to respond to the passenger's complaint, she ended the exchange by tweeting to her followers, "I should have flown Southwest."

Even when American Airlines does respond, its tweets have often failed to address customer issues. For example when one customer recently tweeted to complain that he had been waiting more than forty minutes to check in at an American Airlines business-class ticket counter where one of two agents had just left, the company replied, "We're sorry, we're doing the best we can." In another recent exchange, when a customer tweeted that he was stuck on a plane waiting for takeoff for over two hours, American Airlines tweeted back, "We're sorry. Hang in there."

American Airlines's second social media flaw is unwittingly provoking a public forum for customer criticism. Needless to say, when disgruntled passengers feel further aggrieved by unhelpful responses, Twitter and Facebook sites can become forums for widespread customer anger. For example, American recently provoked a firestorm of social-media criticism after denying parents a refund after their nine-year-old son died just before they were due to take a scheduled

American Airlines flight.[20] The grieving mother posted American's insensitive denial letter on her Facebook page, and the correspondence soon went viral. Social media is thus a two-edged sword, which can enhance or erode a company's brand image, depending on how effectively it is utilized.

Brand Killers

Given the significant contribution of brand equity to business performance, it is important to understand and avoid three unintentional but common management mistakes that can weaken a company's brand image:

1. Breaking a brand promise.
2. Diluting brand meaning through dissonant product-line extensions.
3. Diluting brand value through excessive product complexity.

Breaking a Brand Promise

Strong brands convey a clear promise of what a company and its products stand for, often built up over decades of consistent brand positioning and marketing communications. As such, if a company suddenly reverses course and launches products that break its brand promise, it risks alienating customers, creating brand dissonance, and damaging the brand for years, if not permanently.

One of the most egregious cases of breaking a brand promise involved General Motors, a company that had cultivated the strongest brands in the U.S. car market for decades. Throughout much of the twentieth century, GM had enjoyed market-share leadership in the United States by creating a brand portfolio that delivered "cars for every purse and purpose."[21]

In GM's brand hierarchy,[22] Chevrolet served as the entry-level brand, featuring models with lower power and fewer luxury features than found in GM's other brands. Pontiac was distinguished as GM's performance brand, symbolized by its iconic GTO and Trans Am models, equipped with powerful V8 engines tuned to deliver as much as 350 horsepower.

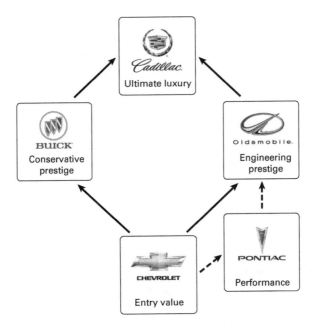

Figure 8.5 An interpretation of General Motors' brand hierarchy

For buyers looking for (and able to afford) more prestige, GM offered two upmarket brands. Buick was aimed at conservative buyers interested primarily in plush riding comfort, while Oldsmobile distinguished itself with sophisticated engineering features, being the first GM division to introduce turbocharged engines and front-wheel drive.

At the top end of the brand hierarchy stood Cadillac, GM's ultimate luxury brand. Cadillac set itself apart from other GM brands with unique comfort and performance features, and often set the world standard for automotive engineering achievement. In its illustrious history, Cadillac became the first carmaker in the world to introduce such automotive breakthroughs as the electric engine starter, electronically controlled fuel injection, power sunroofs, automatic headlamp dimmers, powered seats with memory, automatic interior temperature control, automatic load leveling, electronic seat warmers, and theft-deterrent systems.

General Motors's well-executed brand strategy fulfilled its intent of attracting a large number of entry-level car buyers and then providing logical aspiration paths to retain customer loyalty over successive purchase cycles. By the1960s, GM's U.S. market share exceeded 50 percent, raising antitrust concerns with its apparent corporate invincibility. But GM's success and management insularity fueled corporate arrogance toward its workers, suppliers, and customers. The company's business model drove high levels of product complexity, cost, and internal competition for customers and investment, leaving it far more vulnerable to competition than its management realized.

Following the U.S. gasoline crisis in the early 1970s, high-quality, cheaper, and more fuel-efficient cars from Toyota, Honda, and Nissan began to eat into GM's market share. In response, GM developed its own small cars, starting with the Chevrolet Vega. *Car and Driver* magazine commented that "the Chevy Vega is on everyone's short list for Worst Car of All Time. It was so unreliable that it seemed the only time anyone saw a Vega on the road not puking out oily smoke was when it was being towed."[23]

With the need to improve quality and cut costs becoming more urgent, GM then adopted a disastrously flawed "platform engineering" strategy, spearheaded by CEO Roger Smith, whose background was in finance, rather than marketing or engineering.

The logic behind platform engineering was to cut costs by standardizing the design of major automotive components like chassis and engines for similar-sized cars across its different brand divisions, thereby improving economies of scale. As a result, GM was able to significantly reduce the total number of components required to support its numerous car models. Differentiation between models was primarily maintained by visible styling cues, using brand-specific exterior trim pieces (e.g., front grilles, headlights, and add-on ornaments).

The problem with this approach was that what GM gained from greater economies of scale was more than lost by breaking the strong brand promise of *meaningful differentiation* that had helped it attract and retain customers for decades. General Motors's platform-engineered cars blurred the distinctions between its storied brands, as graphically depicted on the cover of a 1983 issue of *Fortune* magazine.[24] Figure 8.6 shows model variants of GM's midsize cars sold by its Chevrolet, Pontiac, Buick, and Oldsmobile divisions. The cars not only looked alike, but they also shared common performance characteristics, thereby destroying the historical rationale for tiered-brand pricing.

General Motors's brand-killing platform strategy reached its nadir with the 1982 launch of J-body compact cars, with similar-looking

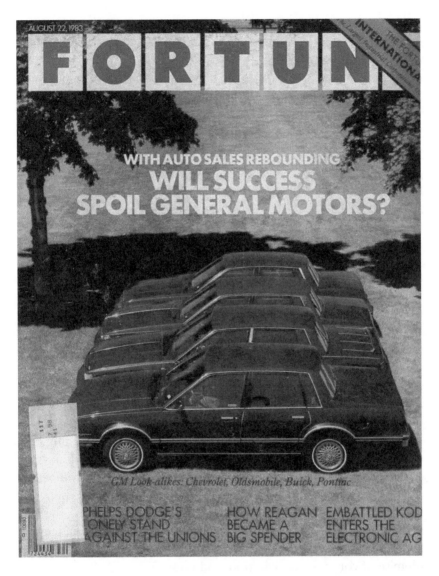

Figure 8.6 GM's midsize cars across four brand divisions. Photo courtesy of *Fortune* magazine. © Time Inc.

variants across all five of its car brands, including Cadillac. After tarnishing Cadillac's image for six years and suffering dismal sales (despite deep discounts), Cadillac's J-body Cimarron was discontinued in 1988. Although GM tried to restore more meaningful brand differentiation in the years that followed, the consequences of breaking its brand promise exacted a heavy toll. General Motors was forced to discontinue two of its brands (Oldsmobile and Pontiac) and declared bankruptcy in 2009. Nearly three decades after discontinuing the Cimarron, Cadillac is still struggling to restore its brand legacy of automotive excellence.

Breaking its brand promise wasn't the only reason GM slid into bankruptcy in 2009, but its brand-killing platform strategy was certainly its most serious and longest-lasting mistake.

Two more recent examples of companies that broke their brand promise and faced serious consequences are Netflix and JCPenney.

In the summer of 2011, Netflix was flying high. Its combined DVD rental and streaming video business was growing strongly, and its stock price had increased by more than 500 percent over the prior two years. The company's main competitor, Blockbuster, had recently declared bankruptcy, and its top executive Reed Hastings had been lauded as *Fortune* magazine's 2010 CEO of the year for leading a company so well attuned to serving its customers.[25]

It thus came as a shock when Hastings announced on July 12, 2011, that the company would soon be splitting into two separate entities. Customers who wanted to continue to use both DVD rental and streaming video services would now have to sign up for two separate accounts and pay $16 per month—a 60 percent increase in subscription rates.

Hastings further infuriated customers by publicly explaining this change in terms of what was best for the company, while dismissing complaints from subscribers. As Hastings noted, the core competencies of the DVD rental and streaming video businesses were quite different, and the company could be best managed by separating the two services. But customers didn't care about Netflix's core competencies; they felt betrayed by a company that broke its longstanding brand promise of convenience, selection, and value.

During the first quarter after the plan was announced, eight hundred thousand Netflix users cancelled their subscriptions. By the time Hastings announced he was abandoning his ill-considered plan on October 10, Netflix's stock had tumbled by nearly 60 percent.

Normally, when a company commits such a severe breach of its brand promise, it costs the CEO his job, does permanent damage to the brand, or both. But Hastings executed a remarkable turnaround, quickly restoring the original service at discounted rates for former subscribers, while taking full personal responsibility for the company's error and accepting a 50 percent cut in his stock option award for the year.

Hastings's genuine mea culpa resonated with consumers, and the company's steadily improving value proposition rebuilt subscriber confidence. Netflix has gone on to become one of the best performing stocks on the S&P 500, increasing nearly five-fold between 2011 and 2015.

Ron Johnson was not so lucky after breaking JCPenney's brand promise. Johnson was recruited as CEO of JCPenney in November 2011 after his remarkably successful run overseeing the growth of Apple's retail store network. Within two months on the new job, Johnson laid out his vision for an ambitious corporate makeover, most notably ending the weekly promotions that had been a signature element of JCPenney's brand promise for over one hundred years.

In its place, Johnson instituted a plan for "fair and square" pricing, where all merchandise was repriced 40 percent less than the prior sticker price. Each month, a new sale theme was introduced, where products related to a holiday or time of year received a "monthly value" discount below the fair and square price. Monthly value items that didn't sell were put on clearance, either the first or third Friday of the month. Consumers found the new scheme confusing and unappealing.

In Johnson's defense, JCPenney's long-standing policy of deep weekly discounts had essentially trained customers to shop primarily on sale days. As a result, the company's financial performance lagged behind Macy's, Target, and other key competitors.

But Johnson made the same mistake as Hastings in trying to address the company's problems without adequate consideration of customer input, compounded by the breathtaking speed with which the transformation was implemented. Within six months of coming on board, Johnson repriced all the merchandise in JCPenney's stores, replaced its ad agency, fired nearly all top executives and thousands of middle managers, and changed the company's logo.

Here's how Johnson explained his strategy:

Customers will not pay a penny more than the true value of the product. We are going to rethink every aspect of our business, boldly pursue change, and create long-term shareholder value, as we become America's favorite store. Every initiative we pursue will be guided by our core value to treat customers as we would like to be treated—*fair and square.*[26]

But customers didn't buy Johnson's vision of how they wanted to be treated or to shop, and they began defecting in droves to competitors still offering traditional promotions and discounts. In the first quarter of 2012, Macy's reported a 38 percent jump in profits, while JCPenney disclosed a big miss, sending its stock plunging 17 percent in a single day.

Over the remainder of 2012, Johnson continued to defend and implement his plan, as consumers continued to revolt. JCPenney's last-quarter 2012 earnings report was perhaps the worst quarterly performance ever recorded in the history of major retail: same-store sales were down 32 percent, to $3.8 billion.[27] By April 2013, with JCPenney's stock down 60 percent during his tenure, the board had seen enough, replacing Johnson after only seventeen months on the job. JCPenney has yet to recover the ground it lost under Johnson's leadership, as their market value declined by another 40 percent over the ensuing thirty months.

In retrospect, both Reed Hastings and Ron Johnson had a sound business rationale to change their companies' strategy. Had consumers gone along with their plans, both Netflix and JCPenney would have improved their efficiency and profitability. But neither CEO anticipated that by breaking their company's brand promise, once-loyal customers would feel betrayed and take their business elsewhere. It takes a long time for a company to build a valued brand promise, but a frighteningly short amount of time to betray the trust of its customers.

Diluting Brand Meaning Through Dissonant Product-Line Extensions

Strong brands have an obvious incentive to launch new products that can exploit their broad consumer awareness and positive reputation. There are numerous examples of successful product-line extensions that have helped companies with strong brands create new profitable growth opportunities.

- After creating a global market for low-price disposable pens, Bic successfully expanded into disposable lighters and razors.
- Planters created a strong brand association with peanuts, and leveraged its reputation to expand into peanut butter, peanut snack bars, and a wide variety of other nut products.

- Procter & Gamble's Tide has maintained detergent market leadership by continuously adding new laundry cleaning products, including liquid detergents, individual pods, and laundry additive enhancements (e.g., bleach, fabric softener, odor removers). To further leverage its brand reputation, Procter & Gamble has also launched a chain of dry-cleaning outlets under the Tide brand name.[28]

Consumer-packaged-goods brands routinely add new flavors, performance enhancements, and packaging varieties to their branded product lineup. For example, Dannon has maintained a strong position in the U.S. yoghurt market by continuously adding flavor varieties to its traditional yoghurt, Greek-style yoghurt, and diet lines.

But if a company ventures too far afield by launching products that fail to deliver meaningful differentiation and create consumer confusion, they can fail in their own right, and, in some cases, weaken the parent-brand image. For every successful product-line extension, there are many more examples of failed launches,[29] some of which provide fodder for lovers of schadenfreude.

Harley-Davidson, known for its rugged motorcycles and related brand accessories (e.g., belt buckles, leather jackets), inexplicably and unsuccessfully waded into the perfume category with an eau de toilette called Hot Road. Ill-advised product-line extensions into perfumes have tempted others as well. Zippo, known more for lighter fluid than perfume, tried its hand with a range of Zippo-branded fragrances. And even Burger King entered the fray with a branded body spray promising "the scent of seduction with a hint of flame-broiled meat."[30]

Coors, struggling to compete with its larger competitors in the U.S. beer market in the late 1980s, tried unsuccessfully to leverage its Rocky Mountain heritage with a line of Coors-branded sparkling water. Unfortunately it became the unconvincing "101st product on the shelf" in an already crowded category and was soon withdrawn.

Guinness, best known for its full-bodied stout beers, could not resist the siren song of the growing appetite for light beers in the late 1970s. With its first new product launch in two hundred years, the company introduced Guinness Light in 1979, supported by a major print advertising campaign carrying the tagline "They said it couldn't be done." But consumers shunned the new entry, suggesting that

Guinness Light *shouldn't* have been done, and the company quietly withdrew the product after less than two years on the market.[31]

After succeeding with product-line extensions into lighters and razors, Bic tried to expand further into panty hose. Bic panty hose didn't resonate with consumers and was quickly dropped.

Can a misguided product-line extension not only fail in its own right but also harm the reputation of its parent brand? Recent research suggests that consumers tend to be relatively tolerant toward strong brands even after they fail to gain market traction with misguided product-line extensions.[32] However, there are circumstances where illogical product launches *can* damage brand image, most notably in cases where a new product introduced within the company's core business undermines established brand values.

For example, few customers seemed to care when GM dabbled briefly and unsuccessfully with a line of personal-mobility devices in partnership with Segway. Consumers apparently shrugged this product failure off as an inconsequential corporate dalliance. However, as previously noted, Cadillac severely tarnished its brand image—self-promoted over the years with hubristic taglines like "Creating a Higher Standard," and "Standard of the World"—with its disastrous Cimarron product-line extension into compact luxury cars.

In a similar vein, many marketing professionals have questioned the wisdom of Starbucks's VIA instant coffee, which was launched with an advertising campaign challenging customers to compare the taste of VIA to the company's store-brewed coffees.[33] Even if VIA's taste were comparable to the store-brewed coffee (a point contested by many published reviews), the broader question remains whether VIA is congruent with the company's reputation for delivering a distinctive customer experience in the luxuriant ambience of its stores.

These examples raise the broader question of the requirements for successful product-line extensions: that they should not only succeed in their own right but also exploit and reinforce the parent brand.

Successful product-line extensions exhibit two fundamental properties: brand leverage and category fit. Brand leverage refers to the strength of specific attributes "owned" by a brand that can be leveraged to successfully extend the brand into new categories. For example, brands can leverage their reputation for functional superiority (e.g., Jeep), category leadership (e.g., Planters peanuts), or prestige intangibles (e.g., Louis Vuitton) to cast a positive halo over new products.

However, consumers have to grant permission for a brand to be accepted in a new category. This is where category fit comes in. Category fit refers to the degree to which a brand's attributes appeal to, and are valued by, consumers in a new product category, i.e., the degree to which an extended brand "fits" consumer expectations.

The brand leverage and category fit concepts help explain the differing market reactions to product-line extensions cited earlier in this chapter. For example, no one doubts that Harley-Davidson "owns" a reputation for powerful motorcycles and the rugged free spirit of its customers. This has served the company well in leveraging its iconic brand to sell a wide array of accessories where its macho brand image is greatly valued—e.g., belt buckles, leather jackets, and manly bling. But Harley's brand leverage is of little value—and in fact, directly clashes with—what consumers are looking for when buying eau de toilette. Ditto Zippo and Burger King.

Strong brands can create brand leverage, but only if consumers in a new category value the same attributes for which the company is best known. For example, consumers did give Jeep permission to enter a decidedly different product category. Jeep enjoys a strong brand reputation for rugged vehicles that can take a beating and safely transport its passengers over any terrain. These brand attributes are also greatly valued by owners of baby strollers, which have become a successful product-line extension for Jeep.

Diluting Brand Value Through Excessive Product Complexity

A third way a company can unwittingly dilute its brand value is by allowing its product lineup to become too complex over time. Not only can excessive product complexity increase costs, reduce quality, and harm profitability, but it can also weaken the foundation of a company's brand image.[34]

A dire example of a company that damaged its brand with excessive product-line complexity is Rubbermaid, a leading U.S. manufacturer of plastic household containers. Rubbermaid had enjoyed double-digit annual growth through the early 1990s on the strength of innovative product design, earning the company recognition as *Fortune*'s Most Admired Company in 1993.

But low-cost foreign competition began to emerge, finding a receptive audience from consumers and big-box retailers who valued "good enough" products at rock-bottom prices. In response, Rubbermaid CEO Wolfgang Schmitt chose to double down on product innovation, announcing that "our objective is to bury competitors with such a profusion of products that they can't copy us."[35]

True to his word, Schmitt guided Rubbermaid through a frenetic level of new product development, resulting in five thousand distinct products in 426 unique colors (including eighteen different shades of black), decentrally managed through ten thousand vendors. This high level of complexity increased the company's costs and caused supply-chain bottlenecks, creating an opportunity for competitors whose quality and efficiency was steadily improving. With viable competitive alternatives, Walmart balked at Rubbermaid's high prices and low (75 percent) on-time delivery and began pulling many of the company's products from its shelves. At other retailers, Rubbermaid was experiencing declining demand, as many customers no longer found the company's product variety justified its premium prices. By 1998, with losses mounting, Rubbermaid opted to sell to Newell Brands—a turnaround specialist—at a price well below its peak stock value.[36]

A more recent example of a company that allowed excessive product-line complexity to weaken its brand image and value proposition is Evernote. Founded in 2008, Evernote is a cross-platform, "freemium" app designed for note taking and organizing and archiving personal information. In other words, Evernote is designed to help individuals and work teams store and retrieve any information in any format on whatever devices they happen to be working on.

By 2013, the company seemed to be on a roll; it had registered eighty million users and attracted over $300 million in investment from venture capitalists who valued the company at one billion dollars.[37] But over the next two years, the company ran into trouble. In 2015, Evernote laid off nearly 20 percent of its workforce, shut down three of its ten global offices, and replaced its CEO.[38]

It turns out that the vast majority of Evernote's users signed up for only the free app and didn't see enough value to upgrade to a paid subscription. Struggling to generate revenue, Evernote lost its focus and continuously released new products that added complexity and often performed poorly. The company developed so many features and functions that it became increasingly difficult to explain to newcomers or even veteran users exactly what the product was.

As Evernote's former CEO Phil Libin explained, "people go and they say, 'Oh, I love Evernote. I've been using it for years and now I realize I've only been using it for 5 percent of what it can do.' And the problem is that it's a different 5 percent for everyone. If everyone just found the same 5 percent, then we'd just cut the other 95 percent and save ourselves a lot of money. It's a very broad usage base. And we need to be a lot better about tying it together."[39] Evernote wound up spreading itself too thin and lost sight of its core identity and primary consumer value proposition.

Why would a company allow itself to undermine its brand value and business viability with such excessive product-line complexity? The tendency to continuously add product variety to economically unjustified levels is actually quite common. To see why, imagine for illustrative purposes that you are the brand manager for a consumer packaged goods product, clawing for fractions of a percent of market share against aggressive national and store-brand competitors.

The pressures to add product-line extensions may seem compelling if your competitors have recently begun to gain market share by launching new flavors, packaging designs, and value-priced variants, supported by increased promotional spending. Your product line may have begun to look stale, and you haven't had a new "story" to tell to retailers or consumers for a while. Perhaps your company's "Big Data" analysts have detected pockets of untapped demand in certain ethnic, gender, and geographic segments that arguably could be better served with targeted new offerings.

Each of these market signals suggests a pressing need for new variants in your product lineup, and as a marketing professional, you would be expected to unleash your creative talents to craft new products to boost demand.

Faced with similar circumstances, marketing executives have proliferated product lines across a range of industries:

- The typical U.S. supermarket now carries from thirty to fifty thousand stock-keeping units (SKUs), up from fifteen thousand just two decades ago.[40]
- The four major U.S. wireless service providers recently offered a total of nearly seven hundred pricing plans.[41]
- Across the automotive, chemicals, machinery, pharmaceuticals, and fast-moving consumer goods sectors, product complexity has

increased by 220 percent over the past fifteen years while product life cycles have shrunk by 30 percent.[42]

- Amazon is putting pressure on manufacturers and brick-and-mortar retailers by putting an apparently limitless array of goods just a mouse click away from consumers. For example, if you're in the market for dog biscuits, Amazon gives you (and Fido) well over one hundred unique choices.

But in adding product variety in search of increased sales, product planners and brand managers often overlook a number of adverse impacts, including increased costs, decreased quality, brand dilution, and customer confusion.

In fact, excessive product proliferation can actually decrease a company's sales for two reasons. First, research studies have found that when confronted by an excessive number of choices, consumers may respond by forgoing a purchase altogether. For example, in one experiment, Columbia Business School professor Sheena Iyengar set out samples of jam on supermarket tables in groups of either six or twenty-four. Iyengar found that while about 30 percent of those who were given six choices went on to actually buy some jam, only 3 percent of those given twenty-four choices did.[43] As psychologist Barry Schwartz explained in *The Paradox of Choice*, an excess of consumer choice leads to angst, indecision, regret, and ultimately, lowered satisfaction with both the purchase process and the products themselves.[44] Too much choice or too much information can be paralyzing.[45]

A second reason that increasing complexity can decrease sales is related to adverse impacts on retailing operations. Product proliferation increases forecast errors and stockouts, and the need for inventory-clearing discounts and obsolescence write-downs.

The difficulty in isolating and measuring these impacts often complicates corporate efforts to reign in the insidious drag of excess complexity. Since the real costs of increasing product-line complexity are widely dispersed across the organization and largely invisible to brand managers, the seemingly free choice of attacking, defending, adapting, and responding to the marketplace often provides an irresistible justification for adding new products.

By this reasoning, one could expect that the In-N-Out Burger restaurant chain would seek to attract new customers by adding a variety of chicken, fish, egg, and sausage food items to compete with the ever-expanding menu at McDonald's. Yet In-N-Out Burger has chosen not to respond to the competitive environment in such a fashion. Why not?

In-N-Out Burger has made a concerted management decision to limit the range of products it brings to market, focusing instead on delivering superior quality within a deliberately limited menu, selling only hamburgers (with or without cheese), a single portion size of fries, and a variety of cold and hot drinks.[46] Limiting product complexity lies at the very core of In-N-Out Burger's business strategy. Its ability to significantly outperform sector competition is driven more by what it is *not* willing to do than by what it is willing to pursue.

In-N-Out Burger attracts a fiercely loyal clientele who evangelically rave about the taste of its cheeseburgers in reverential terms not normally applied to McDonald's. On the surface, both fast-food chains are selling similar products at similar price points. But In-N-Out burgers taste better because its hamburgers are made from fresh patties, delivered daily, with no freezing before use; buns are baked fresh in store, multiple times per day; fresh vegetables are delivered daily from local farms, strictly controlled for product quality; and hamburgers are cooked strictly to order, with no microwave ovens or heat lamps before serving.

If these business practices consistently yield a better-tasting product, why can't McDonald's simply replicate In-N-Out Burger's approach? The reason is that McDonald's has chosen a strategy of high product-line complexity, ubiquitous global locations on a global scale, and extended service hours, and this strategy complicates its logistics and service operations, requiring bulk shipments of frozen food products, in-store freezers, and pre-cooked orders kept warm by heat lamps in each establishment. The resulting quality compromises are very real, caused by structural differences in the underlying product-line strategies.

To add to McDonald's challenges, its growing product-line complexity has also slowed its ability to rapidly fulfill customer orders, compromising the performance of one of the pillars of the company's brand promise: fast food! According to a *Wall Street Journal* article, "Between March and July [2013] alone, McDonald's added Premium McWraps, Egg White Delight McMuffins, blueberry pomegranate smoothies and new Quarter Pounders to its menu. The fast pace of the new-product introductions created challenges for [the company's] franchise operators, making their operations more complex in ways that slowed service."[47]

Determining an optimal product-line strategy is not strictly an analytical exercise to be turned over to technocrats armed with elegant analytical models. While companies should certainly seek to selectively weed out nonperforming product lines over time, a far more important strategic imperative is choosing the basis upon which your company wishes to compete: broad market coverage versus targeted product superiority.

For companies like In-N-Out Burger, Apple, and many others, there is no such thing as a free lunch when it comes to product-line complexity. These companies could not consistently deliver superior products without explicitly choosing to limit the range of their offerings. For them, less can be more.

In summary, effective product strategy and brand strategy are mutually reinforcing. By continuously innovating to create meaningfully differentiated products and services, a company can strengthen its brand promise, build mutual trust, and deepen its customers' symbolic identity with the brand—the hallmarks of great brands.

Companies can further strengthen their brand equity by exploiting effective product personalization, building brand communities, and maintaining a dialogue with customers, while avoiding breaking their brand promise, adding incongruent product-line extensions, or carrying excessive product-line complexity.

CHAPTER NINE

What Makes Products Meaningfully Different?

UP TO THIS point, I have stressed the importance of continuous innovation to deliver meaningful differentiation in the marketplace. But I haven't yet examined how to measure product differentiation, nor identified effective strategies to help companies create products and services that break away from the competitive pack. My task in this chapter, and the one that follows, is to clarify how a company caught in a dogfight can become a cat.

A logical starting point is the question raised in the title of this chapter: What makes products meaningfully different? Marketers and strategists are taught that it shouldn't matter what a company thinks about its products and services. Rather, understanding consumer perceptions is the key to unlocking opportunities to serve unmet needs and to differentiate product offerings.

Product Positioning

The applicable theory for understanding consumer perceptions is *product positioning*.[1] This theory describes the process by which a firm markets its products and brands to occupy a distinct and valued position in a consumer's mind. Positioning theory rests on three principles:

1. Market research can measure how consumers perceive competing products according to tangible and subjective product attributes. (Examples of tangible attributes are digital camera quality in megapixels, car fuel economy in miles per gallon, and product price. Subjective

attributes include "fun to own," "easy to use," "best looking," "best tasting," or "best value," all measured on subjective rating scales).[2]

2. Companies can influence how its products are perceived by altering the "4Ps" that define the presentation of products in the marketplace.[3]

- Product—the design and features of the product or service.
- Place—the physical and online channels through which the product or service is sold.
- Price—the cost and terms associated with purchasing the product, including up-front price, payment terms, and recurring fees.
- Promotion—the mechanisms used to promote the product in the marketplace, including all forms of mass and direct marketing, point-of-sale displays, sales promotions, and public relations.

3. Companies can (and should) develop products and services that differentiate themselves from competitors in ways that are recognized and valued by consumers, i.e., by the creation of a distinct product position.

The basic technique used to analyze differentiation and product positioning is *perceptual mapping*, which evaluates how consumers perceive competing products based on a set of relevant performance attributes. For example, figure 9.1 shows how consumers perceived women's clothing retailers in the Washington, DC, market on two attributes: value for money (from worst to best value) and stylishness (from conservative to current fashion).[4] This perceptual map can be interpreted to develop a number of insights on how consumers perceive competing retailers.

- First, which companies consumers perceived to be the closest competitors, based on specific attributes. For example, Neiman Marcus should concern itself more with competition from Saks than from JCPenney. Based on consumer perceptions, JCPenney has very different performance characteristics, and therefore has a very different customer appeal than that of Neiman Marcus.

- Second, it can be determined whether a retailer has an image deficiency compared to competitors. In this study, for example, JCPenney was considered to be both less stylish *and* a worse value than Hecht's.
- Third, it can be seen if there is a "white space" opportunity not being pursued by *any* competitor. For example, no retailer is positioned above Macy's as both stylish *and* good value.

The next few pages explore the theory underlying a variety product-positioning techniques. Readers who wish to skip directly to a discussion of the common pitfalls and strategic implications of applying these techniques should skip to the next major section, "Common Product Strategy Traps."

How did market researchers obtain the data required to generate the perceptual map depicted in figure 9.1? By simply asking consumers what they thought about competing brands.

Table 9.1 displays the type of the data used in creating the perceptual map shown in figure 9.1. A sample of consumers was asked to rate twenty women's clothing retailers on a scale of 1 to 7 (worst to best) based on fifteen attributes, including value for money and stylishness.

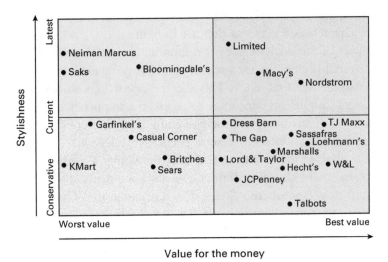

Figure 9.1 Example of a two-attribute perceptual map for women's clothing retailers

TABLE 9.1
Data Collection for Perceptual Mapping

	Saks	Nordstrom	JCPenney	Sears	The Gap
Value for money	2	3	1	5	4
Stylishness	6	7	4	1	6
Customer service	5	7*	3	4	6
Shopping experience	5	6	4	2	4
Convenient locations	3	1	4	4	5
10 other Categories	. . .	. . .	. . .	. . .	. . .
Overall preference Rank	2	1	4	5	3

* "On a scale of 1 to 7, how would you rate Nordstrom for shopping experience?"

As shown in the table, one survey respondent rated Nordstrom a 7 for customer service, while JCPenney was given only a 3 for the same attribute. On the other hand, Nordstrom received a very low rating for convenient locations, while the relatively ubiquitous JCPenney scored higher in this attribute.

By averaging the ratings of each of the twenty retailers for the fifteen attributes, a perceptual map can be created for any pair of performance characteristics, as was the case in figure 9.1.

As part of this analysis, survey respondents were also asked to rank their overall preference for each of the twenty retailers, as shown in the bottom row of table 9.1. This allowed researchers to develop two additional insights on consumer behavior: the importance consumers attach to each attribute, and the size and composition of distinct market segments that differ in these respects.[5]

An analysis of the data from the study on women's clothing retailers found that there were five distinct consumer segments. These are represented by the numbered circles shown in figure 9.2. The size of the circles is proportional to the number of consumers in each segment, while the center of each circle is positioned at the optimal trade-off between value for money and stylishness for consumers within a particular consumer segment.

Figure 9.2 suggests that Neiman Marcus and Saks appeal to a small consumer segment that is willing and able to tolerate high prices

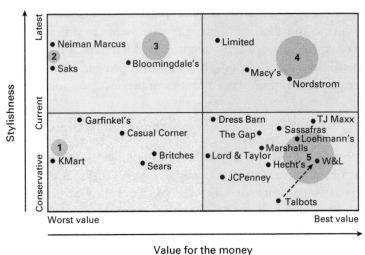

Figure 9.2 Idealized positioning for women's clothing retailers by market segment

(worst value) for the latest trends in women's clothing. At the other end of the spectrum, the largest segment is composed of price-conscious consumers who are best served by a number of competitors that offer conservative styles at an attractive price.

Armed with the results of such an analysis, individual companies can assess their strategic situation and make informed choices about the positioning of their products. As illustrated by the arrow in figure 9.2, Talbots should recognize the need to reposition its merchandise with more stylish clothing at better prices, in order to be perceived as closer to the preferred trade-off between stylishness and value. Sears, Britches, and Casual Corner appear to be in particularly vulnerable positions, seemingly out of touch with consumer preferences in *any* segment, suggesting the need for radical rethinking of their product and market strategies.

These are strategically potent insights. Even rudimentary perceptual maps can inform companies whether their products are sufficiently differentiated from the competition and if they are well positioned to appeal to targeted segments of the market. Armed with such analyses, product planners have the ability to make informed decisions about how to win in the marketplace with highly valued, differentiated products.

However, as I will show, product-positioning analyses may unwittingly lure companies into strategies that yield *less* differentiation in the marketplace. Before exploring these hidden traps, I'll review a few additional perceptual-mapping techniques to provide a more complete picture of the common types and uses of product-positioning theory.

More Perceptual-Mapping Techniques

The previous depiction of product positioning has been limited to two attributes at a time. For example, figure 9.2 displayed how various retailers compare in value for money versus stylishness, even though consumer ratings of many other attributes were available from the data collection effort. I could, of course, construct a new two-by-two positioning chart with, for example, customer service versus value for money on the two axes. However, this too would provide only a partial picture of how competing players are positioned relative to all attributes.

It is possible to depict how multiple products are positioned with respect to multiple attributes through *multivariate* perceptual-mapping techniques. An example of this technique from the beer industry is shown in figure 9.3.[6] Needless to say, when multiple products are positioned relative to multiple attributes, the resulting graphical depiction is complex. However, with suitable explanation, multivariate perceptual maps can provide considerable insight on product positioning.

In figure 9.3, each vector emanating from the center of the chart represents a beer product attribute (or a combination of correlated attributes combined into a single measure).[7] For example, attributes measured in this study include how each beer was rated as being full bodied, light, popular with women, blue collar, premium, and so on. The interpretation of the direction and length of individual vectors can be explained as follows.

The longer the vector, the greater the significance of the attribute in explaining perceived differences between products.[8] For example, in figure 9.3, the factors "popular with men" and "special occasion" are strong differentiators in distinguishing competing beers, whereas "heavy" and "good value" are less discriminating.[9]

Vectors that are polar opposites are inversely correlated. That is, beers that are rated highly for one factor will tend to rate lower on the

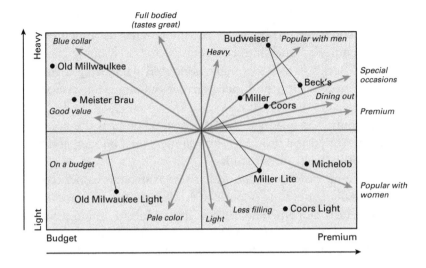

Figure 9.3 Multivariate perceptual map: beer industry

opposing factor(s). For example, the "full bodied" attribute vector is, not surprisingly, the polar opposite of the vectors associated with light and less filling beers.

Vectors that are orthogonal—at right angles to one another—are uncorrelated. That is, beers rating highly for one factor will have no particular tendency to rate high or low on the orthogonal factor(s). Examples of orthogonal attributes in figure 9.3 include "good value" and "heavy."

For convenience, a set of "north/south" and "east/west" axes are generally added to multivariate perceptual maps to highlight particularly important attributes in distinguishing products. In figure 9.3, the attribute vectors are arranged around a heavy/light vertical axis and a budget/premium horizontal axis.[10]

The question remains how to interpret the product positions of the individual beers depicted on a multivariate perceptual map. To see how any given beer is perceived regarding a particular attribute, one needs to draw a line from the position of the beer on the map to a point that intersects a particular vector at right angles. The further out the intersecting line is along the vector, the higher the beer is rated for the specified attribute. Some examples will help to demystify this complex geometry.

In the "northeast" quadrant of figure 9.3, both Budweiser and Beck's are considered to be nearly equally popular with men because their perpendicular lines intercept this vector at roughly the same point. But Beck's is more strongly associated with being a beer for special occasions, as it is positioned farther out along this vector than Budweiser.

In the southwest quadrant, Old Milwaukee Light is the beer most strongly perceived as a product for consumers on a budget, compared to all the other beers in this study.

In the "southeast" quadrant, Miller Lite is strongly associated with being a less filling beer and popular with women. But what about male beer drinkers? The perpendicular line from Miller Lite intercepts the "popular with men" vector, implying that at the time this product-positioning study was conducted, Miller Lite was considered to be decidedly unpopular with men.

Suppose you were the brand manager of Miller Lite, presented with the results of this perceptual map depicting how your beer was seen in the marketplace. It's easy to see that a logical response would be to try to reposition Miller Lite as more appealing to men, without weakening the strong brand affinity for women. After all, men drink the majority of beer in the U.S. market.

This is exactly what the company tried to do with its long-running "tastes great/less filling" ad campaign, which featured burly male sports figures comically extolling the virtues of Miller Lite. The intent of these ads was to change how men perceived Miller Lite in an attribute of keen importance—full-bodied taste—while still retaining the perception of being less filling (and with fewer calories) that had found favor with women. For example, figure 9.4 shows a representative Miller Lite print ad featuring former NFL lineman Bubba Smith. The underlying message is that if Miller Lite is robust enough to appeal to an elite athlete like Bubba Smith, then surely it should be manly enough for the average male beer consumer.

Miller Lite's marketing strategy was successful. For nearly twenty years, Miller Lite ranked as the top-selling light beer in the United States, and its "tastes great/less filling" marketing initiative was chosen as the eighth-best advertising campaign of the twentieth century by *Advertising Age* magazine.[11]

In perceptual-mapping terms, Miller Lite's advertising campaign was trying to reposition how the beer was perceived in the market,

Figure 9.4 The Miller Lite "Tastes Great" advertisements featuring Bubba Smith were representative of the brand (1977). Photo © Miller Brewing Company, MillerCoors.

as hypothetically shown in figure 9.5. In the desired new positioning, Miller Lite would continue to be associated with being less filling, but would now be thought to be popular with both women *and* men.

The desired new positioning would also convey other positive brand associations, including premium status and being a product for dining out or special occasions. This example illustrates how perceptual

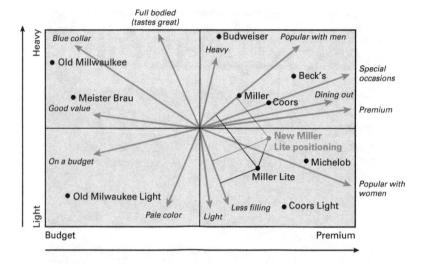

Figure 9.5 Illustrative repositioning of Miller Lite

mapping can help brand managers formulate marketing strategies and help monitor consumer perceptions over time.

Multidimensional Scaling

Perceptual maps can also be developed to assess competing products, even if the exact attributes consumers use to evaluate products are unclear. With multidimensional scaling (MDS) techniques, consumers are asked to rank the degree of similarity between competing products based on whatever criteria they deem relevant to their evaluation.[12] This approach allows consumers to express preferences in their own terms, avoiding the introduction of flaws due to the researcher's preconceptions of marketplace behavior. After the analysis is complete, MDS results can be interpreted to reveal the actual underlying attributes that best explain consumer choices.

For example, Table 9.2 depicts the responses of a survey respondent ranking each of fifteen distinct pairings of U.S. theme parks on the basis of perceived similarity, from 1 (most similar) to 15 (least similar). Figure 9.6 displays the results of an MDS analysis of several hundred such responses, which places each amusement park in a position

TABLE 9.2
Similarity Rankings of Theme Parks

	Universal	MGM	SeaWorld	Magic Kingdom	Epcot
Busch Gardens	11	12	10	6	13
Universal		1	14	2	5
MGM			15	3	6
SeaWorld				8	9
Magic Kingdom					4

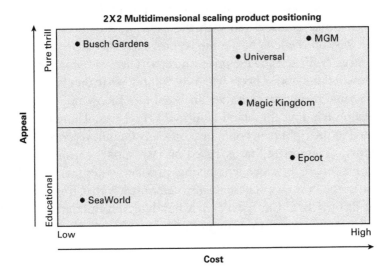

Figure 9.6 Multidimensional scaling analysis of theme parks

that closely replicates the similarity ratings, measured by the distances between data points on the two-by-two grid. Theme parks that are positioned close together on the MDS plot were rated similarly in the underlying data, while those positioned far apart were perceived by consumers to be distinctly different.

For example, consumers thought Universal was similar to MGM, but distinctly different from SeaWorld. Busch Gardens also appears as dissimilar to SeaWorld on the vertical axis, and a polar opposite to Epcot.

In the MDS analysis, it is not known what park attributes are being plotted on the two axes on the chart. However, after examining the pattern of product positioning, researchers can infer that the horizontal axis likely relates to cost, while the vertical axis distinguishes parks by their emphasis on thrill rides versus an educational experience. These hypothesized attributes can be validated by follow-up interviews with survey respondents.

As a final example of product-positioning analysis, consider the results of a two-dimensional MDS analysis of competing beers displayed in figure 9.7.[13] In the left-hand panel, taste-test respondents were asked to rank the similarity of various beers, with prior knowledge of which brand of beer was in each sampling glass. The resulting beer-brand positioning suggests that the horizontal axis of the perceptual map is associated with the robustness of beer taste (with the weakest on the left), while the vertical axis reflects perceived price differences (with the lowest price on top). These results reflect what consumers think about beers when they know what they're drinking.

The same products were then analyzed in a follow-up MDS analysis, this time hiding the brand identity of the beers. These results are depicted in the right panel of figure 9.7. Only Guinness proved to have a distinct, differentiated taste. Based on taste alone, consumers could not differentiate between competing products—despite advertising claims to the contrary. These results demonstrate that marketing can create distinct brand images, even when basic product attributes are difficult for consumers to distinguish.

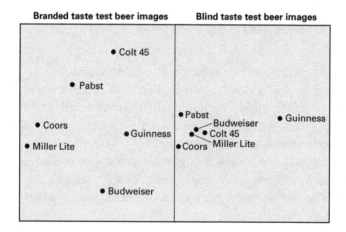

Figure 9.7 Beer product positioning

Common Product-Strategy Traps

These examples illustrate that product-positioning analyses can provide insights on how consumers perceive competing products based on multiple attributes. Thus, perceptual mapping can serve as a valuable tool in developing marketing strategies.[14] But product-positioning techniques have some hidden traps that are important to understand. For one thing, there is nothing proprietary about perceptual mapping. Therefore, it would be prudent for marketers to assume that all major competitors are aware of the product characteristics required to appeal to targeted customer segments. The first company to create value by adding a desirable new feature in any particular product category should expect that the question is only *when*, not whether, competitors will copy (or leapfrog) their temporary advantage. Product-positioning dynamics tend to follow predictable patterns over time, often yielding increasingly *un*differentiated products that all vie for the same customers with similar product features and functions.[15]

To see how these market forces play out, consider the typical life cycle of a new product, from groundbreaking launch to market maturity. In response to the entry of a promising new product or service (e.g., smartphones or wearable fitness trackers), fast followers invariably enter the fray with competing products offering a variety of price/performance trade-offs, in the hope of finding the market's "sweet spot"—i.e., the most appealing consumer value proposition (left-hand panel, figure 9.8). Given the inherent uncertainties in understanding consumer preferences in early-stage markets, competitors experience hits and misses, with some products gaining more market traction than others.

As demand patterns become more apparent over time, each company seeks to find new ways to differentiate its products, while also copying competitors who have beaten them to the punch on desired features or functions (middle panel, figure 9.8). Ultimately, this back-and-forth replication, particularly amongst similarly positioned players, leads to competitive clustering, with little sustained differentiation in key features within clearly defined high- and low-end market segments (right-hand panel, figure 9.8).[16]

For example, ever since Apple ushered in the modern smartphone era in 2007 with its original iPhone, it has played leapfrog with

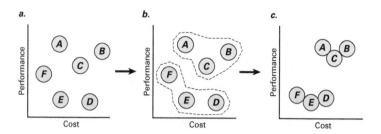

Figure 9.8 Competitive dynamics in product positioning. *a* In the early stages of a new product on the market, competitors typically offer a wide variety of differentiated choices in search of market traction; *b* Over time, the pressure to copy successful positioning moves, especially by those closest on the perceptual map leads to continuous back-and-forth replication among competitors . . .; *c* . . . which ultimately leads to competitive clustering, such that the differentiation within product segments (e.g., high-end vs. low-end) becomes less distinct over time.

Samsung and other companies in a race for superiority on processor speed, screen size, display resolution, camera quality, fingerprint identification, and other technical specifications. However, none of the competitors have been able to sustain technical superiority over successive product cycles.[17] Similarly, in consumer packaged goods such as toothpaste (Colgate versus Crest), diapers (Huggies versus Pampers), and shampoo (Clairol versus Pantene), companies quickly replicate any new product feature that might give a competitor a temporary market advantage. The net result is a blurring of product distinctiveness that often leaves consumers hard-pressed to identify meaningful differences between closely matched competitors. After all, when every product on the market seems to offer "Extra Whitening," "Extra Absorbency," or "Extra Shine," it becomes a challenge for consumers to differentiate them.

Another market dynamic related to this competitive herd instinct is *augmentation*, which refers to the tendency of companies to continuously enhance product performance on well-defined product attributes over successive product cycles (while often also increasing price). Augmentation reflects perfectly rational marketplace behavior. After all, improvements in product technology enable companies to steadily enhance product performance, and consumers are likely to recognize, value, and *expect* improved functionality over time.

The problem is that augmentation often leads to feature–function "arms races" that eventually yield products with more functionality and cost than most consumers want, need, or value. When this happens, companies find themselves in the unenviable position of having overshot real marketplace needs, which usually results in consumer price resistance, stalled growth, and decreasing margins.

Economic theory recognizes that consumer behavior follows the law of *diminishing marginal utility*, which states that each additional unit of consumption of a product yields lower consumer benefit. For example, the tenth bite of chocolate cake rarely seems to be as satisfying as the first. Similarly, the marginal value associated with an attribute of product performance generally declines as performance levels continue to improve.

Consider personal computers, for example. In the early stages of market development, rapid improvements in PC capability propelled strong growth in demand from first-time buyers and repeat purchasers looking for upgraded performance. But while Moore's law[18] projected that producers could double PC processing power every two years, the need for increased PC performance among consumers grew at a more modest pace.

This aligns with my own personal experience. My first home computer—a 1982 IBM PC—was equipped with a 4.8 megahertz processor, a then top-of-the-line 256 kilobyte internal memory, and a low-resolution 11.5 inch green-screen monitor, all of which cost over $3,000 (in 1982 dollars).

Fast-forward to 2016, and a typical midrange home computer now offers a 3.7 gigahertz processor (more than 800 times faster), eight gigabytes of memory (over 31,000 times bigger), and a 27 inch high-resolution touch-screen color monitor—all at a cost 80 percent lower than my original PC.

I've upgraded my PC several times since 1982 but reached a point several product generations ago when my computing needs were more than adequately served by my current computer, rendering further advances in speed or capacity of little value. While there are undoubtedly some power users—e.g., gaming aficionados, graphics designers, and big-data number crunchers—who need and will pay for ongoing improvements in PC performance, ever-increasing PC performance yields little meaningful differentiation or value for the majority of consumers.

Nonetheless, most PC manufacturers have moved in lockstep in augmenting performance levels over successive product generations, which makes it difficult for any one player to stand out—at least on the basic parameters of system capability. Thus, the PC market exhibits the characteristics of a classic competitive dogfight, with each player metaphorically scratching and clawing for advantage, in the futile pursuit of market dominance. If you happen to be in the market for a midrange Windows-based personal computer, you'll find that Asus, Dell, HP, and Lenovo provide numerous competent choices, but little meaningful distinction or differentiation.

Feature–function augmentation is a common competitive dynamic in most product categories. To paraphrase E. F. Schumacher, the renowned twentieth-century British economist, any intelligent fool can make things bigger and more complex, but it takes a touch of genius—and a lot of courage—to move in the opposite direction.[19]

Illustrated by the left-hand panel of figure 9.9, the first generation of any new product is typified by competitors jockeying for advantage by making their entry better on a number of dimensions, e.g., faster, bigger, more effective, or easier to use. But these features of augmented value in any first-generation product are quickly adopted as standard requirements in the next generation of products brought to market (middle panel, figure 9.9). This precipitates a second round of augmentation that, once again, drives each competitor to seek competitive advantage on key elements of product performance.

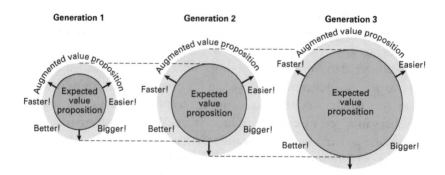

Figure 9.9 Product augmentation trends

Over time, each new generation of products incorporates more baseline functionality, with ever-smaller improvement in perceived consumer value. This is depicted in figure 9.9 by the shrinking size of the "augmented value proposition" outer band, relative to the core value consumers expect in successive generations of product development. This competitive dynamic is exactly what Clayton Christensen identified in his seminal work on disruptive technologies concerning the pervasive tendency of incumbent players to eventually overshoot the needs of mainstream customers. This competitive dynamic opens the door to new entrants, disrupting the market with simpler, lower-cost solutions.[20]

As a case in point, when I ask my MBA students if they would rush to replace their laptop computer if a new model offered 50 percent more speed and storage capacity at a price 25 percent lower than they originally paid, I usually get no takers. For most MBA students, and for most consumers at large, the performance of their home computer is more than adequate to meet current needs, underscoring the decline in PC sales.

Global sales of PCs peaked in 2010 and have been declining ever since, hitting an eight-year low in 2015. By 2007, recognizing that they had overshot the needs of many consumers, several PC makers began defying augmentation trends by offering laptop computers with decidedly *less* performance (in speed, memory capacity, battery life, and screen resolution) at considerably lower prices. These sub-$250 "netbook" models tapped a sizeable segment of consumers who had previously been priced out of the mainstream PC market. Netbooks became the fastest-growing category of the PC market in the ensuing three years.

Apple also defied augmentation trends when it introduced its first tablet computer in 2010. Rather than trying to outmuscle competitors on traditional measures of PC performance, Apple created an entirely new category of personal computing by emphasizing fundamentally different performance attributes, such as wireless connectivity, touch-screen user interface, and access to a broad ecosystem of media and entertainment content. While PC sales were declining, tablet sales grew from less than twenty million units in 2010 to nearly 230 million units in 2014.[21] Becoming a cat in the PC dogfight proved highly rewarding for Apple and its fast followers.

Until recently, the situation has been different in the smartphone market, where ongoing enhancements in product performance and size continued to motivate many consumers to trade up for new models every two years. However, continued feature–function augmentation is now showing signs of overshooting consumer needs in the smartphone market as well, with forecasts calling for lengthening replacement cycles and declines in price realization and growth beyond 2015.[22]

Defying Industry Rules

Consumers play a strong role in promoting product augmentation and competitive clustering because of the self-reinforcing behaviors between companies and their customers. After all, the more firms learn about consumers, the better they can adjust to consumer expectations, attitudes, emotions, and behaviors. In turn, consumers form beliefs about what to expect from companies in a given category, reinforcing product norms and category images.

Taken together, this symbiotic relationship leads to the development of well-defined category images, norms, and structures, which collectively define the rules of the game in a given industry. The following examples help illustrate why so many product categories turn into competitive dogfights, opening opportunities for a few enlightened companies to break away from the pack by offering products with fundamentally different value propositions.

Category Norms

Category norms refer to implicit rules and standards that emerge in a product or service category. Consumers come to accept these norms as "just the way business is done"—at least until a newcomer emerges to challenge what has really been a matter of industry choice, not immutable law. The travel industry is rife with examples. In the hotel industry, in the years before mobile phone ownership was de rigueur, it was expected that business hotels would charge for local landline calls, but provide shampoo, bodywashes, and grooming supplies gratis. There is no compelling reason why the industry had to operate this way, but such were the unwritten, widely followed practices within the hotel industry for decades. Similarly, in the airline industry, it was assumed that a ticket entitled passengers to an assigned seat, free nonalcoholic beverages and meals, inflight amenities (e.g., pillows, blankets), and frequent flyer credits. But low-cost carriers like Spirit Airlines chose to defy all these norms, offering a bare-bones service at rock-bottom fares. Spirit recognized that many consumers are willing to trade comfort for low fares, enabling the airline to achieve impressive, profitable growth.[23]

Well-established industry norms are found in virtually every product category, reflecting implicit assumptions about how consumers value price/performance trade-offs. When most competitors move in lockstep, offering similar products at comparable prices, it opens the door to newcomers to better serve specific market segments that prefer different price/performance trade-offs (e.g., netbook manufacturers and low-cost airlines) or an emphasis on altogether different product attributes (e.g., iPad and Swatch).

Category Structure

As a result of the competitive clustering dynamics described earlier, most industries evolve toward a clearly defined category structure defined in terms of distinct price and product-quality tiers. Take the watch industry, for example. For decades, watchmakers competed in three distinct product segments, as illustrated in figure 9.10. Low-end watches were positioned primarily as disposable functional tools—to reliably and accurately tell the time—sold through mass-merchandising channels at

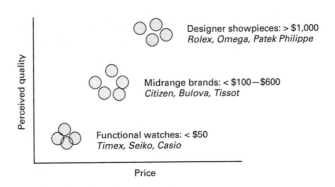

Figure 9.10 Watch industry category structure

low prices. Timex pioneered the development of low-cost mechanical movements in the 1950s, and this was followed by the introduction of low-priced quartz digital watches by Japanese watchmakers in the 1970s.

Midrange watches provided a greater emphasis on durable materials (e.g., stainless steel) and sophisticated design, sold at higher prices through limited retail distribution. At the top of the range, high-end watches distinguished themselves by sophisticated design and the use of precious jewels and metals. These designer showpieces were intended to serve as timeless family heirlooms, best expressed by one watchmaker's advertising tagline: "You never actually own a Patek Philippe watch, you are merely the caretaker for the next generation."[24]

Competing to win as a newcomer in such a highly structured industry against competitors with considerable assets, scale, and brand cachet is a daunting task. Accordingly, when Swatch Group—owner of such distinguished watch brands as Omega, Longines, and Tissot—pondered how to respond to the threat of low-priced quartz digital watches from Japan, it chose to ignore the widely accepted industry structure by seeking to change the rules of the game. The company launched the Swatch brand to create a unique value proposition that did not fit neatly into any of the established watch industry segments. While priced near the low-end watch of the watch market, Swatch positioned its products as boldly styled *fashion accessories*, rather than as functional timepieces.

This strategy not only provided the basis for meaningful and uniquely appealing product differentiation, but it also encouraged many customers to purchase more than one Swatch—not unlike the tendency to own many pieces of costume jewelry or scarves—thus creating a sizeable global market that Swatch dominated for years.[25] More recently, Apple is seeking to redefine the basis of competition in the watch industry by blending elements of classic watch styling with advanced wireless technology. The Apple Watch is yet another metaphorical example of a smart cat avoiding a brutal dogfight.

Category Image

Industry norms, well-defined product segmentation structures, and convergent competitor behaviors collectively shape an image consumers associate with product categories as a whole. Category images are distinctly different from the discussion in chapter 7 on the characteristics of individual product and brand images.

To illustrate this point, I often ask my MBA students to think of the first descriptors that come to mind when I mention a particular product or service category. Table 9.3 reflects the characterizations suggested by my students—both good and bad—affirming that categories as a whole are associated with stereotypical images.

Understanding category imagery is important because it often provides the starting point to identifying opportunities for meaningful product differentiation and competitive advantage. In particular, breakaway strategies reject established industry norms and category images to appeal to customers who are not well served by existing products and services.

In chapter 1, for example, I cited the case of LittleMissMatched that sells socks in sets of three unmatched items in bold colors and designs—the antithesis of the category image of functional, boring products. This sharp departure from the prevailing category image has allowed LittleMissMatched to build a strong and loyal following among tween customers.[26]

As another example, when General Motors launched the Saturn car division in 1990, its most salient distinguishing characteristic was a customer-friendly sales and service process, intended to overcome the strongly negative stereotype that had plagued the industry for decades. Saturn initially succeeded with this markedly different positioning, before inferior product performance ultimately dragged the brand down.

Similarly, it shouldn't be surprising that some insurance companies have sought to break from their negative industry stereotype of boring, complicated products by the use of category-busting advertising

TABLE 9.3
Category Images

Category	Category Image
Socks	Functional, boring
Lingerie	Sexy, indulgent
Car dealers	Sleazy, unpleasant
Insurance	Boring, complicated
Champagne	Special occasion, expensive

spokespersons—such as a talking gecko (Geico) or a perky sales agent (Progressive) to promote simple value propositions in humorous terms.[27]

Finally, when Casella Family Brands was considering whether or not to expand its Yellow Tail product line into the sparkling wine category, it was well aware of the U.S. consumer image of champagne as a luxury/reward product typically associated with special occasions. Rather than trying to compete head-on with prestigious champagne brands in this venerable category, the company chose to sharply break away from the category image. Priced at under $8 per bottle, and whimsically named "Bubbles," Yellow Tail sparkling wines were promoted as casual and refreshing adult beverages intended for everyday consumption. While it is still unclear whether consumers will embrace such a radical departure from the ingrained image of sparkling wines in the United States, Casella Family Brands has clearly and wisely sought to compete as a cat in this category dogfight.[28]

The Essence of Meaningful Differentiation

In each of the examples I have cited, enlightened companies rejected industry norms, structures, and category images by focusing on entirely new product attributes in an attempt to appeal to consumers poorly served by existing products. As shown in figure 9.11, breakout

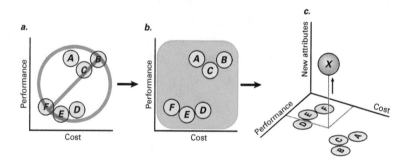

Figure 9.11 Breakout product positioning. *a* Breakout products reject conventional product positioning . . .; *b* . . . by approaching a category holistically, identifying vulnerabilities in *overall* industry norms, structure, and image . . .; *c* . . . to position products differentiated primarily by entirely new product attributes that serve latent unmet consumer needs.

products seek to create entirely new bases of consumer appeal in uncontested product spaces.

Companies that successfully launch breakout products choose not to be bound by conventional category norms, which are inherently based on how current products are perceived by current consumers in terms of current product attributes. Rather, breakout product strategies recognize that the most promising market opportunities may found by competing on *meaningfully different* terms. In other words, by identifying *new* product attributes that create entirely new bases of consumer appeal; attracting *nonconsumers* who have not been well served by current products; creating *new demand* in uncontested new markets; and rendering current competition irrelevant.

This concerted effort to break from current category conventions lies at the heart of all spectacularly successful new product launches, exemplified by Swatch, IKEA, CNN, Southwest Airlines, Nintendo Wii, Apple iPod, iPhone and iPad, Cirque du Soleil, Uber, Snapchat, and Netflix.

CHAPTER TEN

Where Do Great Ideas Come From?

BY NOW, I have made the case that sustained, profitable growth requires continuous innovation to deliver meaningful differentiation, most evidently in products that break away from traditional bases of competition to create entirely new consumer value propositions. But where do great ideas come from? And what tools and techniques can companies use to systematically identify and develop breakthrough product opportunities?

In simple terms, the genesis of all breakthrough products is an innovator's recognition of a better way for consumers or businesses to perform desired tasks. In some cases, successful new products fix a "pain point" associated with using current market offerings to perform routine jobs. This was certainly the case with Swiffer, for example. Launched by Procter & Gamble in the late 1990s, Swiffer proved the dry mop was far more convenient than traditional wet mop cleaning products, including the company's own Mr. Clean brand. The fact that Swiffer replacement pads carry a higher price and margin than traditional liquid household cleaners made this product a win-win solution for consumers and the company alike. Procter & Gamble followed the same playbook when it launched Tide Pods—a single-dose version of its liquid and powder detergents—which reinforced the company's dominance of the laundry detergent market.

In other cases, enlightened entrepreneurs envision products, such as GoPro video cameras, Facebook, and Post-it Notes, that tap latent needs many consumers may not even have realized they had. In 2002, Nick Woodman, an adventure-sports enthusiast, jury-rigged a crude strap-on camera after being unable to find a product on the market that could capture still images of his surfing adventures. Fellow surfers responded enthusiastically to the new product, prompting Woodman to extend his concept to digital video cameras. GoPro cameras unlocked a huge untapped demand among consumers seeking to capture images of their sporting adventures. By solving his *own* consumer need, Woodman laid the groundwork to build GoPro Inc. into a profitable, growing enterprise with a multi-billion dollar market value.[1]

There are two ways to discover new products. Most often, an entrepreneur like Woodman identifies a specific pain point or new value-creation opportunity, and seeks to develop a novel solution to the problem. But there are also notable examples where an entrepreneur starts by serendipitously identifying a novel *solution*, and then searches for a relevant problem to solve.

Take, for example, the inspiring story of Jorge Odón, an Argentine car mechanic, who developed a novel device to assist in difficult birth situations. In 2006, Odón watched a YouTube video demonstrating how to remove a cork stuck inside a glass bottle using nothing more than a plastic bag. During a night out with friends (who had not seen the video), Odón won a dinner bet that he could perform the seemingly impossible feat. Later that night, Odón—a father of five children, with no medical training—found himself dreaming of how the same parlor trick might be adapted to save a baby stuck in the birth canal. At 4:00 a.m., he woke his wife to tell her the idea that had just come to him. His wife, he recalled, "said I was crazy and went back to sleep."[2]

The problem Odón found himself dreaming about—literally and figuratively—is very real. Ninety-nine percent of mothers who die during childbirth live in countries where doctors lack access to the training and tools to assist in difficult deliveries.[3] Odón persisted in following his dream of creating a simple lifesaving device, building a prototype in his kitchen using a glass jar for a womb, his daughter's doll for the trapped baby, and a fabric bag and sleeve sewn by his wife.

With the help of family members, Odón arranged a meeting with the chief of obstetrics at a major teaching hospital in Buenos Aires to demonstrate his prototype. Impressed, the chief helped Odón apply for patents and connected him with officials of the World Health Organization, who eventually embraced the solution. By 2011, Odón's patented solution had been used in thirty successful live trials. In 2014,

Odón quit his automobile-repair job to work full time on his invention. Meanwhile, research continues around the globe toward perfecting the Odón device.

Another example of a solution looking for the right problem can be found in the circuitous path taken in the development of Post-it Notes. In 1968, 3M research scientist Spencer Silver was working on the development of industrial-strength adhesives intended for use in the aerospace industry. Instead of a creating a superstrong glue, Silver stumbled upon an incredibly weak, pressure-sensitive adhesive called acrylate copolymer microspheres (ACM). His new adhesive had two interesting properties: first, when applied to a surface, ACM could be peeled away without leaving any residue; and second, the adhesive was reusable.

However, no one at 3M, including Silver himself, could envision how to exploit these distinctive properties in a marketable product. The best idea that emerged from early brainstorming was for a coated bulletin board, to which plain paper notes could be attached. However, this hardly seemed likely to be a game-changing new business idea. Although Silver continued to proselytize the merits of his unusual discovery within the company, further work on ACM was shelved for five years.

In 1973, a serendipitous event brought what was to become Post-it Notes back to life. Over lunch in the 3M cafeteria one day, a product-development engineer named Art Fry shared with Silver a chronic problem he was experiencing: his hymnal bookmarks kept falling out during church choir practice. Familiar with Silver's discovery from prior company meetings, Fry asked if he could use some of the reusable adhesive to keep his bookmarks in place. Extending the thought further, Fry shared his opinion that 3M had probably been thinking backward about potential ACM product applications. Instead of coating a bulletin board with the reusable adhesive, Fry argued that 3M should apply the adhesive to paper notes, which could then stick to anything. "I thought, what we have here isn't just a bookmark," said Fry. "It's a whole new way to communicate."[4]

To pursue Fry's innovative insight, 3M required further R&D to ensure that the adhesive would only stick to a treated paper note and not to any other surface to which it was applied. With renewed interest in his discovery, Silver and his team were soon able to perfect a reliable formula for ACM that enabled the creation of Post-it Notes.

Despite what now appeared to be a promising new product with the potential for broad market appeal, 3M management remained reluctant to commit to commercial development. After all, producing Post-it Notes at a larger scale would require a sizeable capital outlay for what was still considered to be an unproven concept. To build support, Silver and his team set up a "skunk works" to create batches of Post-it Notes that he shared with 3M employees. This stealthy undertaking had the benefit of providing valuable consumer feedback, as well as building internal support for further project funding. Backed by enthusiastic 3M employee testimonials, Silver and his colleagues were finally able to secure management approval in 1977 to launch a pilot test in four cities of what were then called "Press 'n' Peel" sticky notes.[5]

Unfortunately, the initial pilot tests turned out to be a dismal failure. The company provided relatively little marketing support for the pilot tests, and consumers simply didn't understand or appreciate the value proposition associated with sticky notes. Press 'n' Peel languished on retailer shelves.

Despite this setback, promoters of the new product were determined to give Post-it Notes another chance, this time with more marketing support. So, one year after the initial flop, 3M launched a second pilot test in Boise, Idaho, giving away batches of Post-it Notes so consumers could experience for themselves how useful the new product could be. This time, 3M's reorder rate went from almost zero in the previous pilot to 90 percent, double the best market acceptance rate 3M had ever experienced in a product pilot test.

Two years later, in 1980, Post-it Notes were officially launched nationally and the business has grown steadily ever since. Post-it Notes are currently sold in over four thousand product varieties in more than 150 countries, generating revenues of over half a billion dollars for 3M.[6]

In retrospect, the successes of Post-it Notes, GoPro, and Swiffer seem like slam dunks, given that each delivered a simple and compelling consumer value proposition. The same could be said of Airbnb, conceived by Brian Chesky, a struggling, unemployed industrial designer living in San Francisco, who parlayed the need to rent out a spare bedroom to help pay his rent into one of Silicon Valley's most successful recent ventures.[7] Or Spanx, launched by Sara Blakely, a fax-machine salesperson without any background in fashion, marketing, or retailing, who designed a comfortable shaping undergarment for women, after struggling for years with unflattering and ill-fitting products on the market.[8]

The question remains, where do these breakthrough ideas come from? Does one have to have the rare entrepreneurial instincts found only in geniuses like Chesky, Odón, Woodman, Fry, or Blakely to conjure up winning products? Or can mere mortals working on their own or within a major corporation hope to develop breakthrough products? Extensive research has identified the brain functions that enable the creative spark—or strategic intuition—that allow innovators to imagine breakthrough products and services.[9] While genius undoubtedly helps, any aspiring entrepreneur with intellectual curiosity, open-mindedness, customer empathy and the passion and perseverance to solve problems can come up with game-changing product concepts.

There are two foundational skills underlying successful innovation:

- *Behavioral insight, driven by consumer empathy* The ability to deeply understand consumer behavior, enabling the diagnosis of current pain points or the identification of latent consumer needs.
- *Creative problem-solving ability* The ability to translate behavioral insights into products specifically designed to better serve consumer needs and desires.

The examples I have cited may lead one to conclude that most breakthrough ideas are conceived in a lightning bolt of inspiration, in which an innovator instantaneously envisions a novel product solution to a vexing consumer problem. This view has been reinforced by brilliant innovators like Henry Ford and Steve Jobs, who dismissed the need for market research to guide their innovative thinking. For example, Henry Ford is believed to have once quipped, "If I had asked people what they wanted, they would have said faster horses."[10] And Steve Jobs echoed similar sentiments, noting that "people don't know what they want until you show it to them. That's why I never rely on market research."[11]

Are we to believe that innovators operate in their own creative bubble, without the need to interact with prospective customers? Nothing could be further from the truth. An entrepreneur's inspiration for an innovative new product reflects nothing more than an initial hypothesis and hunch, borne out of personal experience and observation.

This, in turn, requires considerable additional vetting with prospective consumers to validate assumed marketplace behavior and to iteratively optimize final product designs.

Ask any successful entrepreneur to compare his or her initial concept for a breakthrough product with the final version that ultimately achieved strong market acceptance and, invariably, you'll find a considerable product evolution, reflecting the reality that no "business plan ever survives its first encounter with a customer."[12] For example, Pinterest, currently valued at over $10 billion, started in 2009 as Tote, a mobile-shopping app with tools that allowed customers to window-shop and store wish-list items on their smartphone. Tote hit the market a bit too soon to achieve success as a mobile-shopping app. However, founder Ben Silbermann observed how Tote users enjoyed amassing and sharing collections of wish-list items, sparking the pivot from Tote to Pinterest in 2010. Other examples of notable business pivots that evolved from ongoing customer feedback include Flickr, which started as a photo-sharing feature within an unsuccessful multi-player computer game, and YouTube, which started as a video dating site, before expanding into the largest video-sharing platform in the world.

Why Consumers Often Lead Companies Astray

How can we reconcile two opposing views on the genesis of great ideas: a lightning bolt of creativity or the result of carefully assessing and responding to marketplace needs? In reality, the comments of Henry Ford and Steve Jobs on this question reflect *how* and *when* consumer feedback should be used during the product development process, and not whether market research per se has merit. They were correct in recognizing that most consumers generally lack the diagnostic and problem-solving skills required to envision breakthrough product opportunities. As a result, there is little to be gained by using traditional market-research techniques such as focus groups or surveys to troll for new product ideas.

To see why traditional market-research techniques are often ineffective and likely to be misleading in identifying breakthrough product opportunities, consider the following simple example. In a recent MBA class, I asked my students to share their ideas for the design of an innovative measuring cup. Now, this may seem like an unusually prosaic product to waste creative energy on, but remember the everyday floor mop that led to Swiffer, Procter & Gamble's billion-dollar brand.

To get the simulated market-research approach started, I asked one hundred of my MBA students to write responses to two simple questions regarding their personal experience using (or seeing others use) measuring cups:

1. What's wrong with the current design of widely used two-cup glass measuring cups? Specifically, are there any inconveniences or pain points associated with using current products?
2. What features or changes would you like to see in measuring-cup design that would better serve your needs?

These are typical "pains and gains" questions, often asked in focus-group research to uncover new product ideas.

There was no shortage of interesting ideas in response to these questions, and, as noted by the representative answers shown in table 10.1, my students identified numerous current product deficiencies and proposed many solutions.

It is logical to expect that consumers are better at diagnosing current pain points than in proposing innovative solutions. After all, breakthrough product concepts may require new technologies or

TABLE 10.1
Measuring Cup Design Ideas

Identified Problem	Proposed Solution
Hard to read quantities on side of measuring cup.	Use bigger fonts in labeling measurement scale.
Danger of breakage if dropped.	Use plastic instead of glass.
Handle gets slippery when using oily ingredients.	Add rubber sleeve on handle.
Inconvenient when measuring widely different quantities in single size measuring cup.	Create collapsible product design, where measuring cup can be adjusted to different capacities depending on ingredient quantity required.
Cooking ingredients stick to side of measuring cup; awkward to pour ingredients into mixing bowl.	Add "trap door" bottom that would better release ingredients.

design innovations that are far beyond the knowledge or experience of average consumers. But surprisingly, consumers are also quite unreliable when responding to simple questions about their pain points associated with using everyday products.

Why is this? The answer is perhaps best explained by Harvard Business School faculty members Dorothy Leonard and Jeffrey Rayport, who noted that "habit tends to inure us to inconvenience; as consumers, we create 'work-arounds' that become so familiar we may forget that we are being forced to behave in a less-than-optimal fashion and thus we may be incapable of telling market researchers what we really want."[13]

To illustrate this point, at the conclusion of my MBA class discussion on measuring-cup design, I chose two students at random to participate in a simple product-use demonstration.[14] Each student—one male and one female—was asked to show the class how they would go about actually using a standard two-cup Pyrex measuring cup for a cake recipe calling for one cup of water. I advised the students that the recipe cautioned about being precise with the measurement, to ensure the best taste results. For the purpose of the demonstration, I placed a large pitcher of water and a standard two-cup Pyrex measuring cup on a classroom desk, representing a kitchen counter.

The first volunteer—a particularly tall male—carefully poured what he thought to be the correct quantity of water from the pitcher, then bent to examine the measuring cup at eye level. Evidently, he had added too much water on his first attempt, and so poured some of the water back into the pitcher. The student volunteer once again bent over to examine the results, only to conclude that he had been too aggressive. This process of pour-bend-examine-adjust was repeated four times before the student was satisfied that he had accurately met the requirements of the recipe.

Next, I had the female volunteer repeat the same demonstration, which took only three cycles to complete, either because she was shorter or simply because she was more adept at using a measuring cup.

At this point, I asked my class of nearly a hundred students whether anyone had observed an apparent shortcoming with the design of a traditional measuring cup that perhaps had escaped our notice during the preceding class discussion. After a considerable pause, one student tentatively raised her hand to suggest, "Maybe it's the need to repeatedly have to bend down to check the quantity level." Bingo!

The remarkable thing here is that when initially asked to cite mea-suring-cup design shortcomings from their own prior experience, not one of my hundred students mentioned the ungainly pour-bend-examine-adjust cycle. In keeping with Leonard and Rayport's insight, my students had become so inured to a belief that "that's just the way measuring cups work," that none bothered to mention an awkward design constraint. But when given the opportunity to observe and reflect on a demonstration of actual consumer product use, the previ-ously hidden pain point became readily apparent.

This is an important revelation. Unless an innovator accurately understands the relevant shortcomings associated with current prod-ucts, it's unlikely that he or she can devise an effective solution. Since consumers are often unable to recognize and articulate their own product pain points, careful observation of actual consumer product use is a more effective diagnostic tool than asking consumers directly for behavioral insights on product design.

In fact, my classroom exercise replicated the actual product-design approach used by OXO, a New York–based manufacturer of easy-to-use kitchen appliances and housewares. A few years ago, a small toy company submitted a concept for a new measuring-cup design for OXO's consideration as a marketable product. The unusually designed measuring cup featured a horseshoe-shaped plastic insert, imprinted with a graded quantity scale. Because of the steep angle of the horse-shoe insert, a standing user could easily read the quantity of ingredi-ents while looking down on the measuring cup (figure 10.1).

To validate that the novel product actually solved a real consumer problem, OXO used observational research techniques.[15]

One at a time, respondents from a panel of test subjects were asked to describe any shortcomings they perceived with current measuring cups. Next, each respondent was asked to demonstrate how they would use a conventional measuring cup in a simulated kitchen environment. Finally, respondents were asked to repeat the product demonstration, this time using the new measuring cup with the angled insert.

As in my class exercise, consumers initially failed to identify the crit-ical measuring-cup design shortcoming, despite exhibiting repeated pour-bend-examine-adjust cycles in their product demonstration tri-als. Nonetheless, respondents instantly "got it" when asked to try out the new product and enthusiastically endorsed the design concept. Armed with these research results, OXO went on to successfully mar-ket a new product line of angled measuring cups.[16] As OXO found,

Figure 10.1 Angled measuring cup design

consumers can *show you,* if not necessarily *tell you,* where opportunities for innovative new products lie.

The OXO example illustrates that consumers often fail to recognize critical design shortcomings associated with current products and services. But even if they *can* articulate inconveniences or unmet needs, and clearly state their wants and needs for desired product improvements, the information may be misleading because consumers don't understand the design trade-offs inherent in new product development. As a result, companies that redesign their products in response to what consumers claim they want actually run the risk of undermining their overall value proposition.

An example of a company that got snake-bitten by responding to misguided customer feedback (abetted by misguided survey research) is Walmart.

Some historical context helps set the stage for Walmart's epic mistake. Walmart founder Sam Walton recognized from the beginning that low prices and wide selection would attract customers. To deliver this value proposition, Walton designed big-box stores jammed with low-priced merchandise, embodying his operating philosophy of "stack 'em high, watch 'em fly." Merchandising aesthetics took a backseat to everyday low prices in Walmart's dingy, dimly-lit warehouse stores, anchored by the so-called Action Alley—the primary traffic artery from the front to the back of the store, featuring eight-foot shelves stacked high with deeply discounted items.[17]

Walmart's store-design formula proved highly successful in attracting a legion of loyal customers who helped Walmart become not just the largest retailer in the United States, but also the largest company of any kind at the turn of the new millennium. However, as the United States began to emerge from the 2001 recession, sales data showed that Walmart was losing market share to Target, particularly among higher-income shoppers who found Target's stores more inviting and less cluttered. Walmart examined surveys of its own customers and found a common complaint that the cluttered store layouts were difficult to navigate. So Walmart commissioned a special survey where shoppers were specifically asked, "Would you find shopping here more pleasant if we reduced the clutter?" A vast majority responded yes.

To Walmart, this proved to be compelling evidence of the need to act. After all, it was losing customers to a competitor with a cleaner store layout, and its own customers were urging the company to clean up their cluttered stores. Thus Project Impact began, which remodeled Walmart's superstores at a frenetic pace, starting in late 2008. Shelf heights were reduced, aisles were widened, lighting was increased, and video monitors were installed to ease in-store navigation. Walmart had clearly listened and responded to the voice of the customer.

The visual impact was impressive, but the business results were not. Within months of the launch of Project Impact, Walmart's sales began to decline, suffering negative same-store sales growth for eight consecutive quarters, while Target posted positive numbers over the same period. The difference in same-store sales growth between these two companies averaged three percentage points over this period. Now this may not seem like a huge number, but for a company with $400 billion in sales, a 3 percent swing in sales growth represents about $1 billion per month in lost revenue![18]

Walmart's grand plan had clearly backfired. Walmart quietly killed Project Impact in 2011, fired the executive in charge, and began restoring the redesigned stores to their original formats at a cost estimated to exceed $1 billion.[19] The question is, what went wrong with Project Impact? Didn't Walmart give its customers exactly what they asked for?

While it is true that Walmart was losing market share in the five years prior to the launch of Project Impact, Target's success against Walmart reflected the fact that it catered to a very different kind of customer—younger, with average incomes about 25 percent higher.[20] Higher-income customers who defected from Walmart to Target weren't doing so just because Target stores were less cluttered. Target's entire merchandising mix was different, as was their brand image.

As for Walmart, its core customer base still valued the time-tested formula of wide selection at everyday low prices. Walmart asked its customers if they would like a less cluttered shopping environment, but omitted the caveat, *even if it meant lower availability of some of your favorite products.*

Think about it. If you start with a Walmart store of a certain size, remove some aisles, and make the remaining shelves shorter, something has to give. The average Project Impact store wound up eliminating about 15 percent of its branded merchandise. How does such a reduction in available merchandise affect customers? Suppose you prefer Jif peanut butter, but Walmart chose to stock only Skippy and a store brand. Or your baby just had to use Huggies diapers, but now the only choice was Pampers. By the time customers filled their shopping cart at a Project Impact store, virtually all shoppers experienced the loss of some preferred brands. And for customers with strong product brand affinity, this was an unwelcome disappointment. So some shoppers began finding their favorite brands elsewhere, at places like Kroger or Target.

When asked directly—and, as it turned out, improperly—consumers in this case proved to be an unreliable source of what they really wanted. Had Walmart taken the time to develop a more holistic understanding of the preferences and needs of its customers, the company could have avoided a billion-dollar mistake.

How and When Market Research Should Be Used in Developing Innovative Products

Consumer input is pivotal in identifying new business opportunities, provided that the right type of research is conducted at the right time during the product-development process. Every successful new product moves through three phases of development:

- *Inspiration* gives birth to a new product concept.
- *Innovation* translates preliminary ideas into products and services designed to solve real consumer problems at prices consumers are willing to pay.
- *Commercialization* develops a business model that yields attractive returns, deploys resources to bring products to market with competitive advantage, and operates efficiently to drive profitable growth.

As shown in figure 10.2, the type of market research best suited to guide the creation of innovative new products varies by product-development stage.[21]

Behavioral Observation

Also called anthropological[22] or ethnographic research,[23] behavioral observation is perhaps the easiest form of market research to conduct,

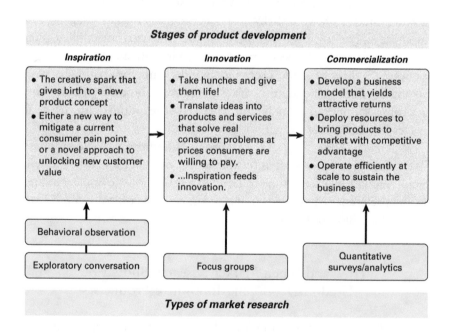

Figure 10.2 Using market research in new product development

and yet it often sparks the initial insights that allow an innovator to envision a breakthrough product. As baseball Hall of Famer Yogi Berra once noted, "You can observe a lot by just watching."[24]

Unlike traditional market research, where respondents are recruited and asked specific, targeted questions about their choices, preferences, and needs, anthropological research is based solely on silently—and often covertly—observing how consumers accomplish various tasks in their homes, offices, or on the go. Thus, behavioral observation research watches what people *actually do* in performing common tasks.[25] The objective of this approach is to understand and empathize with a customer's user experience with current products and services. Behavioral observations can enlighten researchers about the context in which customers would actually use a new product and about the meaning that a product might have in their lives.

In fact, we've already seen numerous examples of this method in practice. The inventors of GoPro, Post-it Notes, and Spanx conceived their ideas based on personal experience. In essence, these innovators were the initial subjects of behavioral observation research. We also saw how OXO confirmed the value proposition for a new type of measuring cup by observing the behavior of a random sample of respondents who volunteered to demonstrate common kitchen tasks.

The singular advantage of behavioral observation methods is in identifying consumer pain points that may be hidden in plain sight from consumers who have simply accepted current product shortcomings as unavoidable inconveniences. In such cases, traditional market-research methods based on direct respondent questioning are unlikely to be fruitful.

Behavioral observation research techniques are derived from the field of anthropology, which has a track record of inferring behavioral insights about subjects that can't articulate their problems or needs—i.e., animals. Like anthropologists, behavioral observation researchers go to natural habitats where consumers are likely to be involved with a product category of interest.

Suppose, for example, that you were responsible for designing a new SUV model, with the objective of incorporating innovative features to enhance customer convenience. A logical starting point would be to determine whether current vehicles have any design shortcomings associated with everyday use. Since SUVs are typically owned by families with children, a shopping mall provides an ideal vantage point from which to observe how owners interact with their vehicles.

Researchers staked out in such a "natural habitat" would undoubtedly observe the challenge faced by a shopper approaching her SUV in the parking lot with a toddler cradled in one arm, two shopping bags in the other, and car keys buried in her purse. Add in some rain and a stream of cars rushing by, and the problem with putting either the child or the bags on the ground while fishing for the car keys becomes even more apparent.

For years, most vehicle owners accepted this liftgate-opening juggling act as an unavoidable inconvenience of modern-day life. The innovator's job is to identify such pain points and to envision effective solutions. In this case, some carmakers responded by adding a remote-control button on the key fob to electronically open the liftgate, but this solution still required vehicle owners to have their car keys in hand. In 2013, Ford introduced an even more novel solution on their Escape SUV, allowing owners to open the liftgate without taking out their keys, simply by gently tapping the underside of the rear bumper with their foot. A remote-control unit in the Escape recognizes the presence of the vehicle owner from radio signals sent from the key fob.[26]

Exploratory Conversation

While behavioral observation is an effective starting point in understanding consumer pain points, it shows only how and what people do, but not necessarily *why*. As such, supplemental conversations with consumers are necessary to probe for underlying mindsets, motivations, and possible sources of confusion or frustration. Unlike other forms of market research, both behavioral observations and exploratory conversations occur in the immediacy of the actual consumer behavior or product use being studied.

Consider, for example, how product developers might go about developing an improved ticketing kiosk for a commuter-rail station platform. Some ideas for improvement might surface simply by observing how consumers interact with current kiosks, while others require further conversational probing (table 10.2).

While researchers can certainly verify their hypotheses regarding the first three observations by talking to users exhibiting the observed behaviors, there is likely to be little doubt about the inferred design shortcomings or logical fixes. The last two observations, however, would require more contextual understanding to discern the reasons consumers acted in this way.

TABLE 10.2
Rail Ticket Kiosk Design Ideas

Observed Behavior	Likely Improvement
Users struggle with where to put their coffee, newspaper, or purse while using the kiosk.	Add storage shelf on kiosk unit.
Users have difficulty using kiosk in bright sunlight or at night.	Add glare shields or better lighting.
Some users seem to repeatedly push touch-screen buttons to initiate an action.	Tactile force on touch screen needs to be adjusted.
Some users hesitate or simply abandon their session.	Indeterminate without further probing.
Wide range in observed time required to complete transaction.	Indeterminate without further probing.

TABLE 10.3
Exploratory Conversations on Kiosk User Experience

Researcher Question	User Response
What type of ticket were you trying to purchase?	*A student-discount, ten-ride, off-peak ticket.*
You seemed to hesitate while trying to complete your purchase; was there something you found confusing?	*Yes, I couldn't figure out how to enter my student-discount status.*
Could you show me the steps you took and explain where you got stuck?	*Sure, the train isn't scheduled to come for another ten minutes.*
What did you find confusing about this particular screen? What would have made the choices clearer?	*I don't know how to go back to the prior screen to change something.*

This is where exploratory conversations come into play. For example, in following up with a kiosk user, a researcher might ask a series of probing questions to determine the root cause of observed user problems, as illustrated by the hypothetical conversation in table 10.3.

Notice that these questions are designed to understand how consumers interact with the ticket kiosk on their own terms and in the actual rail station environment. The consumer dialogue directly identifies sources of user confusion that may not have been apparent to the original product designers. This type of exploratory conversation would help to identify refinements to the kiosk user interface that eliminate common sources of confusion or frustration.

Exploratory conversations of this type differ from the more common product-usability tests, in which respondents are typically given a set of tasks to perform in a laboratory setting and then measured on the speed and accuracy of task completion. The problem with simulated, task-based usability tests (also referred to as user interface, user experience, or UX tests) is that the tasks are prewritten and may not reflect how individual users actually interact with a product. Moreover, laboratory environments are unlikely to accurately account for the messy, but very real, environmental distractions of everyday life, such as bright sunlight, loud background noise, the anticipation of an imminent train arrival, etc.[27]

More importantly, by allowing consumers to frame their actual user experiences in their own terms rather than in response to prewritten scripts, exploratory conversations have the advantage of uncovering unexpected consumer insights that may inspire the idea for a completely different type of product innovation.

Consider how this might play out in the ticket-kiosk redesign example. After spending a week in the field, interviewing and transcribing the responses from several dozen commuters, suppose the ticket-kiosk design team met to interpret customer feedback. In preparation for a brainstorming session, the team displayed the relevant field-research results on Post-it Notes arranged around the wall of their project office, as shown in figure 10.3.

Figure 10.3 Representative user feedback on ticket kiosk use

One can imagine the ensuing brainstorming discussion between team members:

Person1: We heard a ton of specific suggestions for cleaning up the user interface on some of the kiosk screens, but I'm a bit intrigued by these other user comments that speak to more general concerns.

Person2: Yeah, it sure seems like a lot of users really don't like our kiosks very much!

Person3: That's right, but their complaints are all over the map.

Person1: Maybe not. There must be some common themes here.

Person2: Well a few of these comments seem to indicate that some users find using ticket kiosks stressful.

Person3: That's right. And even if we improved the user interface, that still wouldn't eliminate the stress of completing a transaction before the train came.

Person1: In fact, a cleaner user interface wouldn't really address any of these concerns.

Person2: Maybe that's the common link we're looking for. . . . Maybe a kiosk on a commuter-rail platform is actually a terrible place to buy a train ticket!

Person3: If passengers could buy tickets online and print them at home, all of these concerns would go right away.

Person1: That's right. And a system designed for PCs and mobile apps would be easier to use.

Person2: Yeah, but why print the tickets? We could just display tickets digitally on a smartphone. . . . Just like the airlines do.

Person3: But not everyone has a smartphone.

Person1: So maybe those passengers could buy their tickets on the train, which is possible today. I'm sure we could design a scanner device which would both verify digital tickets and process tickets sales on board.

Person2: That's a good idea. And we could pay for the new devices with all the money we save by eliminating ticket kiosks.

Person3: Hey, I thought we were supposed to be redesigning the station-platform kiosk.

Person1: Maybe that's a really bad idea after all!

As I have shown in these examples, behavioral observations and exploratory conversations are well suited to help identify opportunities for innovative new products, which solve real consumer problems. An in-depth exploration of the art and science of well-designed behavioral research goes beyond the scope of this book, but readers interested in pursuing this subject further would be well served by two excellent books devoted to this subject: *Well-Designed: How to Use Empathy to Create Products People Love* by Jon Kolko,[28] and *Customers Included: How to Transform Products, Companies, and the World—With a Single Step* by Mark Hurst.[29]

Focus Groups

Up to this point, I have raised several questions about the value of focus groups, but this technique can definitely play a useful role, if used at the right time and for the right purpose. As many readers may have personally experienced, focus groups involve using a trained moderator to engage a panel of recruited respondents in a group dialogue, while the proceedings are often observed by interested spectators seated behind a one-way mirror. Focus groups have been used for a wide variety of research purposes, such as testing audience reactions to different movie endings or political ads, comparing the taste of different cookie-dough recipes, finding out what customers like and dislike about shopping at different stores, and seeking suggestions for desirable new product features.

What focus groups are good at is capturing consumer *opinions*, particularly when respondents are allowed to see, taste, or try alternative product concepts. In these situations, respondents can provide instant feedback, based on actual observation or trial product use. For example, focus groups have been particularly useful in guiding food companies toward reformulating their recipes. In one celebrated case, Domino's used actual video clips of focus groups criticizing the company's pizzas as the centerpiece of a television advertising campaign, promising viewers that the company was listening and committed to making improvements. In the company's television ads and on its Facebook page, focus-group respondents were shown making disparaging remarks after tasting Domino's pizzas, including the following:[30]

"Your pizza tastes like wet garbage."
"Domino's pizza crust to me is like cardboard."
"Worst excuse for pizza I ever had."

This painful feedback proved to be a win-win application of focus-group research for Domino's and the consumers alike, as it triggered recognition of the urgent need for management action, guiding the development of a tastier pizza, and generating consumer goodwill in response to the company's disarmingly candid public mea culpa. Comparing market performance in the five years before and after Domino's launched its focus-group advertising campaign in 2010, the company's market cap went from losing more than half of its value to increasing more than tenfold. This is quite an endorsement for the value of deploying and responding to focus-group research.

On the other hand, focus groups are generally *not* good at eliciting reliable insights on perceived needs or abstract speculation on desired new product features. In this regard, we've already seen several examples earlier in this chapter that affirm Steve Jobs's assertion that "people don't know what they want until you show it to them."[31]

An additional limitation of focus-group research is the inevitable interpersonal dynamic associated with a group setting. Talkative, dominant, or belligerent respondents may drown out or inhibit dissenting views. And at the very mention of unseen observers behind the fake mirror, some respondents filter their opinions, perhaps unwittingly, according to what they think the hidden audience wants to hear.[32]

So where does that leave us with respect to the value of focus-group research in the development of new products? Focus groups can be a useful approach provided they are used to elicit feedback *after* a product-development team has created working prototypes for innovative new products. Focus groups can provide far more valuable feedback in reacting to specific, tangible product concepts than in opining in the abstract on what they might hypothetically like.

Quantitative Surveys and Analytics

As we have seen, qualitative market research is most useful in the early stages of new product development. But as a promising new product moves closer to full-scale commercial launch or an existing product is reconfigured, there are hard decisions to make that entail significant investment risk. At this point, quantitative research and analytics are most appropriate in helping project teams lock down the final configuration of the product, deploy production and distribution assets in line with the expected size and composition of the market, monitor sales, and detect shifts in the market and competitive environment.

For example, consider the questions facing the developers of Marriott's Courtyard hotel chain, the E-ZPass automated toll-payment system, and JetBlue's airline service, as executives neared the launch of their respective products:

- How much value in terms of willingness to pay do consumers associate with hotel amenities such as room size and decor, type of restaurant and food service, leisure facilities, and guest services?[33]
- What is the relative value for consumers of elements of the E-ZPass system, including number of lanes available, ease of tag acquisition, cost savings, invoicing process, and other uses of the tag?[34]
- When considering JetBlue's service offerings and fare levels, how do consumers trade off the value associated with in-flight amenities (e.g., legroom, entertainment systems) with travel perks such as free bag check?[35]

These are all examples of the design trade-offs required in putting the final touches on a new product or service that can ultimately determine demand, consumer WTP, and profitability.

To optimize their product configuration, all of these companies used conjoint analysis, a quantitative technique for determining the value consumers place on individual product attributes, and how buyers make trade-offs in choosing between competing products. In a conjoint analysis, prospective consumers are presented with descriptions of competing products with distinctly different attributes and asked to rate their likelihood of choosing each alternative. By analyzing the patterns of preferences, conjoint analysis can be used to determine how companies can achieve the most meaningful product differentiation, where they can add the most consumer value at the least company cost, how price affects consumer choices, and what market share can be expected for a range of alternative product configurations.[36]

There are limitations associated with conjoint analysis and other stated-preference models, all of which depend on how accurately consumers rate their preferences among hypothetical product bundles. Consumer intentions and their actual behavior are often markedly different. Nonetheless, quantitative consumer-choice models are valuable tools, once product developers have narrowed their focus to optimize the final launch configuration of a product.

Another important use of quantitative methods in late-stage product development is in refining estimates of the size of the addressable market and the expected level of actual sales. Product-development teams should have undertaken a preliminary assessment of market potential early in the development process. But as the launch date approaches, hard decisions need to be made on manufacturing capacity, sales-channel assets, and marketing budgets.[37] By drawing on early-stage learnings about target market characteristics and how competing products are perceived, analytical rigor should be applied in forecasting expected demand levels prior to full-scale launch.[38]

Finally, even if the launch of a new product has been successful in meeting or exceeding initial business forecasts, it is critical to assess ongoing changes in sales or use. Quantitatively monitoring demand trends can serve as an early indicator of *what* is happening in the market, if not *why*, and point to the need for further targeted research to understand evolving changes in consumer preferences and the competitive landscape.

Estimates of failure rates for new product launches range from 70 percent to over 90 percent, so there is obviously considerable room for improvement in the business processes used to conceive, refine, and launch truly great products.[39]

Putting the Pieces Together— How Honda Developed the Element

Tracing the development of a complex product like Honda's Element SUV effectively illustrates how and when different types of market research should be used to create innovative new products.

The Honda Motor Company has been a paragon of product-development excellence for more than seventy-five years. Born from the devastation of post–World War II Japan, Honda established an early reputation for engineering prowess by launching a reliable and efficient range of small motorbikes and scooters in the late 1940s. By 1960, Honda had extended its product range to larger and more sophisticated models, emerging as the largest motorcycle manufacturer in the world. In the decades that followed, Honda exploited its world-class engine technology by successfully expanding into entirely new product categories, including power products (e.g., tillers, generators, lawn mowers), automobiles and trucks, and eventually, jet aircraft. In each case, Honda started with well-designed, low-priced models before moving progressively upscale to gain additional market share.

As a case in point, Honda entered into the U.S. car market in 1969 and soon achieved success with the Civic, a technologically advanced small car that provided greater fuel economy than competing models from American carmakers. Its next product was the midsize Accord, which won awards as the best sedan from *Road & Track* and *Car and Driver* magazines shortly after its 1976 market entry. Within five years, the Accord became the best-selling car in the U.S. market.

Honda moved further upscale in 1986, becoming the first Japanese car manufacturer to launch a luxury brand in the United States. Its Acura brand featured a line of high-performance, stylish sports cars and sedans carrying premium price tags. From there, Honda expanded its market reach by adding the Odyssey minivan, recognized by *Consumer Reports* as the best minivan in the U.S. market shortly after its 1995 launch. Finally, Honda attacked the SUV category, by once again starting at the low end with the compact CR-V model, before moving progressively upscale with the larger Pilot and Acura MDX models.

By 2002, Honda was selling over 1.2 million motor vehicles in the United States, competing profitably in virtually every segment of the market. Despite such stellar performance, Honda recognized two related brand weaknesses that threatened to limit its future growth.

Honda's brand image was viewed as pragmatic, rather than exciting or aspirational.

From its inception in the U.S. market, Honda's engineers had done a masterful job developing cars that were fuel efficient, reliable, safe, and comfortable. Not surprisingly, these attributes served to associate Honda's brand image with practical, family-oriented, and conservative vehicles. There's nothing wrong with such positioning, as Honda's sales growth attests. While its emphasis on practicality appealed to young families and female buyers, Honda's brand image proved to be off-putting to other segments of the market.

Honda generally did not appeal to young, male first-time car buyers.

In particular, Honda's market penetration among young male drivers was considerably below competitive norms. As one company sales director recalled, "We had products for young women and families, but nothing focused on young men."[40] This was an issue of considerable concern to the company because the young-buyer segment was emerging as a sizeable market opportunity for car companies. When Honda surveyed U.S. demographics as the new millennium approached, it recognized that over half of first-time new-car buyers were less than thirty years old. This age group was likely to grow as the children of baby boomers reached driving age. The company concluded that it simply could not continue to ignore millennial male customers.[41]

Thus began the business imperative for Honda's first vehicle designed specifically to appeal to young men. Honda formed the Element concept-development team in 1998 at its R&D facility in Torrance, California. In keeping with the project mission, most of the design team were relatively young men themselves, charged with the responsibility of creating a compelling design that would resonate with the core values and beliefs of male millennials.

The starting point was to understand the motivations and needs of this new, unfamiliar customer group. Honda certainly had access to numerous market-research studies that profiled the characteristics of millennial customers.[42] While such insights served as an interesting backdrop to the project team's mission, in reality, such broad generalizations—e.g., millennials are idealistic, optimistic, and flexible—provided little guidance on specific design priorities (table 10.4).

The team also obtained detailed data on which vehicles were currently most popular with male millennial drivers, but this information was also of limited use. After all, Honda did not want to merely copy existing design themes; the company was determined to identify the *unmet* needs of its target customer group to guide the design of a unique product with the potential to achieve breakthrough market success that would burnish Honda's image.

Honda realized that simply asking a sample of young males directly what they might be looking for in a new vehicle was likely to be of

TABLE 10.4
Characteristics of Millenials

Demographics	Attitudes and Beliefs

– Born 1980–2000 (80 million).
  a. Also known as echo boomers, millennials.
  b. Children of baby boomers (72 million).
– Notable demographics:
  a. 25 percent live in single-parent households.
  b. 75 percent have working mothers.
  c. Ethnically diverse—34 percent are black, Hispanic, Asian, or Native American.
– Shaping events: O. J. Simpson trial, Monica Lewinsky, Middle East Conflict, Sadaam Hussein, Oklahoma City bombing, Columbine shootings, Reality TV, and 9/11.
– Millenials in popular culture: Hilary Duff, Bow Wow, Mary-Kate and Ashley Olsen, Prince William.
	– Young and trend-conscious.
	– Idealistic, optimistic, and flexible.
	– Hard workers; highly entrepreneurial.
	– Socially responsible; particularly concerned about the environment.
	– Very comfortable with technology; like to multi-task.
	– Have a hunger for feedback and rewards.
	– Spiritually traditional: 89 percent of millennials state that they believe in God.

limited value, and perhaps even misleading. Therefore, Honda appropriately started their project with observational research to better understand how millenial men currently used their vehicles.

The project team decided that the best place to start the "natural habitats" where millenial men were likely to congregate. So, armed with video cameras and tape recorders, the researchers headed to the X Games—an annual ESPN-sponsored extravaganza of extreme sporting events, primarily appealing to young men—and to the beaches and boardwalks of southern California to closely observe how young men interacted with their vehicles.

What emerged from these detailed observations and subsequent exploratory conversations was the persona of a social, active millennial male that Honda dubbed "Endless Summer."[43] The lifestyle of prospective Endless Summer customers placed multiple demands on how their vehicles were used, which began to frame high-level design themes for the still inchoate Element SUV (table 10.5).

With ongoing observational research, Honda's engineers and stylists then began translating their deepening understanding of target customer needs into specific vehicle features that would directly support the diverse lifestyles of Endless Summer males. For example, the project team observed the need to accommodate conflicting vehicle missions, such as hauling mountain bikes or surfboards in the morning and carrying five friends to a party in the evening. To meet these requirements, Honda designed side-folding rear seats that could quickly be flipped up or down.

The team also responded to the target customer need to haul messy recreational equipment, like sandy surfboards or muddy mountain bikes, by adding several unusual design features: pillar-less, wide-opening side doors, a large clamshell tailgate, and a fully waterproof, hose-down interior. No other vehicle on the market incorporated such design features.

After observing how Endless Summer males often ate, lived, and played in their vehicles, the project team included a center-console storage container designed to carry supersized shakes and fries, and a

TABLE 10.5
Preliminary Design Themes for Endless Summer Personas

Personal Characteristics	Vehicle Design Implications
Single	No need to compromise to appeal to spouse's taste. Go all-in on designing a "guy's car."
Social (lots of friends)	Needs to seat four to five. . . . No pickup truck for this persona.
Highly active	Capable of carrying lots of "boy toys"— mountain bikes, surfboards, skis, etc.
Well traveled and nomadic	Spacious enough to serve as a part-time camper and to haul home furnishings for frequent moves.
Educated, hip, and environmentally aware	Exudes edgy styling and features that the target could clearly identify with. No gimmicks.

sound system that amplified bass tones eight times louder than on the staid Honda Civic.

Finally, during exploratory conversations, the project team detected a strong affinity among Endless Summer respondents for products that authentically reflected their lifestyle preferences, and a dislike of gimmicky products that claimed to be hip, but were not. In response, the engineers strove to execute a thoughtful integration of all key design elements: edgy styling, spirited handling, and relevant functionality.

As the engineering effort progressed, the project team recruited focus groups of social outdoor enthusiasts on college campuses across the country to react to sketches of evolving design concepts. After several iterations to refine the design of the Honda Element, the end result emerged as a distinctively boxy SUV, with numerous features that uniquely addressed the needs of the Endless Summer segment of millennial men.[44]

As Honda prepared to launch the Element in model year 2003, the marketing department refined its sales forecasts, based on a quantitative analysis of demand for competing vehicles on the market. Recognizing that the Element was targeting a very specific customer segment with a new, radically styled vehicle concept, Honda's initial

Figure 10.4 Honda Element

U.S. sales forecasts called for relatively modest sales of fifty thousand units per year.

So how did the Element fare, and did Honda achieve its business objective of increasing its market penetration and image strength among millennial male car buyers?

The initial market reaction was positive. In its first year, the Element was named Best Small SUV of the Year by the influential *Automobile* magazine,[45] and U.S. sales of 67,478 comfortably exceeded Honda's initial target. But a closer examination of the sales data revealed that only 20 percent of first-year buyers were young men, accounting for less than 2 percent of all new cars sold that year to millennial males. The remaining Element sales went to older customers, most of whom were over forty. Moreover, sales of the Honda Element peaked in its first year, declining steadily thereafter, and falling below twelve thousand units by 2011, when the model was discontinued.

So what went wrong? Before answering that question, let's first recap what went right. Honda actually did an admirable job of understanding the unmet needs of their target customers and designed the Element to uniquely fulfill real customer requirements. As described, Honda properly sequenced their use of observational research, exploratory conversations, focus groups, and quantitative research to develop and launch a thoughtfully designed vehicle that uniquely met the needs of target customers.

But, as it turned out, Honda missed a few critical red flags.

First, not all millennials are Endless Summer archetypes. When I share a description of Honda's Endless Summer target customers with my MBA students (who themselves are in that target age group), few identify with the Endless Summer persona. The characteristics and lifestyles of students sitting in an MBA classroom in New York City don't align very well with the persona of young men who frequent the X Games in Aspen or the beaches and boardwalks of southern California. The same could probably be said for the majority of millennial men living in Chicago, Atlanta, or Phoenix. The Honda Element project team themselves lived and worked in southern California, and so focused their market research efforts on hard-core outdoor enthusiasts without first pausing to reflect on how small a customer segment that might actually be.

Moreover, Endless Summer customers who worked to live, rather than lived to work, may not have had the disposable income to afford the relatively pricey Honda Element. For example, the Element launched in the U.S. market in 2003 at a base price of $16,100, more than 25 percent higher than Honda's other entry-level vehicle, the Honda Civic, which was priced at $12,800. As such, it is not surprising that Honda Element sales were higher among older, more affluent customers.

If Honda were truly committed to improving its market penetration of millennial customers, it would have developed a broader array of suitable products rather than just focusing on the Element, which aimed at too small a target. In contrast, in seeking to attract more young male customers, Toyota created a whole new brand (Scion) with multiple models to appeal to a broader set of millennial buyers, including the xB model, a small, boxy SUV, comparable to the Element. In retrospect, the Element appealed to only a small subset of male millennials, and the model wound up as an orphan within Honda's broader lineup of practical cars and light trucks.

While there is much to learn from Honda's best practices in applying user-centered design and appropriately sequencing the correct types of market research, the failure of the Element demonstrates the imperative to target new products at a sufficiently large segment of the market. The Element hit the bullseye, but Honda's target was too small.

CHAPTER ELEVEN

Strategies to Break Away from the Pack

THINK OF SOME immensely successful companies that have launched breakout products over the past decade. My starter list is shown in figure 11.1. At first glance, these blockbusters appear to have little in common. The list spans multiple industries, and these companies provide services or products, use sophisticated technologies or off-the-shelf solutions, and sell through Internet or brick-and-mortar facilities. And yet, I would argue that there are strong commonalities explaining how and why each of these companies succeeded in redefining their respective marketplaces.

Each of these companies succeeded by:

- Targeting customers who were poorly served by current products and services.
- Focusing on different performance attributes that addressed unmet consumer needs, rather than mimicking the key product characteristics of incumbent market leaders.
- Substantially changing the "4Ps"[1] that serve to define what, where, and how mainstream products are marketed, priced, and sold.
- Deconstructing and reconstructing prevailing value chains, characterizing the way work gets done.
- Expanding the market by bringing nonconsumers into the category and getting current customers to buy more.
- Making competitors irrelevant (at least temporarily) by fundamentally changing the basis of competition.

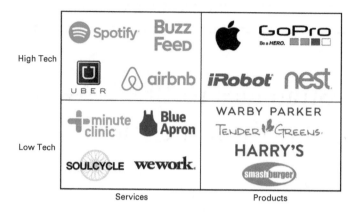

Figure 11.1 Breakout products and services

If you chose other examples of breakout success, see if these new rules of doing business also apply to the companies on your list.

With the benefit of hindsight, it's easy to observe the common conditions underlying successful companies. But it's another (and much harder) challenge to presciently identify promising opportunities and be the first to introduce the "next new thing."

Over the past two decades, three business-strategy frameworks have emerged, all of which provide useful guidance to entrepreneurs and corporate innovators seeking to identify meaningfully differentiated products and services that deliver a compelling consumer value proposition: Youngme Moon's breakout positioning,[2] W. Chan Kim and Renée Mauborgne's Blue Ocean strategy,[3] and Clayton Christensen's disruptive technology.[4]

While each of these approaches adopts a different strategic perspective, they share a clear directive for enlightened companies to reject conventional industry norms, structures, and category images by focusing on new product attributes that appeal to consumers who are poorly served by existing products.

Breakout Positioning

In chapter 9, I showed that competitive dynamics in most industries tend to follow a predictable pattern of tit-for-tat replication and performance augmentation, which, over time, results in increasingly *un*differentiated products targeting and overserving the same customers.

These circumstances create opportunities for an enlightened market entrant to reconceptualize the design of new products and services to better align with the needs of poorly served customers. Two distinct types of breakout positioning strategies warrant attention: reverse positioning and breakaway positioning.[5]

Reverse Positioning

Practitioners of this approach purposely reverse the trend of constant augmentation of product performance on traditional product attributes. This is not to say that reverse-positioning entrants simply "dumb down" product performance in order to offer budget prices, typical of low-end providers within a current category. Rather, purveyors of reverse positioning recognize that a growing number of consumers are simply not well served by traditional high- or low-end industry incumbents (figure 11.2).[6] In such cases, high-end players offer too many

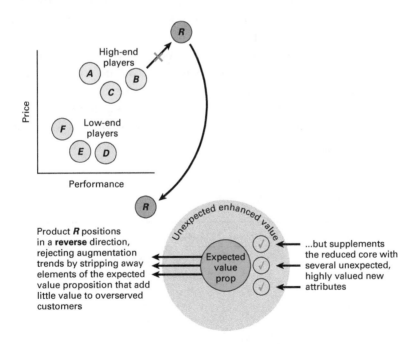

Figure 11.2 Reverse positioning

enhancements that add more cost than real value. (Do you really need more pixels on your smartphone screen than can be detected by the human eye?)[7] But low-end entries simply don't provide enough functionality or convenience to please dissatisfied consumers either. (Are those knee-jamming, nonreclining seats on long-haul budget-airline flights really worth the cost savings?)[8]

In response, successful reverse positioning providers strip out features from high-end offerings that don't add appreciable value for many consumers, and instead add new, unexpected, and highly valued product attributes that were overlooked by existing players. The net result is a far more compelling value proposition for a potentially large segment of consumers whose needs were not served well by any current products on the market.

For example, when JetBlue entered the financially troubled U.S. airline industry in 2000, a number of legacy carriers (like American, United, and Delta) all vigorously competed to outdo each other on high-end amenities: multiple classes of service, full meal service, onboard music and movies, and private lounges for frequent travelers. At the low end of the market, budget carriers (like Spirit and Southwest) stripped out virtually all creature comforts, packed more, smaller seats into their aircraft, and sharply reduced fares.

JetBlue recognized that there was an opportunity to create a better passenger experience for customers who were willing to pay a small premium over budget carriers to enjoy new types of amenities that were simply not available on legacy airlines.[9] In designing its new service, JetBlue started by eliminating costly features typically found on full-service airlines that created little perceived customer value.

TABLE II.I
JetBlue's Reverse Positioning: Eliminated Amenities

Eliminated Amenity	Rationale
Meals	No meals are better than bad meals.
Multiple service classes	Unnecessary for many consumers if coach service is good enough.
Private lounges	Low value proposition for most passengers.
Onboard movies on centrally located monitors	Limited selection to satisfy diverse passenger preferences.

In exchange, JetBlue added a number of unique and highly visible new amenities that were enthusiastically welcomed by many passengers, earning the company a reputation as America's "cheap chic" airline (table 11.2).

A hallmark of reverse-positioned products is that they have the potential to surprise and delight customers with unexpected features not found anywhere else. As a testament to its successful reverse-positioning strategy, JetBlue has received the highest customer satisfaction rating among U.S. low-cost carriers for eleven consecutive years,[10] and has consistently outscored the full-service legacy carriers on customer satisfaction as well.[11]

Another illuminating, but lesser known, case of successful reverse positioning can be found in the hotel industry. As a globetrotting consultant for over three decades, I have had the opportunity to personally experience the consumer value propositions offered in this intensely competitive sector. To simplify an understanding of competitive dynamics in the hotel industry, consider two distinctly different product segments: high-end, business-oriented hotels (such as Marriott, Westin, Ritz-Carlton, and Four Seasons) and budget hotel chains (such as Motel 6, Days Inn, Super 8, and Comfort Inn).

Customers like me are extremely attractive to business hotel operators, as we travel often, have access to generous expense accounts, and participate in business conferences and meetings that generate sizeable revenues. As a result, high-end hotel chains have competed vigorously for our patronage with a rich set of amenities and conveniences, including: prime locations in city centers; luxury dining

TABLE 11.2
JetBlue's Added Surprise and Delight Amenities

Added amenity	Rationale
Increased legroom	Highest in industry; highly valued, tangible benefit.
Leather seats	Previously not offered in coach class.
Satellite TV at each seat with dozens of channels	Unexpected and unique source of customer delight.
Premium snacks	Great snacks more pleasing than bad meals.
Friendly cabin service	Strong differentiator relative to legacy airlines.

and conference center facilities; round-the-clock room service; concierge services; fully equipped fitness centers; pools and spas; spacious, well-furnished rooms; minibars; and complimentary bathrobes and personal-care products. Needless to say, these amenities are costly, driving individual room prices in major metropolitan areas to levels that can exceed $600 per night.[12]

Since all high-end business hotel chains compete on largely the same performance attributes, it is difficult for any one player to stake a claim to unique services or advantaged prices. For example, in one such attempt to break away from the pack in this highly competitive industry, the Westin chain launched a campaign in the late 1990s to develop the world's most comfortable hotel bed. After testing hundreds of beds, pillows, and linens, Westin invested $30 million to equip its hotels with the aptly named "Heavenly Bed." From personal experience, I can attest that they indeed introduced an exquisitely comfortable product. Advantage Westin.

But now put yourself in the shoes of competing hotel chains. Would you allow an archenemy to maintain bragging rights to the most comfortable bed in the industry? In the years following Westin's launch of the Heavenly Bed, Hilton announced the introduction of its own Serenity Bed. Marriott invested a reported $190 million to introduce its Revive Collection. Radisson introduced its Sleep Number bed. Crowne Plaza responded with its Sleep Advantage program. Hyatt rolled out its Hyatt Grand Bed. Westin's competitive advantage was short-lived and precipitated an augmentation war where no one won, except for customers who could afford to pay more for a better night's sleep.[13]

This intense battle for supremacy in sleeping comfort was not fought in the low-end segment of the hotel industry. Budget hotels, more likely to be located at highway intersections than downtown, compete on different terms to attract a different type of customer, where low price is the paramount consumer consideration. As such, budget hotels offer accommodations that are "good enough" for their price-sensitive consumers. That's not to say that budget hotels don't engage in their own form of tit-for-tat replication and augmentation. With nightly rates often below $50, these chains tend to restrict their attention to more prosaic amenities, such as free breakfast and Wi-Fi access.

As it turns out, neither of these two segments of the hotel industry served my needs very well on short solo business trips. More generally, they also fail to address the preferences of high-income, experienced travelers who frequently visit city centers for an urban leisure experience.

First, this sophisticated segment of frequent travelers would certainly reject budget hotels, whose location and lack of panache are antithetical to their needs and values. However, full-service business hotels are also often a poor fit, offering more amenities than these travelers value or are willing to pay for.

For example, savvy and self-sufficient customers are certainly capable of, and may indeed prefer, carrying their own luggage without bellhop assistance (after probably having maneuvered their own suitcases through airports, subways, or taxis). As seasoned travelers, they are likely to be happy to obtain their own room key from an automated kiosk, without waiting in line for assistance from a desk clerk, and to select their own restaurants and theaters without an on-site concierge. (Empowering mobile devices are the norm for sophisticated travelers.)

This customer segment also has little interest in spending much time in their hotel room, and thus puts low value on spacious accommodations with sumptuous furnishings, particularly at prices commensurate with such luxuries. Similarly, when traveling alone, business travelers rarely have the time or interest in dining alone in a fancy hotel restaurant, while leisure travelers often prefer the diverse choices of renowned independent restaurants over hotel fare.

In 2008, serial entrepreneur Rattan Chadha, a retail-clothing company founder and CEO—recognized the opportunity for a reverse positioning strategy to better serve the needs of customers they characterized as "a mix of explorer, professional, and shopper."[14] In creating a new hotel chain called citizenM (M for mobile), he retained the few key features of traditional high-end business hotels that were highly valued by their target customer—most notably, convenient downtown locations, fast free Wi-Fi, high-definition TVs, comfortable bedding, and luxury showers, while stripping out most of the other typical amenities of high-end hotels that added more cost than value.

In place of these eliminated amenities, Chadha introduced unusual hotel design concepts specifically intended to surprise and delight citizenM's target customers. For example, the founder envisioned that solo business travelers would likely prefer to eat a light dinner at a self-service counter or lounge chair, as opposed to sitting at a restaurant table alone and being served by a waiter. While weekend leisure travelers would probably dine at nearby city restaurants, they might

TABLE 11.3

citizenM's Reverse Positioning

Eliminated amenity	Rationale
Bellhops	Customers can/prefer to carry their own luggage.
Front-desk clerks	Key issue and payment can be handled by automated kiosks or via mobile devices.
Concierge services	Target customers are self-reliant on concierge mobile apps.
Hotel restaurants and room service	Most target customers prefer self-serve food service, stocked with healthy, fresh food choices available 24/7.
Large rooms and plush furniture	Not a priority for customers in the target segment, who spend little time in the room.
Conference facilities	Not relevant for most target customers.

welcome a quick snack in pleasant surroundings after a long city walk. Therefore, when guests enter a citizenM hotel they encounter a large downstairs common space named the living room, loosely subdivided by high-end designer furniture and contemporary art. This includes a central area referred to as canteenM, where guests can order coffee or a cocktail and pay for self-serve food items.

Chadha's intent was to create a pleasant, functional shared space attractive enough that guests would prefer spending their downtime there rather than in their rooms. This allowed Chadha to make citizenM's guest rooms unusually small (no wider than their king-sized bed). The citizenM standardized room modules are entirely manufactured off-site and transported to the hotel site during construction. Yet the rooms are luxurious, including a rain-head shower, high-quality bedding, in-room tablets that provide free movies, Internet access, and personalizable mood settings. Once entered, guest preferences are stored in a central database so that rooms can be personalized for subsequent visits (figure 11.3).

This reverse-positioning strategy of citizenM allowed the company to reduce construction costs and staffing levels by 40 percent relative to industry norms. As a result, citizenM can set their prices at less than half the room rate charged by high-end business hotel chains, and citizenM's value proposition has strongly resonated with its target audience. Since its 2008 launch in Amsterdam, citizenM has expanded

a.

b.

c.

Figure 11.3 citizenM reverse positioning: *a*, lobby area; *b*, canteenM; *c*, typical citizenM room. Photos courtesy citizenM.

operations to New York, London, Paris, Glasgow, and Rotterdam, consistently achieving occupancy rates above 90 percent.[15]

Reverse-positioning strategies have also been successfully deployed in many other industries from fast food to furniture retailing. By reconfiguring the design of products and services to surprise and delight customers, as shown in table 11.4, reverse positioning can help companies to profitably break away from the pack in intensely competitive industries.[16]

Breakaway Positioning

The second class of breakout positioning involves "breakaway" products, so named because of the way some companies have chosen to redefine how consumers perceive their products by borrowing features drawn from an entirely different product category. A company might choose such an approach in order to distance itself from the conventional image consumers associate with a given category—which

TABLE 11.4
Additional Reverse Positioning Examples

In-N-Out Burger vs. Fast Food Market Leaders	
Eliminated Feature	Added Surprise and Delight Elements
Breakfast fare.	Freshly baked buns.
Chicken and fish menu items.	Fresh vegetables, delivered daily.
Happy meals and deserts.	All hamburgers cooked to order.
Children's play apparatus.	Secret sauces, known through word-of-mouth.

IKEA vs. Traditional Furniture Retailers	
Eliminated Feature	Added Surprise and Delight Elements
Assembled furniture, built to order.	Full-room solutions, designed for home assembly.
Highly durable construction at commensurately high prices.	Immediate availability and self-delivery at attractively low prices.
Attentive salesperson assistance.	Extremely wide merchandise selection with a variety of self-help tools.
Long wait times for delivery.	Swedish meatballs and babysitting services.

I have shown often limits meaningful differentiation. Companies pursuing a breakaway positioning strategy imbue their products with attributes never before seen, thereby creating a uniquely appealing and sharply differentiated consumer value proposition (figure 11. 4).[17] I've already described a quintessential example of successful breakaway positioning in chapter 6: Swatch.

In the 1980s, Nicolas Hayek, CEO of Société de Microélectronique et d'Horlogerie (SMH), one of Switzerland's largest watchmakers, faced an existential threat from low-cost quartz digital watch imports from Asia, which were gaining global market share at an alarming rate.[18]

Traditionally, Hayek's company competed at the high end of the watch market, selling handcrafted timepieces under the Omega, Tissot, and Longines brand names. These luxury items were sold and repaired in jewelry stores and priced on par with heirloom jewelry.

The advent of lower-cost digital technology in the 1970s spurred rapid growth of a new class of watches, which served as accurate, if not particularly stylish, functional tools. Hayek's problem was that SMH was not well positioned to compete effectively in this rapidly growing segment, which favored competitors with low-cost mass production and distribution through mass merchandisers.

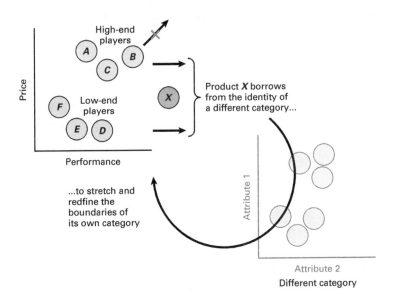

Figure 11.4 Breakaway positioning

To complicate matters, the emergence of quartz digital watches reinforced the category norm that most consumers only needed to own one or two watches, at most. For purely practical purposes, a low-priced entry from Casio or Seiko could reliably serve a consumer's functional timekeeping needs for under $20. At the high end, some consumers with the requisite income might also opt for an additional watch as an aspirational showpiece. Under any circumstances, most adults who required a watch already had what they needed. With high reliability at both ends of the market, replacement demand was relatively low.

Under these circumstances, SMH had to break away from the conventional watch category in which it was poorly positioned to compete. Hayek needed to create a new product that would stimulate significant new consumer demand and distinguish the company from traditional watch manufacturers, enabling SMH to capture a dominant share of this newly created demand.

In other words, rather than join a dogfight in the watch industry against stronger combatants, Hayek needed to become a cat.

To do so, Hayek designed a radically new product, which borrowed heavily from the fashion accessory category. Why fashion? If consumers were prepared to own several scarves, pairs of designer shoes, or pieces of costume jewelry, why wouldn't they similarly choose to own a number of affordable watches from a wide selection of colorful and boldly styled designs?

Everything Hayek did in managing the launch of Swatch was thoughtfully conceived to cultivate a brand image more aligned with the fashion industry than with traditional watches. To understand how Hayek executed his breakaway positioning strategy, consider the 4Ps associated with Swatch's market entry.

Swatch's Product

Swatch was the first watch company to introduce boldly colored plastic casings across its product range. Its Milan-based design studio turned out hundreds of creative styles every year to appeal to a variety of tastes. Swatch rotated its entire product lineup on a seasonal basis and never repeated a design, regardless of popularity (figure 11.5). In addition, Swatch frequently teamed up with globally recognized designers, like Keith Haring and Mimmo Paladino, to introduce special edition models that further piqued consumer interest.[19]

Such product cues, while unheard of in the watch industry, were commonplace in the fashion industry. Not only did Swatch's frequent design changes encourage fashion enthusiasts to purchase multiple watches for their personal collection, but the company also stimulated entirely new demand from consumers historically ignored by the watch industry: tweens.

Swatch's Promotion

Prior to Swatch, Swiss watches were (and to this day, still are) promoted with classy print ads in magazines catering to high-income readers. Since Swatch was intent on shattering the staid image consumers traditionally associated with the Swiss watch industry, it deliberately crafted

Figure 11.5 Representative Swatch watch designs

a radically different marketing approach. Swatch's earliest print ads featured provocatively clad models set against colorful backgrounds to highlight Swatch's unusual product designs. In its television ads that followed, models gyrated to heavy rock music while adorned with colorful Swatches.

To further break from longstanding tradition, Swatch used guerilla marketing to create market buzz when entering a new country. For example, to celebrate its entry into the German market, Swatch created a five-hundred-foot working model of a Swatch watch mounted on the tallest skyscraper in Frankfurt. The message emanating from all of these promotional initiatives was crystal clear: Swatch was not just another watch brand in an already crowded category.

Swatch's Price

Historically, Swiss watches carried high price tags—often topping $1,000—necessitating a deliberate consumer purchase process. At the opposite end of the spectrum, cheap quartz digital watches from Asia, generally priced below $20, were largely viewed as disposable functional tools. For Hayek, neither of these price points was relevant to Swatch's desired positioning. Instead, the company chose to price Swatch on par with stylish costume jewelry, like a colorful bracelet, necklace, or brooch. Accordingly, Hayek initially set the price of a Swatch at $40—low enough to stimulate impulse purchases, but high enough to reflect the product's emotive appeal.

Hayek's pricing strategy also reinforced other distinctive aspects of Swatch's breakaway product positioning. Across the globe, Hayek priced his products in simple round numbers—$40 in the United States, SF 50 in Switzerland, DM 60 in Germany, and ¥7,000 in Japan.[20] Swatch prices were transparent and memorable, and every model carried the exact same price tag, including limited-edition designer pieces, which sold out within hours of launch. Swatch's price strategy signaled that none of its products was more valuable than another. It was up to consumers to express their own preferences in selecting from Swatch's broad and whimsical product line.

Swatch did not change its prices around the globe for over a decade, further reinforcing the company's distinctive brand identity.

Swatch's Place

Not surprisingly, Swatch eschewed traditional channels of distribution. Rather than placing its unusual product line in department stores or jeweler's display cases alongside conventional watches, Swatch opted for unique points of sale. The company opened over two dozen dedicated Swatch stores in the fashion districts of major cities and located boutiques within upscale department stores like Bloomingdales and Neiman Marcus. The company also opened pop-up stores in unusual locations—for example, selling its popular Veggie line of watches in urban fruit and vegetable markets.

Reflecting on Swatch's breakaway positioning strategy, Nicolas Hayek observed that "everything we do and the way we do everything sends a message."[21] Within a decade of its launch, Swatch sold over one hundred million watches worldwide, making it the best-selling watch of all time.

If Swatch's strategic playbook sounds familiar, it should. While Steve Jobs has earned accolades for his visionary leadership of Apple, in many respects Jobs followed the same playbook that proved highly successful for Nicolas Hayek at Swatch, twenty years earlier.

- Both companies were in deep trouble when the CEO took control (in Apple's case, when Steve Jobs returned after a twelve-year absence).
- Both created products that enabled consumers to think in a completely different way about the value proposition in the categories they entered.
- Both utilized elegant design as a key element of the brand promise for every new product release.
- Both developed products which elicited a strong emotive appeal, above technical merits.
- Both relied on "big bang" product launches with tightly choreographed event management and effective public relations. As a result, long lines at company stores greeted each new product release.
- Both CEOs had a healthy disregard for conventional market research.

- Both used simple pricing as a distinguishing element of their product offer: Swatch watches priced at $40 and Apple iTunes songs priced at ninety-nine cents.
- Both tightly controlled all aspects of brand management and consumer touchpoints affecting the consumer experience.
- Both employed high levels of vertical integration, including company-owned and branded retail outlets.
- Both maintained strong brand discipline in order to reinforce their brand promise in the long term.
- Both CEOs were revered within their company.

In addition to Swatch, breakaway positioning has also been successfully deployed in a number of other categories, such as diapers, snack bars, and household liquid cleaners (table 11.5). In each of these cases, an incumbent market leader created a new product by borrowing attributes from an entirely different category. This enabled the company to break away from competition and expand the size of its addressable market.

Take the diaper category for example. For years, Kimberly Clark (Huggies) and Procter & Gamble (Pampers) engaged in a zero-sum game for market-share leadership in a category constrained by the relatively slow growth in the number of babies under two years old. Each product improvement introduced by one competitor was quickly replicated by the other, nullifying the possibility for sustained competitive advantage. Moreover, both companies undoubtedly found it frustrating to compete in a category where buyers (parents) and users (toddlers) couldn't wait to stop using their product.

In 1989, Kimberly Clark launched a breakaway product called Pull-Ups that instantaneously doubled the size of its addressable market and gave the company unchallenged access to new consumer demand. By combining the product attributes of diapers with a different category (children's underwear), Pull-Ups were designed as a potty-training transition product that three- and four-year-old children could use on their own. Toddlers loved Pull-Ups because it made them feel like bigger kids. Parents loved Pull-Ups because they helped to avoid the messy accidents that children experience transitioning from diapers. Kimberly Clark loved Pull-Ups because it took Procter & Gamble over a decade to mount a competitive response. As a breakaway product, Pull-Ups figuratively caught Procter & Gamble with its pants down.

TABLE 11.5
Breakaway Positioning Examples

Original Product	Traditional Basis of Competition	Breakaway Product/ *Borrowed Category*	New Basis of Competition
Huggies Diapers	Absorbency Comfort Ease of application	Pull-Ups Training Pants/ *Children's underpants*	Transition product for entirely new market (children ages 3–4)
Mr. Clean Liquid Cleaner	Cleaning power Price/Value	Swiffer/*Dry and wet mops*	Convenience Effectiveness Speed of use
Special K Cereal	Vitamin/Health benefits Taste	Special K Cereal Bars/*Snack bars*	On-the-go consumption Guiltless snacking

In another category, Procter & Gamble enjoyed its own breakaway product success with Swiffer dry and wet mops. For years, Procter & Gamble was the leading household liquid cleaner provider, led by their Mr. Clean brand. But Mr. Clean faced three problems that constrained its profitable growth.

First, the market for liquid household cleaners was mature and slow growing. Second, consumers dreaded the chores that used Mr. Clean, particularly wet mopping the floor, so household usage rates were low. Third, profit margins for Mr. Clean were depressed by competition from value and store brands.

Procter & Gamble overcame these headwinds by breaking away from the traditional household liquid cleaner category. To do so, it borrowed product attributes from a different category to create the Swiffer floor-cleaning system. With Swiffer, there was no need for buckets, water, or liquid cleaners like Mr. Clean. Instead, a consumer buys a Swiffer mop, designed to be used with proprietary replaceable cleaning pads for dry sweeping or wet mopping.[22]

Given Swiffer's simplicity and ease of use, consumers tended to clean their floors more often, thereby increasing overall demand.

Because of its design and dominant share in the newly created category, Procter & Gamble was able to earn attractive margins from its "razor and blade" business model. The company's breakaway launch of Swiffer redefined the floor-cleaning product category and created a new billion-dollar brand.[23]

As a final example, it should be clear how Kellogg's extended beyond its breakfast cereal roots to create a new line of Special K cereal bars by borrowing the eat anywhere/anytime convenience associated with snack foods. In so doing, Kellogg's created a new demand for guilt-free snacking which reached consumers through new channels of distribution.

The examples in this section illustrate how reverse and breakaway positioning challenges the industry norms that confine most businesses to operate within the boundaries of established bases of competition. New products pursuing *reverse positioning* identify opportunities to attack poorly served segments of the market by reconfiguring product attributes within a given category in different ways. Successful reverse positioning practitioners surprise and delight poorly served customers to gain significant market share at attractive margins.

Strategies grounded in *breakaway positioning* seek to attract new customers by creating hybrid products that combine the attributes of products from different categories. When successful, breakaway positioning can dramatically expand the size of the addressable market and give the pioneer a dominant share for many years.

The bottom line is that when companies find themselves caught in a competitive dogfight, breakout positioning strategies provide an effective way to change the rules of engagement.

Blue Ocean Strategy

The term Blue Ocean conjures up an image of uncharted open waters, which is precisely the connotation that W. Chan Kim and Renée Mauborgne had in mind when they published their acclaimed 2006 book entitled *Blue Ocean Strategy*.[24]

Similarly to breakout positioning, Blue Ocean thinking starts with the recognition that most companies operate according to self-imposed industry norms, where the paramount objective is to steal market share by outperforming competition with better products or lower cost.

Kim and Mauborgne characterize such competitive environments as Red Oceans, symbolizing the bloody battles between sharks (companies) fighting for the same prey (current customers) in well-defined hunting areas (current markets and channels). Most mature products compete in Red Ocean markets that limit opportunities for attractive growth and profitability, as shown in table 11.6.[25]

In contrast, Blue Ocean players consciously reject Red Ocean behaviors by fundamentally reconstructing the basis of competition within their product category. The focal point is targeting new customers who are poorly (or not at all) served by Red Ocean incumbents. Responding to the unmet needs, Blue Ocean entrants design new products and services with the objective of increasing perceived value, while also lowering cost. Unlike conventional industry thinking that assumes companies must choose between best product and lowest cost, Blue Ocean strategies strive to deliver both.[26]

How is this possible? The key lies in recognizing that beauty lies in the eye of the beholder. The definition of "best product" depends

TABLE 11.6
Blue Ocean vs. Red Ocean Strategies

Red Ocean Strategy	Blue Ocean Strategy
Compete in existing market space	Create uncontested market space
Beat the competition	Make competition irrelevant
Exploit existing demand; steal share	Create and capture new demand
Optimize the value/cost tradeoff	Break the value/cost tradeoff
Align the whole system of a company's activities with its strategic choice of product superiority or low cost	Align the whole system of a company's activities with its strategic choice of differentiation and low cost

Red Ocean Characteristics	Blue Ocean Characteristics
Well-defined industry norms and category structure	New rules unlocks new demand, fueling high growth
Low growth, high concentration, and intense competition	Blue Ocean entrant captures dominant share at attractive margins
Low margins (except perhaps for industry leaders and niche specialists)	Incumbents poorly positioned to effectively respond

entirely on the preferences, values, and needs of a particular class of consumer. By designing new product features to appeal to customers who are not interested in current best-in-class offerings, Blue Ocean entrants can deliver extremely high value for the consumer (which may translate into a higher consumer WTP) *and* lower costs.

For example, Kim and Mauborgne cite Cirque du Soleil as an archetype of successful Blue Ocean strategy. At first glance, the circus industry appeared to be an unattractive sector for a new player to enter in the early 1980s. Attendance had been falling for years because of an expanding array of entertainment alternatives and growing consumer concern over the poor treatment of circus animals. High costs and the need to keep ticket prices low to attract a child-centric audience also constrained margins for traditional circus operators.

But Guy Laliberté, a Canadian former street performer, recognized the opportunity to fundamentally reinvent the circus to appeal to types of customers long ignored by traditional circus producers: upscale adults unaccompanied by children, and corporate clientele. To appeal to this mature consumer target, Laliberté eliminated costly, low-value features found in traditional circuses—most notably, animal acts—and added a unique combination of gymnastics, ballet, music, and sophisticated set designs to create an entirely new entertainment experience.

Not only did Cirque du Soleil's customers not miss the signature animal acts of Ringling Bros. and Barnum & Bailey Circus shows, but they actually preferred Laliberté's alternative entertainment genre. As it turns out, the highest-cost activities associated with operating a traditional circus are the care, feeding, training, and transporting of animals. By reinventing the circus, Cirque du Soleil was able to lower costs, charge higher prices, and achieve unprecedented growth. Cirque du Soleil turned a Red Ocean business into a Blue Ocean phenomenon.

How can your company (or entrepreneurial endeavor) identify and create Blue Ocean opportunities? With any successful new product-development initiative, the starting point is to identify the target group of customers that can be better served by a new product or service. The appropriate target is dissatisfied consumers of current products, or those sitting on the sidelines because no available products deliver sufficient value.

Armed with an understanding of unmet consumer needs, the next step is to apply the four-actions framework to fundamentally reconstruct the value proposition offered by products and services currently in the marketplace.[27] The four actions refer to how products can be reconfigured as Blue Ocean entries to unlock untapped demand from target customers:

- *Eliminate* Which elements of current products should be eliminated because they deliver little (or negative) value to target users?
- *Reduce* Which elements should be reduced because, at current levels, they overserve customers, adding more cost than value?
- *Raise* Which factors should be raised because, at current industry levels, they underserve customers, compromising value creation?
- *Create* Which factors should be created, opening an entirely new path to value creation never before offered in the industry?

Table 11.7 illustrates how Cirque du Soleil applied the four-actions framework to transform the Red Ocean circus category into a Blue Ocean market opportunity.[28]

To see another example of how the four-actions framework has been applied to create a Blue Ocean opportunity, consider the fitness center sector. At the beginning of each semester, when I ask my MBA students to identify their favorite brands, one of the most frequent mentions is Equinox, a high-end fitness club featuring sophisticated training equipment, a wide range of fitness classes, plush changing rooms, eco-chic amenities, healthy snacks and smoothies, and inviting

TABLE 11.7
Cirque du Soleil's Four Actions Framework

Eliminate	Reduce
Star performers	Clowns
Wild animal shows	Slapstick humor
Aisle concession sales	Thrill and danger
Multiple show arena	

Raise	Create
Unique venue design	Theme-based shows
	Refined environment
	Multiple productions
	Artistic music and dance

lounge spaces—with commensurately high monthly membership fees. This combination of features plays well in the upwardly mobile and generally fit group of millennials attending Columbia Business School. But what about a different consumer segment, personified by a fictitious persona I'll call Betty?

Betty is a forty-one-year-old homemaker and part-time worker with two young children, living in an inner suburb of a major metropolitan area. Like many of her peers, Betty constantly feels stressed by juggling her many responsibilities and has neither the discretionary budget nor the perceived freedom for much "me-time." Consequently, she hasn't worked out since college and is admittedly out of shape. Her situation has taken a toll on her figure, fitness, and body image.

One day, Betty's friend suggests that she take advantage of a complimentary guest pass for the local Equinox club. With some trepidation, Betty arranges a time to meet, and, upon arrival, is given a tour and sales pitch by the club manager. But, almost immediately, Betty finds that every feature proudly showcased by her Equinox guide leaves her feeling anxious and dispirited, as noted in table 11.8.

Despite its ostensible amenities and charms, the Equinox did not serve Betty's needs well.

After recounting her experience at Equinox, another friend suggests that Betty check out the local Curves fitness club, located in a nearby strip mall. From the instant Betty enters Curves, her experience is

TABLE 11.8

Incongruity Between Value Proposition and Selected Customer Needs

Equinox Feature	Betty's Reaction
Impressively classy and chic lobby design.	Looks expensive.
Large array of sophisticated fitness devices.	Way too complicated and overwhelming.
Muscular men and fit women using exercise equipment, weights, and cardio machines.	I've *never* looked as fit and strong as they do, particularly now.
Mirrors everywhere.	A constant reminder of my pudgy figure.
Healthy-snack bar.	I would never spend $9 for a smoothie.
Plush women's locker room, sauna, and pool area.	I wouldn't feel comfortable here, given my poor body image.

completely different and comfortably reassuring. There isn't a mirror in sight (or men, for that matter), the equipment looks simple and easy to use. A friendly-looking coach is encouraging a small group of women, and most importantly, the club members look just like her (figure 11.6).

Betty learns that the guided workout sessions are designed to last only thirty minutes to accommodate busy schedules, and members come already dressed for their workouts because Curves fitness centers have no changing rooms. By eschewing expensive equipment and amenities, Curves can offer Betty monthly membership fees that are 80 percent lower than those of Equinox.

By understanding the needs of a large segment of consumers like Betty, who were poorly served by traditional fitness centers (and, as a result, were largely ignored by fitness center providers), Curves configured its Blue Ocean entry as depicted in table 11.9. By appropriately eliminating, reducing, raising, and creating fitness center attributes to better serve the needs of women similar to Betty, Curves created an entirely new customer experience, perceived to be better *and* cheaper than available alternatives. As a result, Curves avoided the fitness center dogfight for current customer market share, and instead unlocked new demand in the category. From its founding in 1992, Curves grew to over seven thousand locations within a decade, peaking at nearly ten thousand facilities in eighty-five countries, with more than four million members in 2006.[29] As the Curves example demonstrates, Blue Ocean strategies can create enormous opportunities for growth.

Companies executing effective Blue Ocean strategies are distinguished from traditional competitors by their *focus* and *differentiation*. For an example of these distinctions, imagine conducting a survey of a representative sample of experienced air travelers back in the 1990s to ascertain which airline attributes were most important and how each carrier rated on those factors. The results might, hypothetically, look like those depicted in figure 11.7.[30]

The airline attributes most frequently mentioned as being important to experienced flyers are displayed along the horizontal axis, including price, route coverage, seating-class choices, departure frequency, etc. The red line in figure 11.7 displays how consumers rated one particular legacy airline on a scale of 1 to 5 for each of these attributes. Note that the performance ratings for the highlighted airline all hover around an average score. Seating-class choices and loungers are rated a bit higher than average, while meals and cabin service are rated somewhat lower.

Figure 11.6 Equinox (*top*) vs. Curves (*bottom*)

TABLE 11.9
Four Actions Framework for Curves

Eliminate	Reduce
Men!	Equipment complexity
Mirrors	Time for workout
Changing rooms	Monthly fees
	Intimidation

Raise	Create
Coaching	Supportive/social environment
Ease of getting started	Comfort of working out with
Fun	people "just like me"
Accessibility	New friends

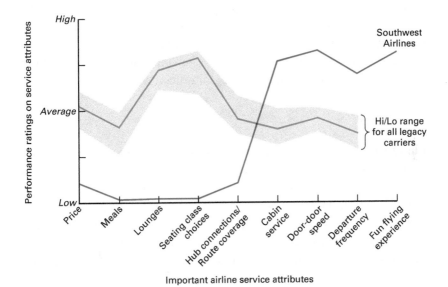

Figure 11.7 Airline industry strategy canvas

Repeating this exercise for the other legacy airlines yields ratings that fall within a relatively narrow range, as shown by the shaded band in figure 11.7. In this example, American Airlines might be rated slightly higher than competitors in departure frequency, but lags behind US Airways on price, United on meals, and Delta on route coverage. In essence, this "strategy canvas" suggests that all airlines compete aggressively on the same performance attributes, but no individual carrier achieves dominant superiority on any single attribute, let alone broad-based market leadership. From this perspective, consumers tend to view all legacy airlines as relatively undifferentiated and mediocre.

The pictorial image conveyed by this strategy canvas is representative of many Red Ocean product categories that conform to tit-for-tat feature replication and performance augmentation across common product attributes. In such circumstances, effective differentiation between incumbent players within the category becomes more blurred over time. Thus, the race toward ever-higher performance on multiple attributes leaves an increasingly large number of consumers poorly served or priced completely out of the market.

Such circumstances create an opportunity for a new entrant to launch a radically reconfigured product or service that addresses the needs of consumers largely ignored by market incumbents. This can be done by incorporating two salient characteristics of effective Blue Ocean strategies: focus and meaningful differentiation.

Focus

Blue Ocean strategies focus on a few select attributes that offer the greatest value to poorly served customers and nonconsumers. As shown in figure 11.7, Southwest Airlines chose to focus on low price, friendly cabin service, door-to-door travel time, and an entirely new attribute: a fun flying experience. Simultaneously, they eliminated many service attributes that had been routinely offered by incumbent airlines, such as meals, seating-class choices (with assigned seats), airport lounges, and hub-and-spoke route networks.

Meaningful Differentiation

By focusing its value proposition, Southwest Airlines could align its entire business model toward operational excellence on selected performance attributes. Southwest achieved competitively advantaged productivity levels by utilizing a single aircraft type on point-to-point flights from secondary airports, with one class of service and no free meals or assigned seating. Thus, Southwest wasn't just more focused than its legacy airline competitors; it was *meaningfully differentiated* by being better on cost, departure frequency, door-to-door speed, and an appealing in-flight experience.[31]

As a result, Southwest has consistently scored at or near the top of customer satisfaction ratings among U.S. airlines while consistently offering the lowest fares, helping the airline to become the largest U.S. domestic carrier. Southwest Airlines successfully executed a Blue Ocean strategy that unlocked significant new demand previously not served by incumbent market leaders.[32]

Companies that remain true to their Blue Ocean roots can build exceptionally strong brand images, reflecting a clear consumer understanding of their strategic intent to deliver meaningful differentiation. For example, both IKEA and CrossFit applied Blue Ocean strategy concepts to develop meaningfully differentiated offerings within their respective categories. While IKEA may not appeal to all consumer tastes, its image for stylish low-priced home furnishings—reinforced since the company's founding in 1943—has established IKEA as one of the most valuable brands in the world.[33] CrossFit, whose Blue Ocean brand promise of "Forging Elite Fitness," is resonating with a growing number of extreme exercise enthusiasts (even as it repels less athletically inclined consumers), propelling strong global growth.[34]

Southwest Airlines has also remained true to its Blue Ocean founding principles and has consistently reinforced its brand image for value and friendly service. For example, in the early 1990s, Southwest's print ads rhetorically asked consumers, "Can you name the airline with low fares on every seat of every flight, everywhere it flies?" Two decades later, Southwest's print ads reinforced the same themes, proclaiming, "Low fares. No hidden fees. What you see is what you pay."

In contrast, legacy airlines have struggled to define a distinct brand promise in the competitive airline marketplace. By attempting to appeal to virtually all consumers, legacy airlines have found it difficult to establish a credible and compelling basis of meaningful differentiation. This challenge is evident in Delta's nondescript advertising taglines over the past forty years, which provide little evidence of distinct competitive advantage.[35]

Delta Airlines Advertising Taglines

1972: Fly the Best with Delta
1974: Delta Is My Airline
1980: Delta Is the Best
1983: That's the Delta Spirit
1984: Delta Gets You There with Care
1986: The Official Airline of Walt Disney World
1987: The Best Get Better
1987: We Love to Fly, and It Shows
1991: Delta Is Your Choice for Flying
1994: You'll Love the Way We Fly
1996: On Top of the World
2000: Fly Me Home
2005: Good Goes Around
2009: Together in Style
2010: Keep Climbing
2012: The Only Way Is Up

I began this section by noting that most companies conceive and execute predictable Red Ocean strategies within well-established business boundaries. Over time, this common management mindset leads to a blurring of meaningful differentiation between companies competing on the same terms for the same customers. The appropriate Blue Ocean response is to break away from the pack by redefining one or more of the boundaries that have historically constrained industry behaviors. There are six pathways to expand strategic scope in formulating Blue Ocean strategies that have been exploited across a wide variety of industries, products, and service categories.[36]

Industry

Rather than compete directly in the hotel sector (as citizenM successfully did), Airbnb challenged the very definition of the hospitality industry, which had always assumed that hoteliers needed to manage dedicated facilities. By creating a platform and business model

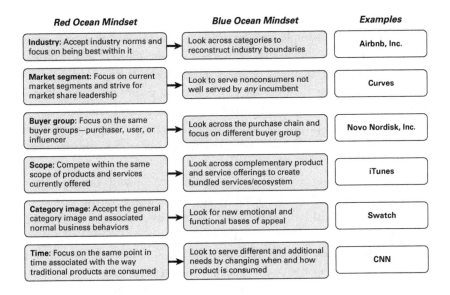

Figure 11.8 Blue Ocean Six-Paths framework

that brings the world's entire housing stock within the address-able scope of a redefined hospitality industry, Airbnb has enjoyed unprecedented growth. Within seven years of its founding in 2008, Airbnb's valuation equaled that of the Hyatt and Marriott hotel chains combined.[37]

Market Segment

I have covered numerous examples throughout this book of new entrants designing a new product or service to appeal to a market segment that had been largely ignored or poorly served by incumbents. Curves, CrossFit, Casella Family Brands, Southwest Airlines, and citizenM all fall into this category.

Buyer Group

A variation on strategies designed to serve a different market segment of customers occurs when a company challenges the defined roles of the individuals who purchase, use, or influence the choice of products. One good example is Novo Nordisk, a Danish pharmaceutical company that has aggressively competed against Eli Lilly in the global market for insulin for many decades. Historically, the two drug giants targeted doctors as the primary customer and promoted their respective products on the basis of their purity, efficacy, and safety. As such, doctors served as product choice influencers by writing prescriptions for patients who rarely knew or cared which company manufactured the product.

But in the mid-1980s, Novo Nordisk recognized the opportunity to change the basis of competition by focusing on the ease with which insulin could be administered by patients. With the company's NovoPen, patients could administer their required dose of insulin with a single click of a pen-like device, providing a significant improvement in convenience over the prior need for syringes and vials.

This change in the basis of competition enabled Novo Nordisk to market directly to consumers, who in turn asked their doctors to prescribe the desired NovoPen product. In the years that followed, Novo Nordisk gained considerable market share against Eli Lilly, who lagged behind in developing improved insulin delivery systems.

More recently, pharmaceutical benefits managers like Express Scripts have redefined the traditional role of drug companies, doctors, and independent pharmacies in the distribution of prescription medications.

Scope

Internet technologies have radically altered the value chain across multiple industries, empowering consumers to be directly involved in the consumption, production, and recommendation of products and services that were once provided by intermediaries.

Historically, the underlying raison d'être for many companies was to sell a product or service that was too complex, inconvenient, or expensive for consumers to provide for themselves. But technology-enabled self-empowerment has already ravaged a number of industries, including travel agencies, record labels, encyclopedias, daily newspapers, accounting, and book publishing.

In each of these cases, jobs that were initially considered too complex for individuals to perform on their own are now easily handled by the average consumer, in ways that are perceived to be better and much cheaper. For example, who needs a commissioned travel agent when Expedia, KAYAK, or TripAdvisor empowers consumers to plan and reserve trips on their own? The same is true for the impact of streaming music providers on record labels and music retailers, Google News and the *Huffington Post* on metro dailies, TurboTax and QuickBooks on accounting, and Amazon and Goodreads on book publishers and retailers.

Category Image

By challenging long-standing category images, such as "socks are boring," "wine is for special occasions," and "watches are for telling time," LittleMissMatched, Yellow Tail, and Swatch unlocked latent demand that had not previously been served by industry incumbents. By breaking down stereotypical category images, Blue Ocean strategies can increase the size of a new product's addressable market.

Time and Place

Changing when and where products are consumed can dramatically alter the competitive landscape. A prime example is CNN's ascendance, which successfully challenged conventional assumptions on when television news could or should be consumed. More broadly, mobile devices and streaming services have freed customers to consume content wherever and whenever they choose, creating enormous growth opportunities for companies such as Netflix, Amazon, Hulu, WatchESPN, Coursera, and edX.

The breadth of these examples suggests that there are numerous opportunities to break from the industry norms and category structures that often confine companies within mature industries to sluggish growth, copycat competition, and tight margins. In such cases, the resulting loss of meaningful differentiation reflects management choices, not inevitable outcomes. Blue Ocean strategies and breakout positioning can enable companies to reignite profitable growth.

Disruptive Technology

Clayton Christensen's disruptive technology framework provides a fitting capstone in my quest to better explain how companies can break away from the pack and achieve long-term profitable growth. In his 1997 book, *The Innovator's Dilemma*, he provided groundbreaking insight on three key questions:

- Why do companies have such a difficult time sustaining market leadership?
- Why is it so often that newcomers, rather than incumbent market leaders, introduce disruptive technologies and business models?
- How can incumbents avoid this innovator's dilemma?

To answer these questions, let's start with Christensen's definition of *disruptive technology*. Despite its name, the disruptive technology framework actually can be applied to many new products or services, whether high or low tech. Under his broad conceptual umbrella, Christensen divided product and service launches into one of just two possible categories. The first, *sustaining technologies*, reflects the routine improvements that every company makes to its products over time in order to appeal to current customers and to respond to competitive pressures. Examples of sustaining technology improvements are echoed in the advertising messages consumers are exposed to every day, like "buy new, improved Crest Toothpaste, now with extra Whitener" or "check out the latest Lenovo desktop computer, now with the 5th Generation Intel Core Processor."

The second class, *disruptive technologies*, is aimed specifically at consumers who are overserved by existing products, and may target nonconsumers who simply have no interest in, or are priced out of, the current marketplace. Developing an understanding of the reason mainstream products do not appeal to a large segment of the current market is exactly what gives new entrants ideas for disruptive product and service opportunities.

In chapter 1, I cited several examples of disruptive technologies, like digital cameras, online travel services, ultrasound, and walk-in medical clinics (see table 1.1). The tendency of incumbent market leaders to relentlessly augment product performance through continuous technology improvements eventually alienates a growing number of overserved consumers, who neither value, nor are willing to pay for, the panoply of features in mainstream products. When this situation emerges, new players recognize the opportunity to attract consumers with simpler, "good enough" solutions, possibly including a few unexpected new features which surprise and delight overserved consumers.

As an example of how low-end disruptive technology dynamics play out, consider the evolution of the personal computer industry, illustrated in simplified terms in figure 11.9.[38] In this schematic, the vertical axis measures product performance, whether storage capacity, screen resolution, or processor speed, while the horizontal axis represents the passage of time, as new generations of products are introduced.

If you happened to be one of the incumbent market leaders in the early stages of the PC business, you probably would have observed at least two large segments of customers in the marketplace. Consumers at the low end of the marketplace didn't really need the most sophisticated PC products and weren't willing to pay huge premiums for top performance. This group is depicted as dotted line B in figure 11.9.

At the opposite end of the market were the high-end power users that expected higher performance and were willing to pay more to obtain state-of-the-art technology. Accordingly, in figure 11.9, dotted line A is positioned above dotted line B, indicative of the differentiated needs of low- and high-end consumers.

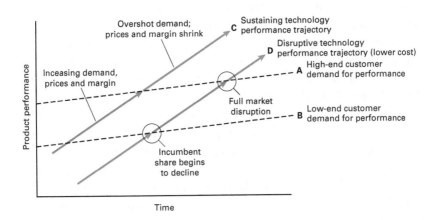

Figure 11.9 Sustaining and low-end disruptive technology dynamics

Another marketplace dynamic that PC providers discovered over time is that customers expect product performance to improve with each new product generation, as a consequence of several factors:

- *Human nature* Across an array of products, marketers have trained consumers to expect each new product to be better than the one it replaces. Personal computers are no exception, as consumers expect continuous improvements in sustaining technology performance.
- *New product uses* As consumers gain more experience with products on the market, they often seek new uses, requiring enhanced product performance. As consumers gained an interest in using PCs for gaming, streaming video, storing photos, and business analytics, demand grew for improved processor speed, storage capacity, and screen resolution.
- *Competitive pressures* With competitors playing leapfrog to gain temporary product performance superiority, the augmentation dynamic I described earlier conditioned consumers to expect continuous improvements in PC performance.

The net result of these marketplace dynamics is depicted in figure 11.9 by the upward slope of lines A and B, which reflects the increase in expected performance by both low- and high-end consumers in the PC market.

One of the breakthrough insights of Christensen's disruptive technology theory is his recognition that in virtually all industries, engineers are capable of improving product performance at a more rapid rate than is demanded by consumers. This dynamic is illustrated in figure 11.9 by the solid line C, which depicts the rate of product performance improvement from an engineering delivery standpoint. The slope of line C is much steeper than the slope of consumer expectations for improved product performance represented by lines A and B. The difference between the inherent supply of, and demand for, product performance in most industries has profound business consequences.

In the early stages of development of a new product category, the ability to rapidly improve product performance helps drive profitable growth. In the PC industry, for example, a pioneering incumbent would benefit by exploiting the steep sustaining technology performance-improvement curve because in doing so it could go from initially serving the performance needs of low-end consumers in the marketplace (where lines B and C intersect), to appealing to high-end power users (where lines A and C intersect). By moving upward to serve the full range of needs in the marketplace, a PC competitor could thus be in a position to increase market share, price realization, and margins.

However, the difference in the rate of performance improvement between what consumers expect and what engineers deliver inevitably leads industry players to overshoot the market. In other words, they provide more PC performance than even high-end consumers need or are willing to pay for. When this happens, incumbents begin to experience a slowdown in demand and increased pressure on price realization and margins. Fewer and fewer consumers value the new performance thresholds.

To see the consequences of an overshot market, consider the computer that you currently own. If you learned that the manufacturer of your PC just came out with a new model that is 50 percent faster, has twice the storage capacity, and sells for $100 less than what you paid for your current computer, would you feel compelled to rush out and buy the improved new product? I suspect not; the reason being that most consumers believe the performance of their PC is sufficient to meet their current needs. The consequences of overshooting the market are already evident in the PC sector: the average selling price and unit sales of PCs have been declining steadily for many years.[39]

When incumbent players overshoot the needs of a significant segment of the market, it opens the door to disruptive entrants who recognize the opportunity to appeal to overserved consumers with simpler, cheaper products. In the PC market, this led to the introduction of netbooks. In 2007, Asus released the first lightweight netbook, with a small screen, a cramped keyboard, and a slow processor. Despite these limitations, it was more portable than the commonly available Windows laptops at the time and was less than half the price of better-featured laptops on the market. Competing netbook models quickly followed from other players at prices below $250, and netbook sales became the fastest-growing segment of the PC market over the next three years, unlocking PC demand from consumers who had previously been priced out of the market.

Once a low-end disruptive technology like netbooks is introduced, it tends to experience rapid sustaining technology improvements, expanding its basis of appeal beyond the least demanding consumers. As shown by line D in figure 11.9, if a disruptive technology improves enough over time to serve even the expectations of high-end consumers, a category can become fully disrupted, wiping out most of the original industry incumbents whose products are generally no longer deemed competitive. This is exactly what happened many times in the computer industry: successive, disruptive waves of new technology transformed the industry from a predominant focus on mainframes, to minicomputers, to PCs, to mobile computing devices. Each disruptive transformation wiped out most of the incumbents wedded to the prior technology, while creating enormous growth opportunities for disruptive entrants. As it turned out, netbooks did not fully disrupt the PC industry; mobile computing became an even more disruptive influence.

The marketplace dynamics described in the previous few pages have broad-based implications for business strategy. As Clayton Christensen has noted, a company that finds itself in an overshot market can't win by staying the course. Either entrants will steal its customers or commoditization will steal its profits.[40]

I've described such scenarios many times throughout this book. For instance, in Red Ocean marketplaces, companies in a mature industry compete on the same terms for the same customers in a slow-growth, low-profit environment. Kim and Mauborgne cited overshot markets in the airline, fitness center, and pharmaceutical industries.[41] Competitors get caught in tit-for-tat product replication and augmentation, causing categories as a whole to lose meaningful differentiation. Youngme Moon's reference to the "bed wars" in the hotel industry and my examples of loss of distinctiveness in the wine, sock, and household cleaning product categories provide additional examples.[42]

Given such widespread industry disruption, a pivotal question arises: why do executives so often mire themselves in such dire circumstances? Ironically, the reason that companies so often overshoot their markets is that managers repeatedly do what good managers are *supposed to do*, like listening and responding to the needs of their best customers. A company's highest-spending and most sophisticated customers are the ones most likely to clamor for (if not necessarily be willing to pay for) better product performance. Since most companies are understandably motivated to respond to power users who are willing to pay the highest prices for top performance, competitive dynamics drives most executives to overshoot mainstream consumer needs.

Low-end disruptive technologies represent one way to avoid this feature–function arms race and create profitable growth by appealing to overserved consumers. Low-end disruptive entries are initially inferior to mainstream products based on traditional performance metrics. However, they deliver a more appealing value proposition to many price-sensitive buyers. For example, the first netbooks performed well below the standards of state-of-the art PCs when they were first introduced, but at a strikingly lower price. Similarly, online travel agency (OTA) sites initially lacked the breadth of coverage and depth of expertise offered by the traditional travel agent industry. Instead, they provided greater convenience, significantly lower fees, and the availability of peer reviews. Over time, the performance of OTAs improved rapidly, and wound up wiping out most traditional travel agencies.

Another way to avoid the consequences of stalemated competition in overserved markets is to pursue new-market disruptive technologies, which attract nonconsumers by focusing on entirely different performance attributes that were previously ignored by industry incumbents. For example, for-profit higher education providers chose not to compete directly against existing colleges on prestige or price. Instead, these new-market disruptors focused on a different attribute: flexible access to education, which allowed students to maintain their jobs while pursuing a college degree. As such, for-profit colleges unlocked a huge untapped, addressable market that had previously been ignored by traditional colleges and universities.

Walk-in medical clinics also unlocked untapped demand by providing more convenient and less expensive access to routine medical services than was traditionally offered by the medical profession. For decades, a patient's only choice to deal with a health issue was to schedule a doctor's appointment during normal business hours or to go to a hospital emergency room. Given the inconvenience and cost associated with either of these alternatives, many consumer ailments simply went untreated, creating a significant untapped opportunity for new-market disruptors. Walk-in medical clinics, located in pharmacies, grocery stores, and other major retailers, now offer access to a wide range of affordable routine medical services seven days a week, including evening hours. By 2015, MinuteClinic (CVS), Healthcare Clinic (Walgreens), and The Clinic at Walmart, among others, were operating more than three thousand walk-in medical facilities in what has become one of the fastest growing sectors of the health-care industry.[43]

As a final example of new-market disruptive technologies, Apple's highly successful iPad (launched in 2010) disrupted the PC industry by appealing to a previously untapped consumer demand for mobile computing and content streaming. As such, Apple expanded the size of the market for computing devices, rather than simply trying to steal market share from existing PC players.

While Christensen is widely acclaimed for introducing a ground-breaking business theory, he has recently been criticized for being too narrowly focused on only two forms of disruptive technologies, low end and new market, which both focus on overserved customers.[44] In fact, as shown in table 11.10, there are four types of disruptive

TABLE 11.10
Different Types of Disruptive Technologies

Disruptive Technology Type	Customer Target	Product Characteristics	Examples
Low End	Overserved consumers	Current products are considerably more sophisticated and expensive than many consumers need.	Southwest Airlines Netbooks
New Market	Nonconsumers	Remove a constraint that previously prevented consumers from participating in the market (e.g., where or when products could be consumed, usually at a more affordable price).	Walk-in Medical Clinics Online Higher Education
High End	Underserved consumers	Breakthrough product performance at a premium price.	iPod FedEx
Big Bang	Mass market	Dramatic improvements in product performance *and* lower prices than current products.	Google Maps Uber

technologies that can fundamentally transform the competitive dynamics of an industry.

In addition to low-end and new-market disruptors, there is a third way to break the no-win stalemate of commoditized markets; by exploiting a technological breakthrough, enabling high-end disruptive technology providers to dramatically improve current performance levels. Such products appeal to consumers who value and are willing to pay a premium for demonstratively superior product performance. Examples in this category include Apple's original iPod and FedEx's overnight package delivery service. Over time, high-end disruptors often seek to expand the size of their addressable market by steadily lowering prices to penetrate the mainstream consumer market.

A current example of a high-end disruptive technology that is rapidly expanding the size of an industry's addressable market is the e-bike. One player in this emerging market, Pedego, focuses on baby boomers seeking recreation or wanting to keep up with their grandkids. As Pedego's CEO noted, "99 percent of our customers would never have purchased another bike in their lifetime, if not for us."[45] The price of many e-bikes on the market in 2015 exceeds $2,000, but similar to the trajectory of other high-end disruptive technologies, e-bike prices are expected to decline in the years ahead, fueling greater market adoption.

A fourth form of highly disruptive technology has emerged in recent years that offers vastly superior performance *and* lower prices over current products. That's precisely the compelling value proposition of "big bang" disruptors that can overwhelm stable businesses very rapidly.[46]

For example, the integrated software and hardware capabilities of smartphones are creating big-bang disruptions in a number of product categories, including cameras, pagers, wristwatches, maps, books, travel guides, flashlights, home telephones, dictation recorders, cash registers, alarm clocks, answering machines, yellow pages, wallets, keys, phrase books, transistor radios, personal digital assistants, remote controls, newspapers and magazines, directory assistance, restaurant guides, and pocket calculators.

The taxi industry is currently experiencing the challenges of big-bang disruption, as many riders perceive Uber as offering better service *and* lower fares. As a measure of the explosive growth potential of big-bang disruption, Uber achieved a valuation of $50 billion within five years, becoming the fastest company ever to reach such a milestone.[47]

Given the huge potential of successful disruptive technologies, why don't more companies disrupt themselves? The consequences of ignoring disruption are grave. Every company is subject to product life cycles that eventually erode the customer appeal, sales, and profitability of products in their business portfolio. Companies like Apple and Amazon have continuously identified and exploited opportunities to disrupt themselves before competition beats them to it, and as a result have achieved the rare feat of sustained profitable growth.[48] Yet continuous disruptive renewal remains the exception, rather than the rule, for a number of reasons.

Customer Focus

As already noted, most companies tend to predominantly focus on the needs of their best customers, leading to continuous sustaining-technology improvements for their current products, rather than disruptive technologies that expand market reach.

Competitor Focus

In the same vein, the tendency of large market incumbents is to look over their shoulder at their traditional competitors. If you're an established player in an industry, you already have a large revenue base, and the fastest way to grow is to steal customers from your closest competitors. But your archenemies are similarly motivated, which reinforces feature–function arms races that open the door for low-end and new-market disruptive entrants. For example, in the luxury automobile market, the Big Three German luxury carmakers—BMW, Mercedes-Benz, and Audi—were so focused on matching each other's product offerings that they ignored the opportunity identified by newcomer Tesla to usher in a new generation of high-performance electric cars. Similarly, Boeing and Airbus have been so absorbed in shadowing each other's jumbo-jet airliner development programs that both missed the opportunity to pursue the rapidly growing regional jet sector, now dominated by Embraer and Bombardier.

Resource Constraints

A third barrier to disruptive technology development is the allocation of corporate resources. Ironically, sustaining technology improvements to existing products often require higher levels of R&D investment than the launch of disruptive technologies. The reason for this is that continuous improvements to mature products often require sophisticated new technologies to push the envelope of achievable performance. In contrast, low-end and new-market disruptive technologies often rely on mashups of off-the-shelf components and low-cost business-model innovations that are cheaper to realize.

In the health-care sector, for example, the leading practitioners of sophisticated CT scanners and MRI equipment—GE, Siemens, and Philips—invested heavily over many years to improve the image quality and accuracy of their advanced diagnostic products. But for many applications, ultrasound (a low-end disruptive technology) provides adequate diagnostic accuracy at a far lower cost. Ultrasound equipment is relatively inexpensive, simpler to use, and allows less-skilled professionals to provide diagnostic services in more affordable, accessible settings. Since GE, Siemens, and Philips were so heavily invested in sophisticated product-development programs, none of them incorporated low-cost ultrasound solutions into their medical-equipment product portfolios for many years, until more recent industry acquisitions.

Similar industry dynamics also played out in the markets for PCs, cameras, photocopiers, steel mills, and many others, where incumbent market leaders continued to invest heavily in sustaining technology improvements, while ignoring the opportunity and need to transition to new disruptive technologies.[49]

Organizational Barriers

A number of common organizational behaviors impede corporate entrepreneurship and obstruct the development of disruptive technologies. For example, monetary incentives typically reward employees who meet short-term business-performance targets, understandably keeping most managers focused on current revenue generators, rather than long-term opportunities for game-changing disruptive technologies. Moreover, most corporations tend to be intolerant of failure, lacking the patience to nurture disruptive product development that can take years before yielding material financial results. Under such circumstances, many would-be *intra*preneurs are reluctant to risk their own compensation and career development by committing to uncertain disruptive product initiatives. Finally, new disruptive technologies that threaten to cannibalize a company's current products usually engender fierce internal opposition.

In addition to these factors, the biggest barriers to disruptive technology development in many companies are management mindsets that are ill-suited to promoting an entrepreneurial spirit of continuous innovation. There are four common dysfunctional management mindsets that warrant particular attention.

Pride in Current Product Technologies

Companies that have achieved market leadership have every right to be proud of their engineering prowess in creating state-of-the-art product performance. But such corporate pride is often accompanied by an attitude of dismissiveness toward early-stage unsophisticated disruptive products that initially exhibit crude performance. The fatal flaw in such thinking is that by design, low-end and new-market disruptive products are not intended to compete head-on in the mainstream market on traditional metrics of product performance. Rather, low-end and new-market disruptive technologies are initially targeted toward customers who are not well served by current state-of-the-art products, but are likely to emerge as a competitive threat in the mainstream market over time.

For example, the first commercially available digital cameras introduced by Sony in the early 1980s did not come close to the image clarity and color vibrancy of industry leader Kodak's film-based cameras at the time. Ironically, nearly a decade earlier, Kodak developed the first digital camera in its research labs. A young Kodak engineer, Steven Sasson, cobbled together a working model of a digital camera from off-the-shelf components, which was capable of displaying color images on a television. Sasson made a series of internal presentations to groups of executives from Kodak's marketing, technical, and business departments. He brought the digital camera into conference rooms and demonstrated the system by taking photos of executives in the room.

Though the picture quality was poor, Sasson assured his colleagues that the image resolution would improve rapidly, and that digital cameras would effectively compete against Kodak's film-based cameras within fifteen to twenty years. Nonetheless, management's response was tepid at best, with the strongest objections coming from marketing and business executives.[50]

In the years to come, Kodak made halting, ambivalent R&D efforts in digital photography, while continuing to refine its film-based camera products. By the time Kodak offered its first digital cameras, eighteen years after Sasson's discovery, Kodak was late to the market, and was ultimately driven into bankruptcy by the industry's transformation to digital photography.

In a similar vein, the top executives of the Big Three U.S. automakers were derisively dismissive of the early imports from Japan's car companies starting in the late 1950s. Toyota's first entry, the Toyopet, was underpowered, uncomfortable, and lacking in basic amenities. By any measure, the Toyopet could not hold a candle to the prestige, power, and comfort of America's flagship car models. Over time, however, the Japanese carmakers rapidly improved their products, which increasingly appealed to value-oriented buyers whose need for fuel-efficient, affordable, and reliable transportation was poorly served by American carmakers. Toyota emerged as the largest car company in the world, while two of the Big Three U.S. carmakers fell into bankruptcy.

More recent examples of management myopia toward the existential threat posed by emerging disruptive technologies can be found in the advertising, telecommunications, publishing, and higher education sectors.

Complacency

Another common trap for executives is complacency with current business results. As I noted in chapter 4, it is typical for companies to experience robust growth right up to a tipping point of prolonged declining sales. In such circumstances, executives often allow their current business success to blind them to existential threats looming on the horizon. That was arguably the case for the BFGoodrich tire company, which enjoyed three years of strong growth before hitting a revenue stall in the late 1970s. The advent of radial-tire technology sent the company tumbling into a decade-long skid that ended in a fire sale. More recently, the U.S. newspaper industry enjoyed strong growth in print-advertising revenues, peaking in 2005 at nearly $50 billion. Since then, growth in digital news delivery has sent the newspaper industry into a tailspin, losing over half of its advertising revenues in the ensuing decade.

Bill Gates is something of an expert on this subject. Though Microsoft has sustained reasonably strong performance in its legacy businesses over the past few decades, it repeatedly missed opportunities to identify and aggressively exploit new growth opportunities in Internet browsers, search engines, mobile computing, social media, and cloud computing. Reflecting on his company's challenges, founder Bill Gates noted, "Success is a lousy teacher. It seduces smart people into thinking they can't lose."[51]

Burden of Proof

The third inhibiting management mindset is the tendency of industry leaders to impose extremely high burdens of proof before committing resources to promising new technologies, particularly those that might threaten the core business. Managers of industry-leading companies generally have access to large strategic-planning and market-research departments, which are capable of churning out detailed studies of market and technology trends. But the problem with such studies is that they often contribute to "analysis paralysis," leading managers to argue endlessly over methodological details and assumptions.

In the meantime, the pace of new technology adoption has been accelerating rapidly. For example, as shown in figure 11.10, it took

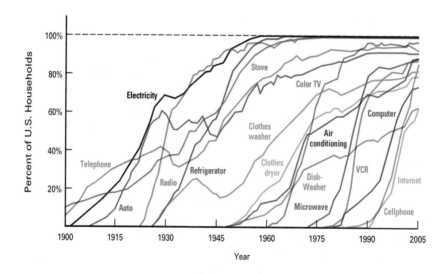

Figure 11.10 Technology adoption rates

over five decades for the telephone to reach 50 percent of U.S. households, starting before 1900. In contrast, it took less than fifteen years for cell phones to accomplish the same market saturation in 2000, and Internet adoption rates have been even faster.[52]

Companies simply don't have the time anymore to dawdle on the sidelines studying market trends before placing bets on emerging technologies. By the time a company knows which disruptive technologies will reshape its industry, it is usually too late to respond. As such, the appropriate management mindset is to commit to constant experimentation aimed at uncovering and gaining experience with emerging disruptive technology opportunities before competitors do.

Overconfidence

All businesses face changes in their market and competitive environments, requiring executives to continuously innovate to maintain meaningful product differentiation. Throughout this book, I have cited examples of dominant industry leaders being toppled by disruptive entrants, often from outside the industry. Yet too many executives remain overconfident in their ability to sustain their company's basis of competitive advantage. They simply live by the adage, "you can't argue with success."

Seth Godin perhaps best captured the dangers of such overconfidence: "You can't argue with success? Of course you can. What else are you going to argue with? Failure can't argue with you, because it knows that it didn't work. The art of staying successful is in being open to having the argument. Great organizations fail precisely because they refuse to do this."[53]

Connecting the Dots

The three strategy frameworks I have reviewed in this chapter provide insightful perspectives on how companies can break away from the pack to create sizeable opportunities for profitable growth, even in industries that are struggling with sluggish demand and slim profit margins. While breakout positioning, Blue Ocean strategy, and disruptive technology frameworks differ in how they characterize competitive dynamics, there are strong commonalities that serve as a checklist for any company seeking game-changing results from new products and services:

- Focus on customers poorly served by mainstream products, including those who have chosen not to consume products in a given category either because of insufficient value or excessive price.
- Identify different performance attributes than those characterizing mainstream products to create a more compelling consumer value proposition for disaffected consumers.
- In doing so, seek to expand the size of the addressable market by unlocking new consumer demand.
- Change the 4Ps—product, price, promotion, and place—underlying how products are brought to market to fundamentally enhance perceived consumer value.
- Make competitors largely irrelevant by reconfiguring products that target previously ignored customers.
- Once a disruptive product has been launched, continuously improve performance and value to expand penetration of the addressable market.
- Be prepared to disrupt your own business when the inevitable onset of Red Ocean market conditions begins to diminish your prospects for continued profitable growth.

CHAPTER TWELVE

Hitting the Bull's-Eye

I WILL END this book where I began, in search of the holy grail of business: long-term profitable growth. I noted at the outset that sustained corporate growth has proven to be an elusive quest, as 87 percent of *Fortune* global 100 companies have been unable to even modestly outperform the market over successive decades.[1]

The problem derives from the inexorable effect of product lifecycles, which erode the sales of all products over time. Unless companies can consistently renew their product and service portfolios to maintain market appeal, their growth, profitability, and even survival are at risk.[2] For example, Nokia and Blackberry are just two of many examples of companies whose once popular products ultimately suffered steep sales declines, without adequate replacements to renew growth. To add to the challenge, product life cycles are shortening across most industries as emerging information technologies continue to streamline product-development processes and replace physical products with digital substitutes.

In the previous three chapters, I presented a number of concepts and techniques to promote the development of meaningfully differentiated products. But I also cautioned that industry incumbents often have great difficulty disrupting themselves and wind up being bested by entrepreneurial newcomers. Nonetheless, long-term profitable growth *is* possible. Just look at high-performing companies like Amazon, Apple, FedEx, Johnson & Johnson, and Starbucks. What can we distill from management best practices that can guide more companies to beat the odds against sustained growth?

Figure 12.1 connects the key themes set forth in this book. Resembling a bull's-eye, the three outer rings establish the requirements for effective corporate leadership: abiding by an appropriate corporate mission, committing to the strategic imperatives for growth, and continuously reinforcing brand equity. As explained below, these management imperatives drive desired business outcomes—the ability to attract and retain customers and competitive resilience—which in turn enables a company to hit the target of long-term profitable growth.

Corporate Mission

As a starting point, a business must establish an appropriate overarching corporate ideology that inspires the organization and provides

Figure 12.1 Strategic imperatives for long-term profitable growth

strategic clarity to all stakeholders on the purpose and priorities of the enterprise. A credible, meaningful, and actionable corporate mission is increasingly important as market environments become ever more dynamic. In every enterprise, new products will come and go, innovative technologies will emerge, customer preferences will shift, management fads will evolve, and new executives will rise up to leadership roles. Despite this dynamism, the core purpose and values underlying the corporate mission of companies that succeed over the long term provide the glue that holds the organization together as it grows, decentralizes, diversifies, expands globally, and develops workplace diversity.[3]

Unfortunately, CEOs often lose touch with the founding corporate vision and instead orient management priorities primarily toward meeting short-term business performance outcomes, like quarterly earnings-per-share targets or near-term sales quotas. As I noted in chapter 3, the problem with such a corporate mindset is that it conflates outcomes with strategy, promoting a decision-making approach in which companies often lose their business—and sometimes even their moral—compass.

For example, a succession of CEOs at Hewlett-Packard (HP) have recently sought to restore growth with ill-considered acquisitions or by propping up short-term profits with R&D cutbacks. The consequence has undermined the company's legacy of technology-driven product superiority and notably failed to restore profitable growth. It is hard to recognize in HP today the clarity of the founders' vision— The HP Way—which cofounder David Packard defined as "a core ideology . . . which includes a deep respect for the individual, a dedication to affordable quality and reliability, a commitment to community responsibility, and a view that the company exists to make technical contributions for the advancement and welfare of humanity."[4] Hewlett-Packard's revenue and profit growth have underperformed its industry peers for more than a decade, as the company has fallen behind in key technologies driving sector growth (e.g., mobile computing and cloud computing), resulting in ongoing waves of corporate downsizing.[5]

Volkswagen (VW) is another example of a company that strayed from what should have been an enduring corporate mission to attract and retain satisfied customers by consistently designing vehicles with superior performance and value. Prior to his resignation, CEO Martin Winterkorn signaled that his top priority was to establish VW as "the world's most profitable, fascinating, and sustainable automobile manufacturer." Winterkorn set extremely ambitious growth targets in an obsessive drive to overtake Toyota and GM as the top-selling automaker, and was well known for his mercurial aversion to performance shortfalls. As one industry analyst put it, "[Winterkorn] doesn't like bad news. Before anyone reports to him, they make sure they have good news."[6]

It is not hard to see how such a management mindset promoted a toxic corporate culture in which the ends justified whatever means were deemed necessary to achieve the CEO's stipulated business outcomes. Volkswagen's resulting widespread fraud over bogus emissions test results has wound up undermining every aspect of the CEO's corporate mandates. In the wake of this scandal, Volkswagen has become unprofitable, demoralized, and the antithesis of a sustainable automobile manufacturer.[7]

Contrast the falls from grace of HP and VW with the corporate missions and managerial focus of companies like Apple, Amazon, and Starbucks, which continue to enjoy profitable growth. Each of these companies has put customers at the center of their corporate mission and has remained committed to their founding ideologies in both good times and bad.

For example, Steve Jobs's original corporate mission for Apple was "to make a contribution to the world by making tools for the mind that advance humankind."[8] Neither Jobs nor his successor, Tim Cook, ever articulated the objectives of becoming the world's most profitable or highest-valued company. Rather, those were the outcomes of Apple's ongoing focus to create beautiful, technologically advanced, easy-to-use products that enrich the lives of consumers, consistent with the company's founding vision.

As another example, Howard Schultz's founding vision for Starbucks was to "inspire and nurture the human spirit, one person, one cup, and one neighborhood at a time." This corporate vision has served as a North Star, guiding Starbucks to create a distinctive and superior customer experience, driving rapid global growth during Schultz's first stint as CEO and again, when he returned to turn around the company after a successor had strayed off course.

As a final example of an enduring commitment to a guiding corporate vision, in his first letter to Amazon shareholders in 1997, Jeff Bezos dedicated his company to "continue to focus relentlessly on our customers and to make investment decisions in light of long-term market leadership considerations rather than short-term profitability considerations or short-term Wall Street reactions."[9]

Bezos has faithfully abided by his founding vision and has led Amazon to achieve the best financial performance of any publicly traded corporation during his tenure as CEO, increasing total shareholder returns by over 20,000 percent.[10] In 2015, Amazon achieved a new milestone: the fastest company ever to exceed $100 billion in sales.

Companies with the best track record of delivering long-term profitable growth have achieved this outcome by executing effective strategies, guided by a customer-centric core mission that creates value for *all* stakeholders—customers, employees, suppliers, shareholders, and the broader communities in which the enterprise operates. Thus an appropriate corporate mission is the logical starting point for achieving the holy grail of business.

Two additional observations are in order to reinforce the importance of an enduring corporate mission, which clearly articulates a company's purpose, values, and core ideology.

North Star or Lip Service?

Of course, virtually every corporation has a corporate mission statement that pushes the right buttons. Hewlett-Packard today continues to affirm its commitment to meaningful innovation, customer loyalty, profit, and growth, even though it has struggled to deliver on any of these aspirations over the past decade.[11] Prior to its bankruptcy, General Motors strived to "develop distinctively designed, high-quality vehicles that truly delight the customer."[12]

Unfortunately, most companies fail to translate their core purpose and values into meaningful actions that bring the corporate mission to life. In chapter 5, I noted that far too many companies can't or don't articulate their strategy clearly to their stakeholders. Or there is a serious disconnect between what senior executives *say* their business strategy and priorities are, and how employees are actually managed and incentivized to behave. This dissonance is almost certain to diminish employee engagement and productivity, detract from customer satisfaction, and undermine long-term business performance.

The 2015 *Harvard Business Review* (*HBR*) ranking of companies with the best long-term financial performance shows that the best performing CEOs have strongly aligned corporate capabilities, assets, incentives, and employee mindsets to execute strategies that reinforce their company's core ideology and corporate mission. For example, I have already cited the management approaches of Amazon (#1) and Starbucks (#37) in this regard. Their financial performance rankings among 907 companies analyzed by *HBR* are shown in parentheses.[13]

Other examples abound. For example, consider FedEx, which ranked thirty-fifth on *HBR*'s list of companies with the best financial performance achieved by current CEOs. Like most companies, FedEx's corporate vision is inspiring and compelling: "FedEx is committed to providing outstanding customer experience, to being a great place to work, a thoughtful steward of the environment, and a caring citizen in the communities where we live and work."

FedEx's corporate mission is genuine and actionable. Over his forty-five-year tenure, founder and CEO Fred Smith has relentlessly reinforced the corporate mission and instilled a clear understanding of corporate priorities across FedEx's workforce of over 250,000 employees. As Smith explains:

> You have to put your money where your mouth is. There isn't a year that's gone by where we haven't invested an enormous amount into trying to make the service better. There have been some years when we could have taken the approach, "You know what? We're not going to try to make the service better. Let's just dial it back by 2 percent. Most people won't notice that, and we can put another 2 percent to the bottom line." We've never done that.
>
> It's also directly related to the culture we've tried to create. Ask any FedEx team member anyplace what the Purple Promise is, and they'll tell you, "I will make every FedEx experience outstanding."[14]

In addition to its track record of long-term profitable growth, FedEx has been consistently included on *Fortune* magazine's lists of the World's Most Admired Companies and 100 Best Companies to Work For.

For companies who have achieved long-term profitable growth like Amazon, Apple, Starbucks, and FedEx, mission statements expressing core ideology and corporate purpose are not just lip service; they serve as a North Star to guide all aspects of the evolving strategic, operational, and management priorities of these enterprises.

Stubbornness versus Flexibility

It seems incongruous, in an era where the pace of change in all aspects of business is shifting so rapidly, to advocate stubborn adherence to a company's core ideology and purpose, which may have been established decades ago. But it is precisely because of, not despite, the rapidly changing business environment that a company needs an anchoring ideology to guide it.

As Jeff Bezos explains:

> It helps to base your strategy on things that won't change. When I'm talking with people outside the company, there's a question that comes up very commonly: "What's going to change in the next five to ten years?" But I very rarely get asked, "What's not going to change in the next five to ten years?" At Amazon we're always trying to figure that out, because you can really spin up flywheels around those things. All the energy you invest in them today will still be paying you dividends ten years from now. Whereas, if you base your strategy first and foremost on more transitory things— who your competitors are, what kind of technologies are available, and so on—those things are going to change so rapidly that you're going to have to change your strategy very rapidly, too.[15]

Amazon's overarching core value is a relentless commitment to superior customer service, whether it's to someone seeking selection, low prices, and fast delivery on Amazon.com, or to a large corporation contracting for cloud storage and data analytics with Amazon Web Services. Amazon's customer-centric core ideology has helped the company make many tough management decisions over the years. For example, many Amazon employees were understandably upset when the proposal to open up Amazon's online store to third-party merchants first surfaced. Amazon's merchandising managers feared such a move would help competitors on Amazon's own website. In another example of a contentious issue, book publishers were anguished when Amazon first proposed replacing curated professional book reviews with user reviews— often negative— on its website.

In explaining Amazon's decision-making approach, Bezos noted that "there's an old Warren Buffett story, that he has three boxes on his desk: in-box, out-box, and too hard. Whenever we're facing one of those too-hard problems, where we get into an infinite loop and can't decide what to do, we try to convert it into a straightforward problem by saying, 'Well, what's better for the consumer?'"[16]

Another principle central to Amazon's core values and to the strategic perspective advocated in my book is the virtue of patience. Companies who strive for long-term profitable growth need to have the patience to invest in products, technologies, and core capabilities that often take years to generate attractive returns. As Bezos notes:

> [W]e are willing to plant seeds and wait a long time for them to turn into trees. I'm very proud of this piece of our culture, because I think it is somewhat rare. We're not always asking ourselves what's going to happen in the next quarter, and focusing on optics, and doing those other things that make it very difficult for some publicly traded companies to have the right strategy. . . . Every new business we've ever engaged in has initially been seen as a distraction by people externally, and sometimes even internally. They'll say, "Why are you expanding outside of media products? Why are you going international? Why are you entering the marketplace business with third-party sellers?" We're getting it now with our new infrastructure web services: "Why take on this new set of developer customers?" These are fair questions. There's nothing wrong with asking them. But they all have at their heart one of the reasons that it's so difficult for incumbent companies to pursue new initiatives. It's because even if they are wild successes, they have no meaningful impact on the company's economics for years. What I have found—and this is an empirical observation; I see no reason why it should be the case, but it tends to be—is that when we plant a seed, it tends to take five to seven years before it has a meaningful impact on the economics of the company.[17]

Summing up the pivotal role of a clear and enduring corporate vision in guiding corporate strategy, Bezos aptly advises to "be stubborn on the vision and flexible on the details."[18]

Strategic Imperatives

Stubborn adherence to a guiding corporate ideology and flexibility in adapting a company's ongoing strategy are the yin and yang of management effectiveness. In Chinese philosophy, the concept of yin and yang refers to how contrary forces are actually complementary.[19] As applied to business, an enduring corporate mission and core ideology helps guide the direction and priorities of an ever-evolving business strategy to drive long-term profitable growth.

Throughout this book, I have advocated three imperatives underscoring effective strategy formulation:

1. *Continuous innovation*, not for its own sake, but to deliver. . . .
2. *Meaningful differentiation*, recognized and valued by consumers, enabled by . . .
3. *Business alignment*, where all corporate capabilities, resources, incentives, and business culture and processes are aligned to support a company's strategic intent.

By delivering innovative and meaningfully differentiated products and services, companies can attract and retain satisfied customers at favorable prices, while making it hard for competitors to replicate their products and practices. These are the essential drivers of long-term profitable growth.

While this prescription for strategic imperatives appears deceptively straightforward, in practice it has proven difficult for most enterprises to execute, underscoring why so few companies can consistently outperform the market. In fact, as I noted in chapter 4, many observers have questioned whether long-term profitable growth is even a realistic goal, given the challenges presented by seemingly immutable forces in the marketplace:

The law of large numbers, which posits the obvious mathematical reality that as a company grows, the incremental revenue required to maintain above-market growth rates becomes ever larger.

The law of competition, which states that companies achieving above-average returns on invested capital will inevitably revert to the industry mean because superior returns will continue to attract new entrants until profit premiums have been competed away.

The law of competitive advantage, which invokes the properties of product life cycles that cause the sales and profit potential of all products to erode over time.

Proponents of intrinsic limits to sustained growth, like Malcolm Gladwell, believe that market leaders have inherent liabilities that make them vulnerable to brash upstarts. In Gladwell's revisionist view of the biblical tale of David and Goliath, dim-witted and ponderous Goliath was actually the underdog in his battle against fearless, agile, and resourceful David.[20]

But as applied to business, this viewpoint is not just flawed, but could become a self-fulfilling prophecy of corporate failure. If management believes that long-term above-market profitable growth *is* impossible, a logical response would be to protect and harvest current assets and customers for as long as possible. But such an approach—playing not to lose instead of playing to win—serves only to hasten the decline of incumbent market leaders. The biblical Goliath may have been a ponderous oaf, but CEOs in large enterprises don't have to be. As numerous examples cited in this book attest, business Goliaths can continue to prosper if they maintain the core values, entrepreneurial spirit, and adaptability that led to their success in the first place.

Brand Equity

In chapter 7, I made the logical connection between the requirements for effective business strategy and brand strategy. As shown in figure 12.1, companies that continuously innovate to deliver meaningfully differentiated products and services can enhance brand equity by reinforcing their *brand promise*, sustaining *mutual trust*, and strengthening the *symbolic identity* that consumers associate with strong brands.

Companies that consistently execute the three pillars of effective business strategy—continuous innovation, meaningful differentiation, and business alignment—generally have the strongest brand equity and outpace their industry peers in delivering superior customer satisfaction. Table 12.1 displays a representative sample of companies who were rated highest in customer satisfaction in 2015 within their industry category, as measured by the American Customer Satisfaction Index.[21] These companies have continued to strengthen their brands and serve customers well despite a decline in the average level of U.S. customer satisfaction in 2015, which plunged to its lowest level in nine years.[22]

I've already mentioned many of these companies earlier in this book as exemplars of successful business and brand strategies. For example, JetBlue built its brand image on a founding corporate vision of "bringing

TABLE 12.1
Customer Satisfaction Leaders by Industry

Industry Sector	Leading Company	Leader Score*	Sector Lowest-Average Score*
Airlines	JetBlue	81	54–71
Autos and light trucks	Lexus	84	73–79
Cellular telephones	Apple	81	71–78
Consumer shipping	FedEx	82	75–81
Health and personal care stores	Kroger	81	75–81
Department and discount stores	Nordstrom	86	68–77
Hotels	Marriott/Hilton/ Hyatt	80	63–75
Internet retail	Amazon	86	77–82
Personal computers	Apple	84	70–77
Specialty retail	Costco	84	75–79
Supermarkets	Trader Joe's	85	71–76

* 0–100 scale

humanity back to air travel."[23] From the airline's inception, consumers recognized and valued JetBlue's innovative approaches to airline service: in-flight entertainment systems, luxurious leather seats with the most legroom room in the industry, premium snacks, and friendly cabin service.

But to renew its brand promise and maintain industry-leading customer satisfaction over the past sixteen years, JetBlue has continued to innovate and reinforce an organizational commitment to core brand values. For example, within the past year, JetBlue added the fastest onboard Wi-Fi, a new premium-class cabin on selected flights, and additional international and domestic routes. To remain true to its brand voice, JetBlue has continued to ensure that its five core values—safety, caring, integrity, passion, and fun—are embraced by each of its more than eighteen thousand employees. To do so, JetBlue holds biweekly orientation programs, where every new employee is personally greeted and trained by C-level executives. Ongoing training with top-level executive participation ensures the airline's organizational mindset remains aligned with its core values, and supports its basis of competitive advantage. JetBlue's strategy is committed to making all company employees ambassadors of the brand. As shown in figure 12.2, customers recognize and value the effort.

Business Outcomes: Hitting the Bull's-Eye of Long-Term Profitable Growth

The mutually reinforcing elements of effective business and brand strategy provide the basis to attract and retain customers and create competitive resilience, which positions leading companies to achieve long-term profitable growth. In its sixteenth year of operation, JetBlue's revenue and operating profit growth significantly outpaced the U.S. airline industry average, and patient investors have seen their shareholder value over the past five years appreciate at a growth rate nearly three times higher than the index of all U.S. airline stocks.[24]

As a final example of how all the elements of effective management combine to hit the bull's-eye depicted in figure 12.1, consider how Costco has achieved exceptional long-term profitable growth and created value for all corporate stakeholders.

Corporate Mission

Costco's mission statement is succinct, easy for all stakeholders to understand, and clearly focuses the company's primary priorities on serving customers and employees. Reinforcing core values yields the desired outcome of rewarding shareholders.[25]

Costco Mission

To continually provide our members with quality goods and services at the lowest possible prices.

In order to achieve our mission we will conduct our business with the following Code of Ethics in mind:

1. Obey the law.
2. Take care of our members.
3. Take care of our employees.
4. Respect our suppliers.

If we do these four things throughout our organization, then we will achieve our ultimate goal, which is to:

5. Reward our shareholders.

As Costco explains:

- Our members (customers) are our reason for being—the key to our success. If we don't keep our members happy, little else that we do will make a difference.
- Our employees are our most important asset. . . . We are committed to providing them with rewarding challenges and ample opportunities for personal and career growth . . . and pledge to provide our employees with competitive wages and great benefits.
- Our suppliers are our partners in business, and for us to prosper as a company they must prosper with us. To that end, we strive to treat all suppliers and their representatives as we would expect to be treated if visiting their places of business.
- Our shareholders are our business partners. We can only be successful so long as we are providing them with a good return on the money they invest in our Company. This, too, involves the element of trust. They trust us to use their investment wisely and to operate our business in such a way that it is profitable.[26]

By clearly articulating the company's purpose, priorities, and values, Costco's mission statement serves as a guide to its ongoing strategy development.

Strategic Imperatives

Costco's strategy embodies the three imperatives of *continuous innovation* to drive *meaningful differentiation* supported by *aligned business practices*, allowing it to deliver on its corporate mission "to continually provide our members with quality goods and services at the lowest possible prices."

Costco's strategy helps drive its competitive advantage. By relying on membership fees for over three-fourths of its operating profits, Costco is able to cap its price markups at half the level typically charged by Walmart, Target, and other big-box retailers. Costco is also in a position to offer lower prices by exploiting competitive cost advantages, driven in part by sharply limiting the number of brands and packaging sizes it carries (for example, four SKUs of toothpaste, versus sixty at Walmart).[27] Costco's limited product variety enables it to increase its purchasing scale and bargaining power while reducing logistics, handling, and stockout costs. Costco also shuns virtually all forms of mass advertising and promotions, saving another 2 percent of revenue compared to other grocery chains and big-box retailers.

To enhance profit margins, Costco has been steadily expanding the number of categories covered under its private-label Kirkland brand, which currently accounts for over 20 percent of sales. Its overall assortment strategy generally skews toward higher-quality merchandise, which appeals to its upscale customer base. Costco members reportedly have twice the average income of Walmart shoppers, giving them the discretionary spending power to afford annual membership fees and to buy staple items in bulk. In summary, the key elements of Costco's strategy are well suited to the needs of its target upscale market, fulfilling its enduring mission of consistently delivering a demonstrably superior consumer value proposition.

Costco's strategy has also faithfully fulfilled its corporate mission to take care of its employees. The warehouse retailer pays its workers roughly twice the hourly wage of Walmart employees, and provides superior health-care coverage, retirement-account contributions, and vacation-time allowances.[28] In 2014, Costco ranked second (behind Google) as the company whose employees were most satisfied with their compensation, and sixteenth overall in Glassdoor's ranking of Best Places to Work.[29] The company's generosity toward workers has yielded significant business benefits. Relative to its parsimonious competitors, Costco employees are more engaged, productive, and loyal. This reflects Costco's ability to attract and retain higher-caliber employees to deliver higher-quality service, while allowing the company to reduce the costs and operational problems associated with high turnover rates. Despite its higher wage rates and superior benefits, Costco generates nearly three times the sales per employee and 40 percent higher profits per employee than Walmart.[30]

Brand Equity

By consistently delivering on its brand promise, Costco attracts and retains highly satisfied customers (see table 12.1), who trust and identify with the brand. Word-of-mouth referrals from customer evangelists have helped Costco boost its membership base. Despite its aversion to advertising and a recent increase in annual dues, Costco has grown its membership by 35 percent over the past five years and enjoys a 91 per-cent customer renewal rate in the United States.[31] These are indicative validators of Costco's exceptionally strong brand.

Hitting the Bull's-eye

Costco is an exemplar that embraces all the requisites for long-term profitable growth illustrated in figure 12.1. From its inception, Costco established an actionable corporate mission that clearly articulated its purpose and customer- and employee-centric core values. While Costco has remained true to its founding vision, its strategy has evolved through continuous innovation to renew and strengthen its basis of meaningful differentiation. Costco's business model is strongly aligned with the company's core mission, helping to drive consistently strong business outcomes.

Costco has hit the bull's-eye of long-term profitable growth. Figure 12.2 shows the growth in Costco's revenues, operating profits, and shareholder value relative to its two primary competitors between 2010 and 2015. In addition to delivering exceptional returns to sharehold-ers, Costco has also created considerable value for all its stakeholders— its customers, employees, and suppliers, and the growing number of communities in which it operates.

The holy grail of long-term profitable growth may be elusive, but it is not beyond reach. I hope this book will prove to be a useful guide for your quest.

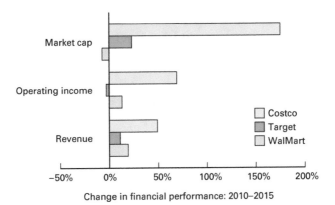

Figure 12.2 Business outcomes: Costco vs. Walmart and Target

Notes

Preface

1. Toni C. Langlinais, and Marco A. Merino, "How to Sustain Profitable Growth," *Accenture Outlook*, September 2007, http://www.accenture.com /SiteCollectionDocuments/PDF/OutlookPDF_FutureGrowth_03.pdf.

2. Audio file available at http://www.bain.com/bainweb/media/breeze /five-pillars-of-sustainable-growth.

3. Matthew S. Olson, Derek van Bever, and Seth Verry, "When Growth Stalls," *Harvard Business Review*, March 2008.

1. The Origins of Modern Business Strategy Thinking

1. Michael E. Porter, "How Competitive Forces Shape Strategy," *Harvard Business Review* 57, 2 (March–April 1979): 137–145.

2. Martin Reeves, Sandy Moose, and Thijs Venema, "BCG Classics Revisited: The Growth Share Matrix," *BCG Perspectives,* June 4, 2014.

3. Buffett made this observation in 1989. See Carol J. Loomis, "The Wit and Wisdom of Warren Buffett," *Fortune Magazine,* November 19, 2012.

4. Lee Dranikoff, Tim Koller, and Antoon Schneider, "Divestiture: Strategy's Missing Link," *Harvard Business Review,* May, 2002.

5. Jack Welch was CEO of GE from 1981 to 2001. See "There's Just One Word For Jack Welch," *Knowledge@Wharton,* September 13, 2001.

6. Since Welch's retirement in 2001, GE's market capitalization has declined by more than 40 percent. Whether the company's declining valuation reflects weak performance by Welch's successor or that GE's historical success was built on risky, overleveraged forays into financial services is open to debate. Under any circumstances, there is no question that Welch aggressively reconfigured GE's business portfolio during his tenure as CEO.

7. *In Search of Excellence* sold over three million copies, becoming the first business book to reach a mass audience. See http://tompeters.com/writing /books.

8. From Jim Collins's author website. See http://www.jimcollins.com /about-jim.html.

9. Extracted from the following Jim Collins books: *Built to Last* (New York: HarperCollins, 1994) and *Good to Great* (New York: HarperCollins, 2011).

10. Jim Collins acknowledges that based on his research, he cannot claim a definitive causal relationship because the rigorous experiments required to establish true causality simply do not exist in the real world of management. Rather, he asserts that "the variables we identify in our research are correlated with the performance patterns we study, and we cannot claim a definitive *causal* relationship." But as noted in this chapter, strong "halo effects" associated with his data render his results more tautological than correlative, and therefore have questionable value. For a more complete description of Collins's research methods, see http://www.jimcollins.com/books/research.html.

11. An excellent explanation of this phenomenon is described in IMD professor Phil Rosenzweig's *The Halo Effect . . . and Eight Other Business Delusions That Deceive Managers* by IMD professor Phil Rosenzweig, (New York: Free Press, 2009). Also, the halo effect is more broadly discussed in behavioral economics terms in Daniel Kahneman's *Thinking, Fast and Slow*, (New York: Farrar, Straus, and Giroux, 2011).

12. Michael V. Copeland, "Reed Hastings: Leader of the Pack," *Fortune Magazine*, November 18, 2010.

13. For an example of subsequent criticism, see Dave Smith, "Netflix Earnings Release: Why Reed Hastings Needs to Go," *International Business Times*, "October 24, 2011.

14. Adam Lashinsky, "How Tim Cook Is Changing Apple," *Fortune*, May 24, 2012.

15. Al Gore, "The World's 100 Most Influential People," *Time*, 2012.

16. Nick Bilton, "Disruptions: Will Apple Be the First to Break $1 Trillion?" *New York Times*, September 23, 2012.

17. Ian Sherr and Evan Ramstad, "Has Apple Lost Its Cool to Samsung," *Wall Street Journal*, January 13, 2013.

18. Greg Satell, "The Problem with Tim Cook," *Forbes*, February 13, 2013, http://www.forbes.com/sites/gregsatell/2013/02/13/the-problem -with-tim-cook.

19. An excellent analysis of the analytical flaws in Collins's books is covered by Michael E. Raynor, Mumtaz Ahmed, and Andrew D. Henderson, "Are 'Great' Companies Just Lucky," *Harvard Business Review*, April 2009.

20. Judith H. Dobrzynski, "Rethinking IBM," *Bloomberg Businessweek*, October 4, 1993, http://www.businessweek.com/stories/1993-10-03 /rethinking-ibm.

21. James C. Collins and Jerry I. Porras, *Built to Last: Successful Habits of Visionary Companies* (New York: HarperCollins, 1994), and James C. Collins and William C. Lazier, *Beyond Entrepreneurship: Turning Your Business into an Enduring Great Company* (Paramus, NJ: Prentice Hall, 1995).

22. Clayton M. Christensen, *The Innovator's Dilemma: When New Technologies Cause Great Firms to Fail* (Boston, MA: Harvard Business School Press, 1997).

23. The term "sustaining technology improvement" in Christensen's book refers to the continuous improvement all companies make to their core products over time. For example, each new generation of personal computer has a faster processor, more storage, and a higher resolution screen. At some point, the state-of-the-art PC becomes more than good enough for most consumers, opening opportunities for disruptive newcomers to find more cost-effective products to satisfy the needs of overserved customers.

24. The term "creative destruction" was first popularized by Austrian economist Joseph Schumpeter in the 1940s. The term refers to the process of industrial transformation that incessantly revolutionizes the economic structure from within, incessantly destroying the old one, incessantly creating a new one. Christensen recognizes that the forces underlying his disruptive technology theory have been present for centuries. His theory attempts to explain why such forces are so pervasive and inevitable.

25. In his original book, *The Innovator's Dilemma*, Christensen focused primarily on explaining his theory of disruptive technology, drawing on a wide range of industry examples. But he offered little advice on how incumbent companies could avoid becoming victims of disruption. His next book, *The Innovator's Solution*, co-authored with Michael Raynor in 2003, showed how businesses can effectively disrupt themselves to sustain long-term growth. Christensen then co-authored *Seeing What's Next: Using the Theories of Innovation to Predict Industry Change* with Scott Anthony and Erik Roth in 2004 to predict how disruptive changes might impact the future development of several dynamic industries, including education, aviation, telecommunication, semiconductors, and health care. Christensen also applied his framework to explain the dynamic growth or stagnation of national economies as discussed in Clayton M. Christensen, Thomas Craig, and Stuart Hart, "The Great Disruption," *Foreign Affairs*, March/April 2001.

26. Thinkers50 has been dubbed the Oscars of management thinking, recognizing the most influential contribution to business theory every two years. Clayton Christensen earned the top award in 2011 and 2013. See http://www.thinkers50.com.

27. *Brandchannel*, May 2, 2014, http://www.brandchannel.com/home/post/2014/05/02/140502-Taco-Bell-Disruption.aspx.

28. For example, TBWA Worldwide, a unit of Omnicom, has conducted hundreds of "Disruption Days" with its clients, which are intended to brainstorm

new disruptive business ideas. See http://www.the-chiefexecutive.com/features/feature71671.

29. Jill Lepore, "The Disruption Machine: What the Gospel of Innovation Gets Wrong," *New Yorker*, June 23, 2014. Former Harvard Business School professor Clark Gilbert responded to Lepore in a defense of the validity of Christensen's work. See http://www.forbes.com/sites/forbesleadershipforum/2014/06/30/what-jill-lepore-gets-wrong-about-clayton-christensen-and-disruptive-innovation.

30. Frederick E. Allen, "Is Clayton Christensen's 'Disruptive Innovation' a Myth?" *Forbes*, June 17, 2014, http://www.forbes.com/sites/frederickallen/2014/06/17/is-clayton-christensens-disruptive-innovation-a-myth.

31. Larry Downes and Paul Nunes, *Big Bang Disruption: Strategy in the Age of Devastating Innovation* (New York: Portfolio, 2014).

32. Steve Denning, "Business's Worst Nightmare: Big Bang Disruption," *Forbes*, January 7, 2014, http://www.forbes.com/sites/stevedenning/2014/01/07/businesss-worst-nightmare-big-bang-disruption.

33. Downes and Nunes, *Big Bang Disruption*.

34. Rita Gunther McGrath, *The End of Competitive Advantage: How to Keep Your Strategy Moving as Fast as Your Business* (Boston, MA: Harvard Business School Press, 2013).

35. Youngme Moon, *Different: Escaping the Competitive Herd* (New York: Crown Business, 2010).

36. Ibid.

37. See http://littlemissmatched.com/t/category/girls-socks.

38. W. Chan Kim and Renée Mauborgne, *Blue Ocean Strategy* (Boston, MA: Harvard Business School Press, 2005).

39. John R. Graham, Campbell R. Harvey, and Shiva Rajgopal, "The Economic Implications of Corporate Financial Reporting," *National Bureau of Economic Research*, Working Paper 10550, June 2004, http://www.nber.org/papers/w10550.

40. Phil McKinney, former chief technology officer of Hewlett-Packard, observed that a high percentage of new project ventures in large corporations are terminated after eighteen months. McKinney's "Rule of Eighteen Months" posits that a new venture typically starts halfway through a fiscal year with funding cobbled together from existing budgets, based on high, and likely unrealistic, expectations for project results. When the next full budget cycle comes around, the project is well underway and the funding is all but assured, given that no one expects the project to have any impact—yet. The next funding decision is a different issue. When the second budget cycle comes around, new priorities often crowd out ongoing development efforts, particularly those saddled with unrealistic financial targets. Phil McKinney, "Why Projects are Cancelled for the Wrong Reasons," *Forbes*, March 10, 2011,

http://www.forbes.com/sites/philmckinney/2011/03/10/why-projects
-are-cancelled-for-the-wrong-reasons.

41. PwC, "Unleashing the Power of Innovation," July 2013, http://press
.pwc.com/GLOBAL/innovation-a-top-priority-for-business/s/918ccaab
-2d82-4889-bc41-9905b3a4b9ec.

42. Joanna Barsh, Marla M. Capozzi, and Jonathan Davidson, "Leadership
and Innovation," *McKinsey Quarterly*, January 2008.

43. Ibid.

44. Karen Brettell, David Gaffen, and David Rohde, "As Stock Buybacks
Reach Historic Levels, Signs That Corporate America Is Undermining
Itself," *Reuters Investigates*, November 16, 2015, http://www.reuters.com
/investigates/special-report/usa-buybacks-cannibalized.

45. William Lazonick, "Profits Without Prosperity," *Harvard Business
Review*, September 2014.

46. Quote attributed to Chris Bouffard, chief investment officer of Mutual
Fund Store overseeing $9 billion, as quoted in http://www.bloomberg
.com/news/2014-10-06/s-p-500-companies-spend-almost-all-profits-on
-buybacks-payouts.html.

47. Booz Allen Hamilton has gone through two metamorphoses since
my employment there. In 2008, the corporate consulting group was spun
off from the government consulting practice under the new name Booz &
Company. In 2013, Booz was acquired by PricewaterhouseCoopers, taking
on the new name Strategy&.

48. C. K. Prahalad and Gary Hamel, *Competing for the Future* (Boston,
MA: Harvard Business School Press, 1994).

49. Another strong proponent of capabilities-driven strategy was advo-
cated by Paul Leinwand and Cesare R. Mainardi, *The Essential Advantage:
How to Win with a Capabilities-Driven Strategy* (Boston, MA: Harvard
Business Review Press, 2010).

50. Chris Zook and James Allen, *Profit from the Core: A Return to Growth
in Turbulent Times* (Boston, MA: Harvard Business School Press, 2001), and
Chris Zook, *Beyond the Core: Expand Your Market Without Abandoning Your
Roots* (Boston, MA: Harvard Business School Press, 2003).

51. George S. Day and Christine Moorman, *Strategy from the Outside In:
Profiting from Customer Value* (New York: McGraw-Hill, 2010).

52. James Womack and Daniel Jones, *The Machine That Changed the
World* (New York: Free Press, 1990).

53. W. Edwards Deming, *Out of the Crisis* (Cambridge, MA: MIT Press,
1986).

54. Larry Bossidy and Ram Charan, *Execution: The Discipline of Getting
Things Done* (New York: Crown Business, 2002).

55. Bossidy and Charan, *Execution*.

56. Casella Family Brands in New South Wales, Australia, and Deutsch Family Wine & Spirits in White Plains, New York, co-launched Yellow Tail wine in the U.S., which will be the focus of chapter 2.

2. There's No Such Thing as a Bad Industry

1. Merrill Research & Associates, Wine Trends and Market Analysis.

2. Market research has shown that wine consumers are far more likely to shop for a wine varietal (e.g., merlot or chardonnay) than a country of origin. Imagine how odd it would be to shop for a television in a store that had separate display areas for televisions from Korea, Japan, and the United States, rather than aggregating all televisions by size or price class.

3. Internet Wire, "New Survey Shows 'Wine Anxiety' Is Widespread, Canyon Road Winery Tracks Consumer Wine Fears, Offers Solutions," August 23, 2002, https://business.highbeam.com/436102/article-1G1-90703907 /new-survey-shows-wine-anxiety-widespread-canyon-road.

4. Quote from James T. Lapsley, a winemaker, author, and member of the faculty of University of California, Davis Viticulture and Enology Department. Quote cited in W. Chan Kim, Renée Mauborgne, Jason Hunter, Brian Marks, and Wayne Mortensen, "Crafting Winning Strategies in a Mature Market: The US Wine Industry in 2001," *Harvard Business Review*, July 2009.

5. Unless otherwise indicated, quotes attributed to Bill Deutsch in this chapter are taken from conversations with the author.

6. Frank J. Prial, "The Wallaby That Roared Across the Wine Industry," *New York Times*, April 23, 2006.

7. Quoted verbatim from bottles of Château de Fontenille, Grand Vin de Bordeaux (2005), Château D'Arcins, Haut Medoc (2006), and Yellow Tail Shiraz (2001).

8. Kim et al., "Crafting Winning Strategies."

9. Frank J. Prial, "The Wallaby That Roared Across the Wine Industry," *New York Times*, April 23, 2006.

10. It's important to note that the notion of wine being a product for everyday, casual consumption as opposed to a beverage reserved for special occasions is not at all unusual elsewhere. Yellow Tail achieved its most notable meaningful differentiation in the United States. Although Casella Family Brands exports Yellow Tail wine throughout Europe, Asia, and South America, the United States accounts for twice the consumption of the rest of the world combined.

11. AC Nielson, Yellow Tail Impact Study, 2004.

12. Prial, "The Wallaby That Roared Across the Wine Industry."

13. MIT Global Airline Industry Program, Airline Data Project, http:// web.mit.edu/airlinedata/www/Traffic&Capacity.html.

14. Brian Pearce, "Profitability and the Air Transport Value Chain," International Air Transport Association Briefing No. 10, June 2013, https://www.iata.org/whatwedo/Documents/economics/profitability-and-the-air-transport-value%20chain.pdf.

15. Michael E. Porter, "The Five Competitive Forces That Shape Strategy," *Harvard Business Review*, January 2008. Figure 2.5 depicts a subset of the industries shown in the analysis presented in the article.

16. For example, in surveys conducted by Glassdoor on employee satisfaction across all industries, Southwest ranked numbers 1 and 2 in 2010 and 2011 respectively. Southwest has also been consistently at or near the top of airline customer satisfaction rankings, based on research conducted by ACSI and J. D. Power & Associates.

17. Pat Cataldo, "Focusing on Employee Engagement: How to Measure It and Improve It," *UNC Kenan Flagler Business School*, 2011.

18. "The Twelve Greatest Entrepreneurs of Our Time," *Fortune*, April 2012, http://archive.fortune.com/galleries/2012/news/companies/1203/gallery.greatest-entrepreneurs.fortune/index.html.

19. Total shareholder return is the percentage increase in stock price appreciation including reinvested dividends achieved over a specified time period.

20. Evan Hirsh and Kasturi Rangan, "The Grass Isn't Greener," *Harvard Business Review,* January–February 2013.

21. Andrew Goldman, "Bubble? What Bubble?" *New York Times*, July 7, 2011, http://www.nytimes.com/2011/07/10/magazine/marc-andreessen-on-the-dot-com-bubble.html?_r=1&.

22. J. L. Pfeiffer, "Their Careers Hint at Where Not to Go: A Tip from Harvard MBAs," *New York Times*, January 29, 1994.

23. William Vijverberg, "MBA Job Placement and Stock Market Performance," Stanford University Economics Department, May 10, 2010, https://economics.stanford.edu/sites/default/files/publications/vijverberg_hthesis2010.pdf. This paper demonstrates that job choices are a reliable indicator of past industry performance, but not of future performance.

24. "Banks? No thanks!" *The Economist*, October 11, 2013.

25. Barefoot Cellars was founded in 1986 by industry newcomers Michael Houlihan and Bonnie Harvey. Long before Yellow Tail hit U.S. shores, Houlihan and Harvey had the idea that it was time for a wine that didn't take itself too seriously. They chose the name Barefoot because it was easy to pronounce and used the foot imprint of one of their founders as the brand logo. They initially ran the company out of their home on a shoestring budget, relying heavily on word-of-mouth referrals and "cause marketing" (trading wine supplied to non-profit organizations at fund-raising events for free publicity) to gain consumer awareness. After twenty years of operation, Barefoot was selling about five hundred thousand cases, primarily in the western United

States. Since being acquired by Gallo in 2005, Barefoot sales have grown to over ten million cases nationally. See Michael Houlihan and Bonnie Harvey, "The Barefoot Spirit: How Hardship, Hustle, and Heart Built America's #1 Wine Brand," *Evolve*, 2013.

26. Data provided by Deutsch Family Wines & Spirits.

27. Data provided by Deutsch Family Wines & Spirits.

28. Analysis based on data from the Airline Data Project, MIT Airline Industry Program, http://web.mit.edu/airlinedata/www/Expenses&Related.html.

29. Southwest's average pilot wage in 2013 was 66 percent higher than the industry average. Nonetheless, by operating at high productivity levels, Southwest is able to serve 72 percent more passengers per flight crew than the U.S. airline average. After adjusting Southwest's costs for stage-length differences, as shown in figure 2.11 Southwest maintains a considerable (33 percent) cost advantage over larger legacy airline rivals on an adjusted cost per available seat mile basis.

3. Why Are We in Business?

1. Michael Jensen and William Meckling, "Theory of the Firm: Managerial Behavior, Agency Costs and Ownership Structure," *Journal of Financial Economics* 3, 4 (October 1976): 305–360. By the end of 2014, this article had been cited in almost forty-six thousand academic articles.

2. Friedman was the head of the Economics Department at the University of Chicago and won the Nobel Prize for Economics in 1976. He has been described by the *Economist* as the "most influential economist of the second half of the twentieth century . . . possibly all of it."

3. Milton Friedman, "The Social Responsibility of Business Is to Increase Its Profits," *New York Times*, September 13, 1970.

4. "The Jack Welch MBA," *Economist*, June 23, 2009.

5. Geoffrey Colvin, "The Ultimate Manager," *Fortune*, November 22, 1999.

6. Francesco Guerrera, "Welch Condemns Share Price Focus," *Financial Times*, March 12, 2009.

7. Jack Welch and John A. Byrne, *Jack: Straight from the Gut* (Business Plus, 2001), 224–225.

8. Roger Martin, "The Age of Customer Capitalism," *Harvard Business Review*, January–February 2010.

9. Clayton M. Christensen, "Are Investors Bad for Business," *Harvard Business Review*, June, 2014. Christensen's primary concern is with the inappropriate financial metrics used by many senior executives in managing the

business with an overly short-term focus. His views are strongly related to but not specifically directed at MSV doctrine per se.

10. William Lazonick, "Profits Without Prosperity," *Harvard Business Review*, September, 2014.

11. Jeff Bezos, "Letter to Shareholders," [], 1997, Amazon Investor Relations Website http://media.corporate-ir.net/media_files/irol/97/97664 /reports/Shareholderletter97.pdf. Bezos's primary concern is with the short-term orientation of many CEOs who are trying to maximize shareholder value. He also subordinates the interests of Amazon shareholders seeking short-term gains to an enduring commitment to deliver superior customer service.

12. Caroline Fairchild, "Starbucks CEO Howard Schultz: 'Profitability Is a Shallow Goal,'" *Huffington Post*, June 28, 2013. Schultz's primary concern is with the need for broader societal objectives, beyond MSV, in managing the enterprise.

13. Martin Wolf, "Opportunist Shareholders Must Embrace Commitment," *Financial Times*, August 26, 2014.

14. Steve Denning, "The Dumbest Idea in the World: Maximizing Shareholder Value," *Forbes*, November 28, 2011.

15. Wolf, "Opportunist Shareholders."

16. William Lazonick pointed out that companies have generally timed their stock purchases poorly (Lazonick, "Profits Without Prosperity"). Stock buyback activity tends to be highest when a company's stock price is high and lowest when its stock price is depressed. This pattern contradicts a commonly cited rationale for stock buybacks as occurring when a company believes its stock is undervalued.

17. Eric Olsen, Frank Plaschke, and Daniel Stelter, "Avoiding the Cash Trap: The Challenge of Value Creation When Profits Are High," *BCG Perspectives*, September 2007.

18. Olsen et al., "Avoiding the Cash Trap." In the referenced study, BCG found that investors preferred that companies seeking to return profits to shareholders do so in the form of dividends rather than share buybacks.

19. Clayton M. Christensen and Derek van Bever, "The Capitalist's Dilemma," *Harvard Business Review*, June 2014.

20. Ibid.

21. Alyssa Davis and Lawrence Mishel, "CEO Pay Continues to Rise as Typical Workers Are Paid Less," *Economic Policy Institute*, June 12, 2014.

22. Lazonick, "Profits Without Prosperity."

23. Peter F. Drucker, *The Practice of Management* (HarperBusiness, 2006). Originally published in 1954.

24. Telis Demos, "Alibaba IPO Biggest in History as Bankers Exercise 'Green Shoe' Option," *Wall Street Journal*, September 21, 2014.

25. Ryan Mac, "As Alibaba's IPO Approaches, Founder Jack Ma Pens Letter to Potential Investors," *Forbes*, September 5, 2014.

26. Bezos, "Letter to Shareholders."

27. Through the end of 2015, Amazon has executed only four share repurchases, amounting in aggregate to approximately 3 percent of its float. These targeted share repurchases, executed during periods of low stock-market valuations, have delivered triple-digit returns to shareholders, based on subsequent stock price movements. See J. Allen Capital Management, Investor Newsletter, October 14, 2014, http://jallencapitalmanagement.com/posts/amzn-amazons-share-repurchases.html.

28. Matthew Yglesias, "Amazon Profits Fall 45 Percent, Still the Most Amazing Company in the World," *Slate*, January 29, 2013.

29. American Customer Satisfaction Index, http://www.theacsi.org/customer-satisfaction-benchmarks.

30. Harvard Business Review Staff, "The Best-Performing CEOs in the World," *Harvard Business Review*, November 2015, https://hbr.org/2015/11/the-best-performing-ceos-in-the-world.

31. "The Institutional Yes: An Interview with Jeff Bezos," *Harvard Business Review*, October 1, 2007.

32. J&J company website, accessed June 1, 2016, http://www.jnj.com/about-jnj/jnj-credo.

33. Denning, "The Dumbest Idea in the World."

34. Ed Wallace, "When GM First Messed Up," *Bloomberg Businessweek*, June 4, 2009.

35. Mike Spector and Christopher M. Matthews, "U.S. Charges GM with Wire Fraud, Concealing Facts on Ignition Switch," *Wall Street Journal*, September 17, 2015.

36. Rachel Abrams, "Lumber Liquidators Chief Robert Lynch Resigns," *New York Times*, May 21, 2015.

37. "About IKEA," IKEA United Kingdom website, accessed June 1, 2016, http://www.ikea.com/ms/en_GB/about_ikea/the_ikea_way/our_business_idea/a_better_everyday_life.html.

38. "IKEA Group Yearly Summary FY15," IKEA U.S. website, accessed June 1, 2016, http://www.ikea.com/ms/en_US/pdf/yearly_summary/IKEA_Group_Yearly_Summary_2015.pdf.

39. Howard Schultz and Joanne Gordon, *Onward: How Starbucks Fought for Its Life Without Losing Its Soul* (Rodale Books, 2011), 273–274.

40. John H. Ostdick, "Rekindling the Heart and Soul of Starbucks," *Success*, March 6, 2011.

41. Nancy F. Koehn, Kelly McNamara, Nora N. Khan, and Elizabeth Legris, "Starbucks Coffee Company: Transformation and Renewal," *Harvard Business School Publishing*, Case 9-314-068, June 2, 2014.

42. Drucker, *The Practice of Management.*

43. "Benchmarks by Industry," American Customer Satisfaction Index, accessed [June 1, 2016], http://www.theacsi.org/index.php?option=com _content&view=article&id=148&Itemid=213. The two industries at the very bottom of the American Customer Satisfaction Index are (cable) subscription television services and Internet service providers. Most customers of companies in these industries would gladly and instantly switch providers if and when a viable alternative emerges.

4. The Search for the Holy Grail of Business: Long-Term Profitable Growth

1. A company's market valuation at any given time reflects the discounted value of expected future cash flows, not profits or margins per se. But cash flows are derived from a company's revenues and profit margins, which in turn are directly influenced by management action throughout the enterprise. The point of this section is to decompose the drivers of shareholder value into specific management actions that individually and collectively affect shareholder value.

2. Peter F. Drucker, *The Practice of Management* (New York: HarperBusiness, 2006). Originally published in 1954.

3. Comments by Rob Maruster, chief operating officer of JetBlue, at the employee orientation session, August 28, 2013.

4. JetBlue Airways, "Customer Bill of Rights," http://www.jetblue.com /flying-on-jetblue/customer-protection.

5. Christopher Elliott, "If You Want Decent Customer Service, These Are the Airlines to Fly," *Fortune,* May 13, 2015, http://fortune.com/2015/05/13 /airlines-jd-power-survey/.

6. This definition is somewhat simplified for clarity. Other factors added in the calculation of enterprise value are the equity value of preferred shareholders and minority interests, while cash equivalents (e.g., accounts receivable) are usually subtracted along with cash.

7. Free cash flow is defined as a company's cash from operating activities net of capital expenditures required to sustain current operations. For ease of calculation, free cash flow is often computed by netting total capital expenditures from operating cash flow.

8. Jason D. Schloetzer, Matteo Tonello, and Melissa Aguilar, "CEO Succession Practices: 2014," *The Conference Board,* Report Number: *TCB _R*-1544-14-R, April 9, 2014.

9. Matthew S. Olson, Derek van Bever, and Seth Verry, "When Growth Stalls," *Harvard Business Review*, March 2008. The CEB study focused on revenue rather than profit or earnings growth. The authors note that no

company can sustain profitless growth over the long term, so focusing on topline performance is a reliable indicator of long-term business performance.

10. To be more specific, the CEB study established three criteria to define a stall. First, real revenue growth in the prior decade had to be at least 2 percent. Second, real growth after the stall had to be less than 6 percent. That is, companies who continue to enjoy greater than 6 percent real revenue growth are not considered to have stalled, even if prior decade growth was in double digits. And finally, the difference in revenue growth in the decade before and after the stall had to be at least 4 percent.

11. Richard Foster, "Creative Destruction Whips Through Corporate America," Innosight, "Executive Briefing, Winter 2012," http://www.innosight .com/innovation-resources/strategy-innovation/upload/creative-destruction -whips-through-corporate-america_final2015.pdf.

12. John Hagel III, John Seely Brown, Tamara Samoylova, and Michael Lui, "Success or Struggle: TOA as a True Measure of Business Performance," Report 3 of the 2013 Shift Index Series, Deloitte University Press, October 30, 2013, http://dupress.com/articles/success-or-struggle-roa-as-a-true-measure -of-business-performance.

13. Malcolm Gladwell, *David and Goliath: Underdogs, Misfits and the Art of Battling Giants* (Boston: Little, Brown, 2013).

14. Lily Tomlin skit on Saturday Night Live, Season 2, Episode 1, September 18, 1976, Video: https://www.youtube.com/watch?v=CHgUN _95UAw. Text transcript: http://snltranscripts.jt.org/76/76aphonecompany .phtml.

15. Paul Ingrassia, *Crash Course: The American Automobile Industry's Road to Bankruptcy and Bailout—and Beyond* (New York: Random House, 2011).

16. Jerry Kim and Bruce Kogut, "General Motors 2.0: What Happened? What's Next?" *Columbia Business School Caseworks*, 2010.

17. Clayton M. Christensen, "Key Concepts," http://www.clayton christensen.com/key-concepts.

18. Paul Krugman, "On the Symmetry Between Microsoft and Apple," *New York Times*, August 24, 2013.

19. Cromwell Schubarth, "Disruption Guru Christensen: Apple, Tesla, VCs, Academia May Die," *Silicon Valley Business Journal*, February 7, 2013.

20. Yukari Iwatani Kane, *Haunted Empire: Apple After Steve Jobs* (New York: HarperBusiness, 2014).

21. Stefan Schultz, "The Apple Crash," *Spiegel Online*, January 24, 2013, http://m.spiegel.de/article.do?id=879352.

22. Susan Decker and Adam Satariano, "Apple Seen Losing Innovation Magic by 71 Percent in Global Poll," *Bloomberg*, May 16, 2013, http://www

.bloomberg.com/news/2013-05-17/apple-seen-losing-innovation-magic-by -71-in-global-poll.html.

23. Bruce Greenwald, "Competitive Advantage," presentation at Columbia Business School Th+nkCBS lecture series, November 7, 2013, YouTube video, https://www.youtube.com/watch?v=zsvnvV3wDgc.

24. Daisuke Wakabayashi, Eva Dou, and Lorraine Luk, "Can Apple Crack the Smartwatch Code," *Wall Street Journal*, June 20, 2014.

25. Paul Lamkin, "Apple Watch Sales Hit Seven Million," *Forbes*, November 5, 2015, http://www.forbes.com/sites/paullamkin/2015/11/05/apple-watch -sales-hit-7-million.

26. For 2015 sales estimates, see Paul Lamkin, "Apple Watch Sales Hit 12 Million in 2015," *Wareable*, February 9, 2016, www.wareable.com /smartwatches/apple-watch-sales-hit-12-million-in-2015-2279. The Apple Watch revenue estimate in this paragraph generously assumes that Apple sells all watches through its own stores, capturing all retail proceeds as revenue. In fact, Apple is also selling its watches through selected retail partners, reducing the value of its unit sales to wholesale price levels. Julia Love, "Average Apple Watch Sells for $529, at Top End of Estimates," *Reuters*, September 30, 2015, www.reuters.com/article/us-apple-watch-idUSKCN0RU1AA201 50930#pQd5246hh4KokrKW.99.

27. "Gartner Says Worldwide Video Game Market to Total $93 Billion in 2013," *Gartner*, http://www.gartner.com/newsroom/id/2614915.

28. Lucas Mearian, "Mobile Health Device Market to Grow Eightfold to $42B," *Computerworld*, July 2, 2014.

29. Don Reisinger, "Apple Is Buying Lots of Space for Self-Driving Cars: Report," *Fortune*, May 6, 2016, http://fortune.com/2016/05/06 /apple-self-driving-cars/.

30. Jean Baptiste Su, "Why Apple Lost Its Innovation Spirit with New iPads," *Forbes*, October 23, 2013, http://www.forbes.com/sites/jeanbaptiste /2013/10/23/apple-lost-innovation-spirit-with-new-ipads/#3ff4b9ba3296.

31. Vanessa Friedman, "Reviewing Google's Smartwatches—The LG G and the Samsung Gear Live," On the Runway, *New York Times*, June 26, 2014.

32. Andrew Hoyle, "Samsung Galaxy Gear Review," *CNET*, September 27, 2013.

33. Geoffrey A. Fowler, "Apple Pay Review: Easy to Use, but Still Hard to Find," *Wall Street Journal*, October 28, 2014.

34. Note that the product life cycle depicted in figure 4.8 displays the typical sales trend for a successful product. Most new product launches fail before hitting the growth phase.

35. Sharon Reier, "Half a Century Later, Economist's 'Creative Destruction' Theory Is Apt for the Internet Age: Schumpeter: The Prophet of Bust and Boom," *New York Times*, June 10, 2000.

36. Larry Downes and Paul Nunes, *Big Bang Disruption: Strategy in the Age of Devastating Innovation* (New York: Portfolio, 2014). See chapter 1 of this book for a description of the dynamics underlying big bang disruptions, which can dramatically shorten product life cycles.

37. Hannah Karp, "Apple iTunes Sees Big Drop in Music Sales," *Wall Street Journal*, October 24, 2014.

5. Do You Know What Your Strategy Is?

1. Harvard Business Review Staff, "When CEOs Talk Strategy, Is Anyone Listening?" *Harvard Business Review*, June 2013.

2. Dominic Barton and Mark Wiseman, "Where Boards Fall Short," *Harvard Business Review*, January, 2015.

3. American Customer Satisfaction Index Press Release, May 20, 2014, http://www.theacsi.org/news-and-resources/press-releases/press-2014/press-release-telecommunications-and-information-2014. Surveys from other market research organizations, including the YouGov BrandIndex and J. D. Power surveys of consumer satisfaction, also rate Comcast and Time Warner Cable lowest in customer satisfaction among hundreds of companies from dozens of industries.

4. Comments by Brian Roberts, Comcast CEO in the Q3 2014 Comcast earnings call.

5. Daniel B. Kline, "Time Warner Cable Inc Admits Its Customer Service Faults: 'We Can Do Better,'" *The Motley Fool*, October 18, 2015, http://www.fool.com/investing/general/2015/10/18/time-warner-cable-admits-its-customer-service-faul.aspx.

6. Kim Wagner, Eugene Foo, Hadi Zablit, and Andrew Taylor, "The Most Innovative Companies 2013: Lessons from Leaders," *BCG Perspectives*, September 26, 2013.

7. Joanna Barsh, Marla M. Capozzi, and Jonathan Davidson, "Leadership and Innovation," *McKinsey Quarterly*, January 2008.

8. For suggestive evidence, it should be noted that Time Warner Cable and Comcast have lost almost seven hundred thousand pay-TV subscribers between 2013 and 2014. http://www.ibtimes.com/comcast-time-warner-cable-bleeding-cable-subscribers-pay-tvs-worst-third-quarter-ever-1723870. And in Barsch et al. "Leadership and Innovation," McKinsey reported that two-thirds of executives surveyed were "somewhat," "a little," or "not at all" confident about the innovation decisions they make.

9. Jeff Bercovici, "Rewriting the Definition of Success, Twitter Gets Eccentric," *Forbes*, October 27, 2014. Of the three eccentric circles, one circle

was meant to represent core users of the social-media service; another denoted those who visited the site but didn't log in; and the third circle was for people who saw Twitter content embedded on other sites.

10. Yoree Koh and Kirstin Grind, "Twitter CEO Dick Costolo Struggles to Define Vision," *Wall Street Journal,* November 6, 2014.

11. David J. Collis and Michael G. Rukstad, "Can You Say What Your Strategy Is?" *Harvard Business Review,* April 2008. In this article, the authors propose three components for strategy formulation: scope, advantage, and objective, where the latter specifies financial targets. For the simplified exercise described in this chapter, financial objectives have been omitted from the thirty-five-word strategy statement, but should of course be included in any statement of corporate or business unit strategy.

12. Coors lost its basis of competitive advantage when competitors attacked its market-share leadership in the western United States and Miller led the market shift towards light beers. In response, Coors expanded to national distribution and added new products, which weakened its distinctiveness against stronger competitors, Anheuser-Busch and Miller.

13. Pankaj Ghemawat, "Adolph Coors in the Brewing Industry," *Harvard Business School Publishing,* Case 9-388-014, June 23, 1992.

14. In this example, cost to serve is equivalent to operating costs, which include the cost of goods sold, plus the allocated unit costs to attract and retain customers and to invest in product renewal over time.

15. Airline fees are hidden in the sense that it takes a fair amount of digging through an airline website's fine print to understand all the types and levels of fees charged. On the other hand, when a consumer uses an online booking service like KAYAK or CheapTickets to purchase a ticket, the primary basis of comparison between competing fares is base price, which is boldly displayed, with no distinction between free and fee-based service perks.

16. Tom Huddleston, Jr., "People Love These Airlines the Most," *Fortune,* May 11, 2016, http://fortune.com/2016/05/11/alaska-airlines-jetblue-jd -power/.

17. Jeremy Reimer, "Total Share: 30 Years of Personal Computer Market Share Figures," *Ars Technica,* December 15, 2005, http://arstechnica.com /features/2005/12/total-share/5/.

18. Orit Gadiesh and James L. Gilbert, "Profit Pools: A Fresh Look at Strategy," *Harvard Business Review,* May 1, 1998.

19. Jad Mouawad, "Pushing 40, Southwest Is Still Playing the Rebel, *New York Times,* November 20, 2010.

20. Luca Ciferra, "BMW Development Chief Diess Says Internal Synergies Key to Premium Strategy," *Automotive News Europe,* February 4, 2014.

21. Brad Smith, "Intuit's CEO on Building a Design-Driven Company," *Harvard Business Review*, January-February 2015.

22. Willie E. Hopkins, Paul Mallette, and Shirley A. Hopkins, "Proposed Factors Influencing Strategic Inertia/Strategic Renewal in Organizations," *Academy of Strategic Management Journal* 12, 2 (2013): 77.

23. Rita Gunther McGrath, *The End of Competitive Advantage: How to Keep Your Strategy Moving as Fast as Your Business,* (Harvard Business Review Press, 2013): xi.

24. Stephen Hall, Dan Lovallo, and Reinier Musters, "How to Put Your Money Where Your Strategy Is," *McKinsey Quarterly*, March 2012.

25. Richard H. Thaler, Amos Tversky, Daniel Kahneman, and Alan Schwartz, "The Effect of Myopia and Loss Aversion on Risk Taking: An Experimental Test," *Quarterly Journal of Economics* 112, 2 (May 1997): 647–661.

26. Lovallo and Musters, "How to Put Your Money Where Your Strategy Is."

27. Dynamic capital reallocation need not compromise short-term financial performance. Ideally, in an enterprise with multiple business units, a company can manage its portfolio of new product investments, such that in any given year, the resulting mix of products at varying stages of their life cycle can yield attractive overall financial performance.

28. Dan Lovallo and Olivier Sibony, "The Case for Behavioral Strategy," *McKinsey Quarterly*, March 2010.

6. Getting Strategy Right

1. The events recounted here are based on a confidential consulting engagement that I led with Audi. While the account is accurate, respecting corporate and personal confidentiality, I have refrained from identifying the real names of client executives.

2. Unless otherwise noted, Audi of America will be referred to as Audi.

3. In Audi's vehicles, the accelerator and brake pedals were closer together than in typical American-designed cars, which may have contributed to drivers mistakenly depressing the wrong pedal.

4. Paul Niedermeyer, "The Best of TTAC: The Audi 5000 Intended Unintended Acceleration Debacle," *The Truth About Cars*, March 7, 2010, http://www.thetruthaboutcars.com/2010/03/the-best-of-ttac-the-audi-5000-intended-unintended-acceleration-debacle.

5. Subaru offered the only other AWD car on the market at the time but promoted their version as a utilitarian vehicle for adverse weather, rather than as sporty vehicle intended for everyday high-performance driving.

6. Ian Austen, "In Canada, the Torch Is Passed on a Quiet but Profitable Legacy," *New York Times*, July 3, 2006.

7. Michelle Krebs, "Good-Bye Pontiac, Saturn, Saab, Hummer," *Edmunds Auto Observer*, April 27, 2009.

8. Jai Singh, "Dell: Apple Should Close Shop," *CNET*, October 6, 1997, http://www.cnet.com/news/dell-apple-should-close-shop.

9. Brad Stone, "Steve Jobs: The Return, 1997–2011," *Bloomberg Businessweek*, October 6, 2011. Jobs was referring not only to the need to streamline Apple's product line but also to the need to partner with rather than compete against Microsoft.

10. Mark Gottfredson, Steve Schaubert, and Hernan Saenz, "The New Leader's Guide to Diagnosing the Business," *Harvard Business Review*, February 2008.

11. A. G. Lafley, "What Only the CEO Can Do," *Harvard Business Review*, May 2009.

12. Brian Christian, "The A/B Test: Inside the Technology That's Changing the Rules of Business," *Wired*, April 25, 2012.

13. SMH—Swiss Corporation for Microelectronics and Watchmaking Industries Ltd.—was renamed Swatch Group in 1998.

14. Seth Godin, "On Making a Ruckus in Your Industry," *Seth's Blog*, April 7, 2012, http://sethgodin.typepad.com/seths_blog/2012/04/on-making-a-ruckus-in-your-industry.html.

15. "Benchmarks by Industry," American Customer Satisfaction Index, accessed [date], http://www.theacsi.org/customer-satisfaction-benchmarks/benchmarks-by-industry.

7. Creating Strong Brands

1. "2014 Ranking of Best Global Brands," Interbrand, http://interbrand.com/best-brands/best-global-brands/previous-years/, and "BrandZ Top 100," Millward Brown, http://www.millwardbrown.com/docs/default-source/global-brandz-downloads/global/2014_BrandZ_Top100_Report.pdf.

2. Interbrand (2014).

3. "The Harris Poll 2013 Reputation Quotient," Harris Interactive, http://www.rankingthebrands.com/PDF/The%20Reputations%20of%20the%20Most%20Visible%20Companies%202013,%20Harris%20Interactive.pdf.

4. For background on the Axe ad, see http://theinspirationroom.com/daily/2012/axe-anarchy-for-him-and-for-her. For background on the Federal Express ad, see http://www.creativebloq.com/inspiration/print-ads-1233780.

5. Thomas Oliver, *The Real Coke, the Real Story* (New York: Random House, 1986).

6. Robert Klara, "Perspective: Generation Appreciation," *Adweek*, October 13, 2011.

7. Coca-Cola's market share would have been even lower, were it not for its dominant position in exclusive distribution contracts with major restaurant chains (e.g., McDonald's) and vending-machine distribution.

8. Oliver, *The Real Coke*, 181.

9. Mark Pendergrast, *For God, Country, and Coca-Cola* (New York: Basic Books, Second Edition, 2000), 360.

10. Ionut, Arghire, "It Doesn't Take a Genius to Choose Galaxy S III over iPhone 5, Says Samsung," *Softpedia*, September 17, 2012, http://news.softpedia.com/news/It-Doesn-t-Take-a-Genius-to-Choose-Galaxy-S-III-over-iPhone-5-Says-Samsung-292580.shtml.

11. Ewan Spence, "Apple's Amazing iPhone Conquers China with Spectacular Q1 2015 Results and 74.5 Million Sales," *Forbes*, January 27, 2015.

12. Philip Elmer-DeWitt, "How Apple Sucks the Profit Out of Mobile Phones," *Fortune,* February 14, 2016, http://fortune.com/2016/02/14/apple-mobile-profit-2015.

13. Kevin Lane Keller, *Strategic Brand Management: Building, Measuring, and Managing Brand Equity*, 4th ed. (Upper Saddle River, NJ: Prentice Hall, 2012).

14. Ted Wright, *Fizz: Harness the Power of Word of Mouth Marketing to Drive Brand Growth* (New York: McGraw-Hill, 2014).

15. Tanzina Vega, "Ad About Women's Self-Image Creates a Sensation," *New York Times*, April 18, 2013.

16. Kendra McGowan, "Dove Real Beauty: PR In Practice," *University of Oregon Blogs*, June 10, 2013, http://blogs.uoregon.edu/j350doverealbeauty.

17. http://realbeautysketches.dove.us.

18. http://www.eonline.com/news/409073/dove-real-beauty-sketches-campaign-gets-women-to-rethink-their-looks.

19. Peter Evans, "Procter & Gamble and Unilever Escalate Big-Hair War," *Wall Street Journal*, February 24, 2014.

20. "Global Revenue Of The Unilever Group From 2005 To 2015, By Product Segment," *Statista*, 2016, http://www.statista.com/statistics/269200/revenue-of-the-unilever-group-worldwide-by-product-segment, and "Procter & Gamble's Net Sales Worldwide From 2013 To 2015, By Business Segment," *Statista*, 2016, http://www.statista.com/statistics/238771/sales-of-procter-und-gamble-by-sector-in-2009/.

8. Brand Builders and Killers

1. "Brandshare 2014," Edelman, http://www.edelman.com/insights /intellectual-property/brandshare-2014.

2. Ibid.

3. "Guru: Alfred Sloan," *Economist*, January 30, 2009.

4. Robert Hutchins, "New Dimensions: Is Toy Retail Ready for 3D Printing?" *Toy News*, February 3, 2015.

5. Lisa Koivu, "5 Best Beauty Reward Programs," The Frugal Shopper (blog), *U.S. News & World Report*, August 13, 2014, http://money.usnews.com/money /the-frugal-shopper/2014/08/13/5-best-beauty-rewards-programs.

6. Pandora company website, About section, http://www.pandora.com /about.

7. Spotify company website, About-us section, https://www.spotify.com /us/about-us.

8. James H. Gilmore and B. Joseph Pine II, "The Four Faces of Mass Customization," *Harvard Business Review*, January 1997.

9. Richard Teerlink and Lee Ozley, *More Than a Motorcycle: The Leadership Journey at Harley-Davidson* (Boston, MA: Harvard Business Review Press, 2000).

10. James R. Hagerty, "Harley Goes Lean to Build Hogs," *Wall Street Journal*, September 21, 2012.

11. USAA website: https://www.usaa.com/inet/pages/why_choose_usaa _main.

12. "USAA, Kaiser Permanente, Amazon.com, Pandora, Costco, Wegmans, Apple, TracFone, Southwest and Westin Among the Highest in Customer Loyalty in the 2014 Satmetrix® Net Promoter® Benchmarks," *PR Newswire*, March 5, 2014.

13. "World's Most Admired Companies 2015," *Fortune*, http://www.ranking thebrands.com/The-Brand-Rankings.aspx?rankingID=118&year=908, accessed June 7, 2016.

14. GoPro YouTube channel page, https://www.youtube.com/user /GoProCamera/about.

15. Nick Wingfield, "GoPro Sees Opportunity in Its Amateur Daredevils," *New York Times*, January 30, 2014. All clips on GoPro's YouTube channel indicate the model of GoPro camera used to shoot the video. The referenced fireman video can be found at https://www.youtube.com/watch?v=CjB _oVeq8Lo.

16. While GoPro gets high marks for brand building, it has been unable to overcome structural weaknesses in the category in which it competes. Action

video cameras represent a niche consumer discretionary product, and growth in category sales showed signs of slowing by 2015, despite the entrance of several low-price competitors. As a result, GoPro's recent financial results have weakened, sending its stock price tumbling 90 percent below its peak in late 2014. See Tim Bradshaw, "GoPro Shares Dive 27 Percent on Revenue Warning," *Financial Times*, January 16, 2016.

17. JetBlue YouTube channel. Comments by CEO David Neeleman, February 19, 2007, https://www.youtube.com/watch?v=-r_PIg7EAUw.

18. Figure 8.4 was compiled from data provided by Twitter as of February 20, 2014.

19. Gregory Karp, "JetBlue, Southwest Top-Rated Carriers for Customer Experience," *Chicago Tribune*, March 19, 2015.

20. "The American Way," Gulliver Business Travel, *Economist*, March 16, 2015.

21. Quote attributed to Alfred Sloan, who was president, CEO, and/or chairman of General Motors from 1923 to 1956.

22. The descriptions in this section refer to GM's brand strategy up to the 1970s. As noted in the text, GM radically changed its approach to product positioning in the 1980s and discontinued the Pontiac and Oldsmobile brands in 2004 and 2009 respectively.

23. *Car and Driver* editors, "Dishonorable Mention: The 10 Most Embarrassing Award Winners in Automotive History," *Car and Driver*, January 2009.

24. Paul Niedermeyer, "Will Success Spoil General Motors," *Fortune*, August 22, 1983.

25. James B. Stewart, "Netflix Looks Back on Its Near-Death Spiral," *New York Times*, April 26, 2013.

26. "JCPenney's Transformation Plans Revealed at Launch Event in New York City," *PR Newswire*, January 25, 2012, http://www.prnewswire.com /news-releases/jcpenneys-transformation-plans-revealed-at-launch-event-in -new-york-city-138045223.html.

27. Jim Edwards and Charlie Minato, "How Ex-CEO Ron Johnson Made JCPenney Even Worse," *Business Insider*, April 8, 2013.

28. Andrew Martin, "Smelling an Opportunity," *New York Times*, December 9, 2010.

29. Estimates of product-line extension failures range from 60 percent to 90 percent. See for example, David Aaker, "Brand Extensions: The Good, the Bad, and the Ugly," *MIT Sloan Management Review*, July 15, 1990, and Laura Ries, "How Crocs Crashed," *Ries' Pieces*, October 2009, http://ries .typepad.com/ries_blog/crazy_lineextensions.

30. Hadley Freeman, "A Tasty Little Present for Men—Burger King Body Spray," *Guardian*, December 16, 2008.

31. David Hughes, *"A Bottle of Guinness Please"*: *The Colourful History of Guinness* (Wokingham, UK: Phimboy, 2006).

32. Kevin Lane Keller and Sanjay Sood, "Brand Equity Dilution," *MIT Sloan Management Review*, Fall 2003.

33. See for example, James Poniewozik, "VIA Taste Test: Grading Starbucks' New Instant Coffee," *Time*, October 2, 2009, and Barry Silverstein, "Starbucks Favors, Flavors Instant Coffee," *Brandchannel*, May 17, 2010, http://content.time.com/time/arts/article/0,8599,1927544,00.html.

34. Mark Gottfredson and Darrell Rigby, "The Power of Managing Complexity," *Harvard Business Review*, January 12, 2009.

35. Sydney Finkelstein, *Why Smart Executives Fail* (New York: Portfolio, 2004).

36. Ibid., chap. 5.

37. Scott Austin, Chris Canipe, and Sarah Slobin, "The Billion Dollar Startup Club," *Wall Street Journal*, February 18, 2015.

38. Eugene Kim, "The Inside Story of how $1 Billion Evernote Went from Silicon Valley Darling to Deep Trouble," *Business Insider*, October 3, 2015.

39. Chris O'Brien, "Evernote's 5 Percent Problem Offers a Cautionary Lesson to Tech Companies," *VentureBeat*, January 5, 2016.

40. Johan Sjöström Bayer, Mikael Hilding, Antal Kamps, Gustaf Sahlén, and Robin Sparrefors, "When Product Complexity Hurts True Profitability," *Accenture Outlook*, February 2013.

41. Thomas Gryta, "Inside the Phone-Plan Pricing Puzzle," *Wall Street Journal*, July 31, 2013.

42. "Mastering Product Complexity," Roland Berger Strategy Consultants, November 2012, http://www.rolandberger.us/media/pdf/Roland_Berger_Mastering-Product-Complexity_20121107.pdf.

43. Sheena Iyengar, *The Art of Choosing* (New York: Twelve, 2010).

44. Barry Schwartz, *The Paradox of Choice* (New York: HarperCollins, First Edition 2004).

45. Subsequent research has raised questions as to whether the choice paradox always holds true. Benjamin Scheibehenne and colleagues examined multiple studies of the impact of complexity on consumer choice and found the net effect to be zero, sometimes increasing demand and sometimes not. See Benjamin Scheibehenne, Rainer Greifeneder, and Peter M. Todd, "Can There Ever Be Too Many Options? A Meta-Analytic Review of Choice Overload," *Journal of Consumer Research* 37, October 2010.

46. In-N-Out Burger does offer a number of condiments not listed on its menu to add flavor to its burger fare. This is a good example of "versioning," wherein a company sharply limits its core product line (to control costs and enhance quality) but still caters to varying consumer tastes with low-cost

add-ons and accessories, which are relatively simple and cheap to provide. Chipotle has followed a similar versioning strategy.

47. Julie Jargon, "McDonald's Acknowledges Service Has Suffered," *Wall Street Journal*, November 14, 2013.

9. What Makes Products Meaningfully Different?

1. Al Ries and Jack Trout, *Positioning: The Battle for Your Mind* (New York: McGraw-Hill, 2001).

2. Anil Kaul and Vithala R. Rao, "Research for Product Positioning and Design Decisions: An Integrative Review," *International Journal of Research in Marketing* 12, 4 (November 1995): 293–320.

3. Yoram Wind, "Beyond the 4Ps: A New Marketing Paradigm Emerges," *Harvard Business Review*, April 1, 2014.

4. Orville C. Walker and John W. Mullins, *Marketing Strategy: A Decision-Focused Approach*, 6th ed. (New York: McGraw-Hill/Irwin, 2008), 159.

5. There are several analytical techniques that can be used to add these additional insights. The relative importance of each attribute can be determined by a *revealed preference analysis*. For example, by running a regression on preference rankings as the dependent variable and the attribute ratings as the independent variables, researchers can analytically determine the relative importance of each attribute in explaining the observed overall rankings of preferred retailers. Alternatively, survey respondents could be asked directly to rank the importance of each attribute. Finally, researchers could choose to perform a *conjoint analysis*, to quantitatively measure the value associated with each retailer attribute. Under any of these approaches, the research can be used to identify distinct market segments within which consumers tend to exhibit common behavioral traits in the perception of the relative importance of product attributes.

6. Adapted from William L. Moore and Edgar A. Pessemier, *Product Planning and Management: Designing and Delivering Value* (New York: McGraw-Hill, 1993), 145.

7. The technique used to reduce the number of factors used in a perceptual map to combine highly correlated attributes is called factor analysis. For a description of factor analysis, see John R. Hauser and Frank S. Koppelman, "Alternative Perceptual Mapping Techniques: Relative Accuracy and Usefulness," *Journal of Marketing Research* 16 (November 1979): 495–506.

8. The length of the vector is related to the magnitude of the underlying variance in perception ratings for a given factor. The greater the variance, the more significant the factor is in explaining the perceived difference between beers. Thus the length of the vectors gives a visual cue as to which factors are most important in distinguishing competing beers.

9. In this case, the consumers rated competing beers very differently with respect to being popular with men (or not), whereas all beers were rated similarly on being good value.

10. The orientation of the vectors and product positions can be rotated as a set without changing the interpretation of the perceptual map. In figure 9.4, the perceptual map was oriented so that heavy/light vectors were positioned around the vertical axis and budget/premium vectors aligned with the horizontal axis.

11. "Ad Age Advertising Century: Top 100 Campaigns," *Advertising Age*, March 29, 1999.

12. Ingwer Borg and Patrick J. F. Groenen, *Modern Multidimensional Scaling: Theory and Applications* (New York: Springer, 2005), 37–41.

13. Kevin Lane Keller, *Strategic Brand Management*, 3rd ed. (Upper Saddle River, NJ: Prentice Hall, 2007), 49–51.

14. A recent paper has suggested that business performance measures can also be added to perceptual-mapping analyses to more directly link product positioning to business strategy. See Charan K. Bagga, "A Better Way to Map Brand Strategy," *Harvard Business Review*, June 2015.

15. Many of the observations in this section were inspired by Youngme Moon, *Different: Escaping the Competitive Herd*, (New York: Crown Business, 2010).

16. Youngme Moon, "Rethinking Positioning," Harvard Business School Module Note 506-025, October 2005 (rev. March 2006).

17. Despite close parity on technical smartphone specifications, Apple has gained considerable market share at Samsung's expense as a result of its ease of use, tactile and visual elegance, and ecosystem strength, all of which are more difficult to emulate.

18. A description of the origin and interpretation of Moore's law can be found at http://www.mooreslaw.org.

19. Ernst Friedrich "Fritz" Schumacher was a renowned economic thinker, statistician, author, and economist in Britain, serving as chief economic advisor to the UK National Coal Board for two decades. His complete quote is: "Any intelligent fool can make things bigger, more complex and more violent. It takes a touch of genius—and a lot of courage to move in the opposite direction," Goodreads website, http://www.goodreads.com/quotes/1199046-any -intelligent-fool-can-make-things-bigger-more-complex-and.

20. Clayton M. Christensen, *The Innovator's Dilemma: When New Technologies Cause Great Firms to Fail* (Boston, MA: Harvard Business School Press, 1997).

21. "Worldwide Tablet Shipments From 2nd Quarter 2010 to 1st Quarter 2016," *Statista*, 2016, http://www.statista.com/statistics/272070/global-tablet -shipments-by-quarter.

22. Brett Molina, "IDC: Smartphone Growth to Continue Slowing Down," *USA Today*, May 26, 2015.

23. For the four years following its IPO on May 22, 2011, Spirit's stock appreciated by 447 percent, while the industry as a whole appreciated by 127 percent. For this comparison, Spirit's stock price (ticker SAVE) was compared to the airline stock index (ticker ^XAL) between May 31, 2011, and May 31, 2015.

24. Maria Doulton, "'You're Just Caretaker of This Watch,'" *Financial Times*, April 4, 2008.

25. W. Chan Kim and Renée Mauborgne, "Strategy, Value Innovation, and the Knowledge Economy," *MIT Sloan Management Review*, April 15, 1999.

26. Luke Williams, *Disrupt: Think the Unthinkable to Spark Transformation in Your Business* (Upper Saddle River, NJ: FT Press, 2010), 32–33.

27. Stuart Elliott, "Geico's Lizard Offers a New Message of Reassurance," *New York Times*, February 18, 2009, and Ashley Rodriguez, "Flo's Progressive Evolution," *Advertising Age*, November 12, 2014.

28. Category images vary widely by country. In Italy and Spain, for example, prosecco and cava sparkling wines are widely considered to be appropriate for casual, everyday consumption, particularly in hot summer months.

10. Where Do Great Ideas Come From?

1. Ryan Mac, "The Mad Billionaire Behind GoPro: The World's Hottest Camera Company," *Forbes*, March 25, 2013.

2. Donald G. McNeil Jr., "Car Mechanic Dreams Up a Tool to Ease Births," *New York Times*, November 13, 2013.

3. Sydney Brownstone, "The 100 Most Creative People, 2014—#17: Jorge Odón," *Fast Company*, June 2014.

4. http://www.post-it.com/3M/en_US/post-it/contact-us/about-us/, accessed June 10, 2016.

5. Michael Szycher, *How to Create Wealth for Your Company and Stakeholders* (Productivity, 2014), 21.

6. Andrew Adam Newman, "Turning 30, an Office Product Works at Home," *New York Times*, July 27, 2010. The 3M Company does not release revenue data for individual products. The estimated Post-it Notes revenue of over $500 million is based on author estimates from published figures on Post-it Notes unit volumes and prices.

7. Jessica Salter, "Airbnb: The Story Behind the $1.3bn Room-Letting Website," *Telegraph*, September 7, 2012.

8. Clare O'Connor, "How Spanx Became a Billion-Dollar Business Without Advertising," *Forbes*, March 26, 2012.

9. William R. Duggan, *Strategic Intuition* (New York: Columbia University Press, 2007).

10. Patrick Vlaskovits, "Henry Ford, Innovation, and That 'Faster Horse' Quote," *Harvard Business Review*, August 29, 2011.

11. Walter Isaacson, *Steve Jobs* (New York: Simon & Schuster, 2011).

12. Steve Blank, "No Plan Survives First Contact with Customers— Business Plans Versus Business Models," *Steve Blank*, April 8, 2010, http://steveblank.com/2010/04/08/no-plan-survives-first-contact-with-customers-%E2%80%93-business-plans-versus-business-models.

13. Dorothy Leonard and Jeffrey F. Rayport, "Spark Innovation Through Empathic Design," *Harvard Business Review*, November-December 1997.

14. This exercise was adapted from a description of the actual process used to design the innovative OXO measuring cup, as described in Marc Hurst, *Customers Included: How to Transform Products, Companies and the World—With a Single Step*, 2nd ed. (New York: Creative Good, [2015]), Kindle edition.

15. Ibid. On this project, OXO worked with Smart Design Worldwide for customer research and product design.

16. The angled measuring cup that OXO marketed also featured some of the other product design suggestions shown in figure 10.2, including plastic construction, rubber handle, and multiple product sizes.

17. Brian O'Keefe, "Meet the CEO of the Biggest Company on Earth," *Fortune*, September 9, 2010.

18. Krystina Gustafson, "Time to Close Wal-Mart Stores? Analysts Think So," *CNBC.com*, January 31, 2014.

19. "Wal-Mart Lost Billions by Listening to Customers," *Keith Dawson (blog)*, The CMO Site, April 25, 2011, http://www.thecmosite.com/author.asp?section_id=1200&doc_id=205973, accessed June 10, 2016.

20. Hayley Peterson, "Meet the Average Wal-Mart Shopper," *Business Insider*, September 18, 2014.

21. Behavioral observation and exploratory conversation are schematically shown as overlapping, since they are often conducted simultaneously. Also, both these market-research types could also be beneficially used in succeeding stages of product development, but the reverse is generally not true.

22. Gary King, Robert O. Keohane, and Sidney Verba, *Designing Social Inquiry: Scientific Inference in Qualitative Research* (Princeton, NJ: Princeton University Press, 1994).

23. Ken Anderson, "Ethnographic Research: A Key to Strategy," *Harvard Business Review*, March 2009.

24. Brainy Quote website, http://www.brainyquote.com/quotes/quotes/y/yogiberra125285.html, accessed June 10, 2016.

25. Jon Kolko, *Well-Designed: How to Use Empathy to Create Products People Really Love* (Boston, MA: Harvard Business School Press, 2014), 73.

26. Byron Pope, "Ford Escape Auto Liftgate," *Ward's Auto*, May 30, 2012.

27. Mark Hurst and Phil Terry, *Customers Included: How to Transform Products, Companies and the World—With a Single Step* (New York: Creative Good, 2013), 70.

28. Kolko, *Well-Designed*.

29. Hurst and Terry, *Customers Included*.

30. Paul Farhi, "Behind Domino's Mea Culpa Ad Campaign," *Washington Post*, January 13, 2010.

31. Isaacson, *Steve Jobs*.

32. Janet Smithson, "Using and Analysing Focus Groups: Limitations and Possibilities," *International Journal of Social Research Methodology* 3, 2 (2000): 103–119.

33. Jerry Wind, Paul E. Green, Douglas Shifflet, and Marsha Scarbrough, "Courtyard by Marriott: Designing a Hotel Facility with Consumer-Based Marketing Models," *Interfaces* 19, 1 (January 1989): 25–47.

34. Paul E. Green, Abba M. Krieger, and Yoram Wind, "Thirty Years of Conjoint Analysis: Reflections and Prospects," *Interfaces* 31, 3 (May 2001): 56–73.

35. JetBlue's use of conjoint analysis for configuring service elements based on communication with Marty St. George, executive vice president, commercial and planning, December 10, 2015.

36. Anders Gustafsson, Andreas Herrmann, and Frank Huber, "Conjoint Analysis as an Instrument of Market Research Practice," in *Conjoint Measurement: Methods and Applications*, 3rd edition, ed. Gustafsson, Herrmann, and Huber, (Berlin: Springer, 2003), 5–46.

37. The logic—and indeed the imperative—of framing the expected market size of an entrepreneurial venture at a very early stage of product development is covered at length in two excellent books. The first, focused on startup ventures, is Steve Blank and Bob Dorf, *The Startup Owner's Manual: The Step-By-Step Guide for Building a Great Company* (Pescadero, CA: K&S Ranch Consulting, 2012. Early-stage market sizing in the context of corporate entrepreneurship is covered in Rita Gunther McGrath and Ian C. MacMillan, *Discovery-Driven Growth: A Breakthrough Process to Reduce Risk and Seize Opportunity* (Boston, MA: Harvard Business Review Press, 2009).

38. Paul Saffo, "Six Rules for Effective Forecasting," *Harvard Business Review*, July-August 2007.

39. Joan Schneider and Julie Hall, "Why Most Product Launches Fail," *Harvard Business Review*, April 2011.

40. Marc H. Meyer, "Perspective: How Honda Innovates," *Journal of Product Innovation Management* 25, 3 (May 2008): 261–271.

41. Generation Y, also referred to as millennials, is generally defined as those born between 1980 and 2000. There have been three generations of population spurts since World War II: baby boomers, generation X, and millennials.

42. The data shown in table 10.4 represent a composite of several market research studies on characteristics of millennials. As an example, see "A Portrait of Generation Next," *Pew Research Center,* January 9, 2007, http://www.people-press.org/2007/01/09/a-portrait-of-generation-next, accessed June 10, 2016.

43. In user-centered design and marketing, personas are fictional characters created to represent the different user types that might react to a site, brand, or product in a similar way. For a critique of personas, see Hurst and Terry, *Customers Included,* 5–59.

44. Phil Patton, "Honda Element; Young Man, Would You Like That in a Box?" *New York Times,* December 15, 2002.

45. "2013 Honda Model Recognition," Honda Automobiles Press Information, October 5, 2003, http://automobiles.honda.com/news/press-releases-article.aspx?Article=2003100848363.

11. Strategies to Break Away from the Pack

1. The 4Ps refer to how products and services are brought to market in terms of product configuration, price, promotion, and place (i.e., sales channels).

2. Youngme Moon, "Rethinking Positioning," Harvard Business School Module Note for Instructors, March 22, 2006. In her published work, Moon uses the term disruptive positioning. To distinguish her work from Christensen's "disruptive technologies" terminology, I have renamed Moon's concept to breakout positioning.

3. W. Chan Kim and Renée Mauborgne, *Blue Ocean Strategy* (Boston, MA: Harvard Business School Press, 2005).

4. Clayton M. Christensen, *The Innovator's Dilemma: When New Technologies Cause Great Firms to Fail* (Boston, MA: Harvard Business School Press, 1997).

5. Moon, "Rethinking Positioning" actually identified three forms of breakout positioning. In addition to reverse positioning and breakaway positioning covered in this chapter, Moon covers stealth positioning, wherein a company seeks to establish a product in an entirely different category than the one for which it was originally intended. The rationale behind stealth positioning is that under some circumstances, a product can achieve a better outcome by adopting the category image characterizing an entirely different type of

product. For the sake of clarity, I have omitted stealth positioning in this chapter; such cases are relatively rare and fleeting, as they usually apply to situations where an immature product has yet to achieve adequate performance to serve its originally intended purpose.

6. Adapted from Moon, "Rethinking Positioning."

7. Jessica Colcourt, "Phones with Ultra High-Res 4K Screens Are Serious Overkill. Seriously," *CNET,* September 2, 2015, http://www.cnet.com/news/phones-with-ultra-high-resolution-4k-screens-are-serious-overkill.

8. Ed Perkins, "Which Airline's Seats Are the Most Uncomforatble?" *Huffpost Travel,* January 19, 2013, http://www.huffingtonpost.com/smartertravel/worst-legroom-airlines_b_2482315.html.

9. The term "legacy carrier" refers to the large full-service airlines whose operations began prior to deregulation of the U.S. airline industry in 1978. These airlines include United, American, Delta, Continental, Northwest, US Airways, and TWA.

10. Tom Huddleston, Jr., "People Love These Airlines the Most," *Fortune,* May 11, 2016, http://fortune.com/2016/05/11/alaska-airlines-jetblue-jd-power. It is important to note that JetBlue has continued to innovate over the past decade to ensure a meaningful differentiated product. Starting in 2014, JetBlue began introducing first-class service and the industry's fastest Wi-Fi service on selected flights.

11. "Benchmarks by Industry," The American Customer Satisfaction Index, http://www.theacsi.org/index.php?option=com_content&view=article&id=147&catid=&Itemid=212&i=Airlines, accessed June 13, 2016.

12. On a randomly chosen Tuesday night in October 2015, the lowest-priced room rates in midtown New York for the four referenced business hotel chains ranged from $634 to $1,350.

13. Youngme Moon, *Different: Escaping the Competitive Herd* (New York: Crown Business, 2010), 89.

14. Freek Vermeulen, "3 Steps to Break Out in a Tired Industry," *Harvard Business Review*, May 1, 2015, and email correspondence with Rattan Chadha, CEO, and Robin Chadha, Chief Marketing Officer, citizenM Hotels, April and June 2016.

15. Ibid.

16. It is important to note that reverse positioning strategies are not intended to appeal to all consumers, but rather to a specific target segment of consumers identified as being poorly served by traditional competitors. As a case in point, IKEA generates a highly polarized reaction in the marketplace, with large numbers of both loyal brand proselytizers and viscerally opposed brand haters.

17. Moon, "Rethinking Positioning."

18. Société de Microélectronique et d'Horlogerie changed its name to the Swatch Group in 1998.

19. Alice Pfeiffer, "Contemporary Design and the Pop Swatch," *New York Times*, March 23, 2011. Limited-edition watches by famous designers, originally selling at retail for $40, later commanded resale values in excess of $20,000 at Christie's auctions.

20. Hayek's simple, transparent pricing strategy was later used by Apple in pricing all iTunes songs at ninety-nine cents, and Amazon's original pricing of Kindle bestselling books at $9.99.

21. Youngme Moon, "The Birth of Swatch," *Harvard Business School Publishing*, Case 9-504-096, November 22, 2004.

22. For wet mopping, the consumer buys a Procter & Gamble brand solvent in a special non-spill sealed bottle that clips into the Swiffer mop handle.

23. Alexander Coolidge, "Which Will Be P&G's Next Billion-Dollar Brand?" *Cincinatti.com*, July 19, 2014, http://www.cincinnati.com/story /money/2014/07/19/procter-gamble-billion-dollar-brand/12882917.

24. Kim and Mauborgne, *Blue Ocean Strategy*.

25. Ibid., 18. Adapted from figure 1.3.

26. The assumption that winning strategies must inherently choose between best product or low cost derives from Porter's Five Forces framework, reviewed in chapter 1.

27. Kim and Mauborgne, *Blue Ocean Strategy*, 29.

28. Ibid., 36.

29. As it turned out, Curves faced management challenges in managing its extraordinarily rapid growth and has reduced its number of locations over the past decade. Nonetheless, its early success validates the potential of a properly executed Blue Ocean strategy to unlock new demand. See Karsten Krauss, "Crash Diet: After Shedding Thousands Of Locations, Can Curves Get Back in Shape?" *Forbes*, May 27, 2014.

30. Adapted from Kim and Mauborgne, *Blue Ocean Strategy*, 38. Note that the ratings of each airline could be determined from consumer surveys or from actual data measuring airline industry performance (e.g., average fare level, number of scheduled departures per day).

31. Michael E. Raynor, "Disruptive Innovation: The Southwest Airlines Case Revisited," *Strategy & Leadership* 39, no. 4 (2011): 31–34.

32. For a comparison of customer satisfaction ratings by U.S. airline, see "Net Promoter Industry Report—Airlines," *Satmetrix*, 2014, http:// cdn2.hubspot.net/hub/268441/file-518418683-pdf/Benchmarks_PDFs /Satmetrix_2014_US_Consumer_NPS_Benchmark-Airlines.pdf.

33. "2014 Ranking of Best Global Brands," Interbrand, http://interbrand .com/best-brands/best-global-brands/previous-years, accessed January 13, 2016.

34. Mike Ozanian, "How CrossFit Became a $4 Billion Brand," *Forbes*, February 25, 2015.

35. Delta Airlines corporate website, About Delta; Corporate Information; Trademarks & Slogans, http://www.delta.com/content/www/en_US /about-delta/corporate-information/trademarks-slogans.html, accessed June 13, 2016.

36. Kim and Mauborgne, *Blue Ocean Strategy*, 79.

37. Rolfe Winkler and Douglas MacMillan, "The Secret Math of Airbnb's $24 Billion Valuation," *Wall Street Journal*, June 17, 2015.

38. While this example traces product development in the technology sector, the same dynamics play out in virtually any product category.

39. Personal Computer Shipments (Desktop and Portable/Notebook) Worldwide from 2009 to 2020, *Statista*, 2016, http://www.statista.com/statistics /269049/global-pc-shipment-forecast-since-2009. Average Selling Price of Desktop PCs Worldwide From 2005 to 2015, *Statista*, 2016, http://www .statista.com/statistics/203759/average-selling-price-of-desktop-pcs-worldwide.

40. Clayton M. Christensen and Michael E. Raynor, *The Innovator's Solution: Creating and Sustaining Successful Growth* (Boston, MA: Harvard Business Review Press, 2003), 152.

41. Kim and Mauborgne, *Blue Ocean Strategy*.

42. Moon, "Rethinking Positioning."

43. Martha Hamilton, "Why Walk-In Health Care Is a Fast-Growing Profit Center for Retail Chains," *Washington Post*, April 4, 2014.

44. Ben Thomson, "What Clayton Christensen Got Wrong," *Stratechery*, September 22, 2013, http://stratechery.com/2013/clayton-christensen-got -wrong.

45. Stephen Shankland, "Electric Boost Puts E-Bikes on the Fast Track," *CNET*, October 15, 2015, http://www.cnet.com/news/electric-boost-puts -e-bikes-on-the-fast-track.

46. Larry Downes and Paul Nunes, *Big Bang Disruption: Strategy in the Age of Devastating Innovation* (New York: Portfolio, 2014).

47. Eugene Kim, "Uber Has Grown Faster in Its First Five Years Than Facebook Did," *Business Insider*, June 1, 2015, http://www.businessinsider. com/uber-vs-facebook-valuation-in-years-one-through-five-2015-6.

48. No one doubts the extraordinary success of Apple over the past fifteen years. Apple has repeatedly disrupted itself, with the iPhone launch cannibalizing iPod sales, the iPad cannibalizing laptop sales, and larger iPhones eating into iPad sales. But overall high rates of profitable growth have helped Apple become the highest-valued public corporation in the world, with a market cap topping $700 million in 2015. Amazon has also amassed an admirable record of disruptive technology launches, from Internet retailing to e-book ecosystems to cloud computing. Amazon has chosen to aggressively reinvest its cash from operations in new growth initiatives, propelling the company to become the fastest ever to achieve $100 billion in revenues. Despite its

lack of profitability, at the end of 2014, Amazon's stock had achieved a total shareholder return of over 20,000 percent since its IPO in 1997.

49. Christensen and Raynor, *The Innovator's Solution*, 56–65.

50. James Estrin, "Kodak's First Digital Moment," Lens (blog), *New York Times*, August 12, 2015.

51. Bill Gates, *The Road Ahead* (New York: Viking, 1995).

52. Rita Gunther McGrath, "The Pace of Technology Adoption is Speeding Up," *Harvard Business Review*, November 25, 2013.

53. Seth Godin, "You Can't Argue With Success," *Seth's Blog*, November 11, 2012, http://sethgodin.typepad.com/seths_blog/2012/11/you-cant-argue-with-success.html.

12. Hitting the Bull's-Eye

1. The Corporate Executive Board (CEB) studied the long-term revenue growth of about five hundred Fortune 100 and comparable international companies over the past half-century. The study defined a revenue "stall" as being a point in time when a company could no longer sustain a real annual revenue growth rate of as little as 2 percent over a ten-year period (and in many cases, stalled companies actually experienced a decade or longer of declines in revenue). The CEB study found that 87 percent of the companies hit a stall point at least once over the past half-century. Some, like Apple and 3M, were able to recover, but the majority (e.g., RCA, Motorola, and Kodak) continued to struggle in ensuing decades, usually ending in bankruptcy or forced sale at extremely low valuations relative to their historical peak. See Matthew S. Olson, Derek van Bever, and Seth Verry, "When Growth Stalls," *Harvard Business Review*, March 2008.

2. In fact, from 1983 to 2013, roughly 60 percent of the nonfinancial companies then in the S&P 500 were acquired. As a recent *McKinsey* report on corporate growth patterns suggested, "it's grow or go, and they have gone." http://www.mckinsey.com/Insights/Growth/Why_its_still_a_world_of_grow_or_go?

3. Bob de Wit and Ron Meyer, *Strategy: Process, Content, Context*, 4th ed. (Andover, UK: Cengage Learning, 2010), 629.

4. David Packard, *The HP Way: How Bill Hewlett and I Built Our Company* (New York: HarperBusiness, 1995).

5. Laura Lorenzetti, "This Is How HP Lost Its Way," *Fortune*, September 16, 2015. Note that on November 2, 2015, Hewlett-Packard split into two companies. HP Inc. contained the PC and printing business and continued trading on the New York Stock Exchange under the ticker symbol HPQ. A new company, HP Enterprises, is now devoted to networking and enterprise solutions and services.

6. Joann Muller, "How Volkswagen Will Rule the World," *Forbes*, April 17, 2013, http://www.forbes.com/sites/joannmuller/2013/04/17/volkswagens -mission-to-dominate-global-auto-industry-gets-noticeably-harder.

7. William Boston and Sarah Sloat, "Volkswagen Emissions Scandal Relates to 11 Million Cars," *Wall Street Journal*, September 22, 2015.

8. "Mission Statement," *Economist*, July 2, 2009, http://www.economist .com/node/13766375.

9. Jeff Bezos, "Letter to Shareholders," Amazon Investor Relations Website: Annual Report and Proxies—1997, March 30, 1998, http://media.corporate -ir.net/media_files/irol/97/97664/reports/Shareholderletter97.pdf. Amazon has included Bezos's first letter to shareholders to every annual report since the company's founding.

10. Harvard Business Review Staff, "The Best-Performing CEOs in the World," *Harvard Business Review*, November, 2015, https://hbr.org/2015 /11/the-best-performing-ceos-in-the-world.

11. Hewlett-Packard Corporate Website: About Us, http://www8.hp.com /us/en/hp-information/about-hp/corporate-objectives.html, On November 2, 2015, accessed June 13, 2016. Hewlett-Packard split into two separate entities, presumably committed to the same core ideology as the original company.

12. Motors Liquidation Company: Investor Information, "General Motors 2003 Annual Report," http://www.motorsliquidationdocket.com/invest_info .php3, accessed June 13, 2016.

13. Harvard Business Review Staff, "Best-Performing CEOs." The rankings reflect an average of each company's performance on industry-adjusted TSR, country-adjusted TSR, and growth in market capitalization over the CEO's tenure.

14. Brian Dumaine, "FedEx CEO Fred Smith on . . . Everything," *Fortune*, May 11, 2012, http://fortune.com/2012/05/11/fedex-ceo-fred-smith-on -everything.

15. Julia Kirby and Thomas A. Stewart, "The Institutional Yes," *Harvard Business Review*, October 2007, https://hbr.org/2007/10/the-institutional -yes.

16. Ibid.

17. Ibid.

18. Ibid.

19. "Yinyang," *Internet Encyclopedia of Philosophy*, accessed June 13, 2016, http://www.iep.utm.edu/yinyang.

20. Malcolm Gladwell, *David and Goliath: Underdogs, Misfits and the Art of Battling Giants* (Boston, MA: Little, Brown, 2013).

21. American Customer Satisfaction Index, Benchmarks by Industry, http://www.theacsi.org/customer-satisfaction-benchmarks/benchmarks-by -industry, accessed June 13, 2016.

22. American Customer Satisfaction Index, U.S. Overall Customer Satisfaction, http://www.theacsi.org/national-economic-indicator/us-overall-customer-satisfaction, accessed June 13, 2016.

23. Joel Peterson, "Just What Are You Trying to Say?" *Forbes*, November 13, 2012, http://www.forbes.com/sites/joelpeterson/2012/11/13/just-what-are-you-trying-to-say.

24. Stock values, revenues, and profit figures in the U.S. airline industry were compared as of November 16, 2015.

25. http://media.corporate-ir.net/media_files/NSD/cost/reports/our_mission.pdf.

26. Ibid.

27. Ashley Lutz, "This Formula Made Costco the Anti-Walmart," *Business Insider*, November 27, 2012, http://www.businessinsider.com/costco-is-the-anti-walmart-2012-11.

28. Melissa Campeau, "'A Stick and a Carrot at the Same Time': Why Costco Pays Twice the Market Rate," *Financial Post*, October 30, 2014, http://business.financialpost.com/executive/cfo/a-stick-and-a-carrot-at-the-same-time-why-costco-pays-twice-the-market-rate.

29. "Best Places to Work, and Best Compensation and Benefits Rankings," *Glassdoor*, accessed June 13, 2016, https://www.glassdoor.com/List/Top-Companies-for-Compensation-and-Benefits-LST_KQ0,43.htm.

30. Wayne F. Cascio, "The High Cost of Low Wages," *Harvard Business Review*, December 2006.

31. Demitrios Kalogeropoulos, "Just How Many Americans Are Costco Wholesale Corporation Members?" *Motley Fool*, June 22, 2015, http://www.fool.com/investing/general/2015/06/22/just-how-many-americans-are-costco-wholesale-corpo.aspx; Andrés Cardenal, "The Main Reason Costco Is Outperforming Wal-Mart and Target," *Business Insider*, June 25, 2014, http://www.businessinsider.com/costco-is-outperforming-competitors-2014-6.

Index

Page references indicated by italicized page references indicate figures and tables. Page references followed by *n* indicate notes.